At-Risk Youth in Crises

At-Risk Youth in Crises
A Team Approach in the Schools

SECOND EDITION

Sharon R. Morgan

pro·ed

8700 Shoal Creek Boulevard
Austin, Texas 78757

pro·ed

© 1994, 1985 by PRO-ED, Inc.
8700 Shoal Creek Boulevard
Austin, Texas 78757-6897

Morgan, Sharon R., 1942–
    At risk youth in crises : a team approach in the schools / Sharon
R. Morgan. — 2nd ed.
        p.   cm.
    Rev. ed. of: Children in crises. 1991.
    Includes bibliographical references (p.) and index.
    ISBN 0-89079-574-6
    1. Teacher participation in educational counseling—Case studies.
2. Peer counseling of students—Case studies.   3. Children of
divorced parents—Education—Case studies.   4. Abused children—
-Education—Case studies.   5. Mentally ill children—Education—Case
studies.   6. Problem children—Education—Case studies.   I. Morgan,
Sharon R., 1942– Children in crises. II. Title.
    LB1027.5.M567   1994
    371.4'6—dc20   93-41948
                                                                          CIP

Production Manager: Alan Grimes
Production Coordinator: Adrienne Booth
Art Director: Lori Kopp
Reprints Buyer: Alicia Woods
Editorial Assistant: Claudette Landry

Printed in the United States of America

1 2 3 4 5 6 7 8 9 10   98 97 96 95 94

CONTENTS

Preface

The greatest amount of effort in the schools now is aimed at youths who are at risk in the area of learning—those likely to fail and/or drop out. However, there are an ever increasing number of children and adolescents who are at risk for emotional problems. Some of these youths are receiving attention in a preventative way, but the majority of them still are not getting the help they need. These are the children I write about in this book.

My hope in using the particular style in this book is to sensitize the reader to what it is like to be a young person under stress. I have tried to do this through the use of fictional vignettes, thinking that literature, rather than dry case studies, will somehow get us in touch with how youths think and feel. If we do that then we come to understand why youths behave as they do in the classroom. They do not seem so bizarre to us.

There always have been stresses in growing up, but some areas have reached crisis proportions for both young children and adolescents. The overwhelming pressures of certain life events on the youth of our society is the theme of this book. The approach is boldly humanistic.

I have had, during my lifetime, more benefactors than one person deserves:

The late Sister Rose Anthony Schmitt, my undergraduate advisor. God bless you, Sister. I'll always love you.

Dr. William C. Morse, my doctoral advisor and mentor. He is dynamite and I am still, 20 years later, under his influence.

My loving friends. All of you. You know who you are: Connie Kane, Pam Botts, Esther Monty Gomez, Shelby Smith, Catherine Medina, Yvette Sams, Elaine Huffman, Connie Paulson, Anna Alphonse.

My developmental editors, Dr. Jim Patton and Rebecca Fletcher, who gently kept pushing me to finish this project and who provided important and timely suggestions.

My mother. After all was said and done, she did help me get through a major part of my life, and I love her.

I wish all children had the people, the breaks, the second and third chances, the help, the forgiveness, the empathy, the understanding, the poking and prodding, and the hoists that I have had. If only they could all find you, dear reader. Good luck to you and be careful out there.

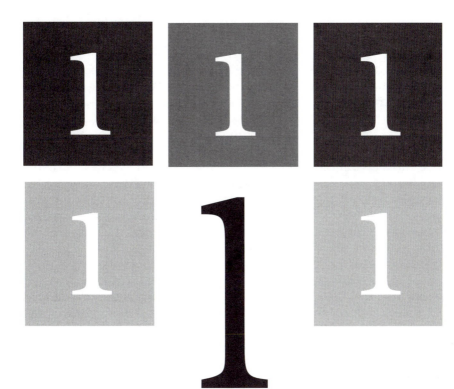

Through the Experiences of At-Risk Youth

The term *at risk* means different things to different people. School professionals are developing "at-risk programs" and hiring special personnel to run these programs. Each program that is called an at-risk program may have a slightly different focus and target different populations. Some professionals define *at risk* in broad terms to mean primary-age children who are failing and will be retained even though they have the intellectual potential to succeed. Other school programs target the at-risk program to focus on adolescents who are most likely to drop out. Other programs focus on children in danger of developing emotional and/or behavioral problems to the extent that they would no longer be eligible to attend school in a mainstream classroom. Finally, there are districts that take the shotgun approach and target their programs at pre-K through 12th-grade youths who would be at risk for developing learning, behavioral, and emotional problems that would lead to school failure, dropping out, delinquency (gangs, prison, and murder), and suicide potential.

Some children who have the potential to succeed do not succeed because they are trying to cope with a major life crisis. All of us, at one time or another in our lives, confront crises and are challenged to cope with them. Most of us do cope—not without some pain and disruptiveness—but we manage to get through what we need to and go on with our lives. Many children face some of the same tragedies that adults find difficult to manage. It is not surprising when children respond to painful life situations by developing emotional and behavioral problems and failing in school. What is amazing is that there are some young persons who experience crises and manage to maintain themselves without an emotional reaction that causes intrapsychic distress, interpersonal problems, and school failure. No one knows for sure why some children are able to cope with stress more successfully than others. The best explanation in the offering right now is that we are all individuals born with basic personality characteristics and preset limitations in our ability to tolerate frustration. Some, by their nature, can tolerate greater amounts of stress than others. The focus of this reading is on the youths who are in jeopardy because they do not have the means to cope with their problems. Issues such as homelessness, divorce, loss, abuse, dropping out, delinquency, and the tragic endings to these at-risk crises are everyday occurrences. These are not rare incidents: divorce is on the rise; loss is a part of life; a child is abused every 2 minutes somewhere in America; and suicide is the second leading cause of death among adolescents. It seems obvious that professionals in the schools should be knowledgeable in these areas, but many are not.

This book presents those issues that impair the emotional development of young persons to such an extent that they are at risk for greater mental health problems, failure to have successful lives, and suicide. Numerous children and adolescents are failing in school and becoming dropouts even though they are intellectually capable. These are the youths who do not qualify for services in special education because they do not have disabling conditions that can be formally categorized. As you will see in this text, there are stringent criteria that must be met before a youth can be labeled as having a disability. Nevertheless, there are many children in today's schools who have problems of such magnitude that their functioning is impaired. These children, and the fact that they were receiving no help, were identified several years ago by Morgan (1985). At that time there were virtually no programs in place and relatively few people in the schools to help these young persons. In the past, these subjects were neglected in teacher education programs for several reasons: it was assumed that these were anomalous events; that they were the responsibility of only the most specialized professionals; that the schools, even if they wanted to, were not equipped to take on such problems; and that school professionals were not knowledgeable about these problems—they had not been informed or trained. Today, however, numerous programs are being developed and trained professionals (teachers and counselors) are being hired specifically to work with these students. Now there is hope; there is reason to feel encouraged. Once people recognize there is a problem that can be corrected with some effort and money and they make the commitment to help all children, then the schools are on the way to the recovery of some of their ills and our children will be preserved.

Over the last 3 decades, special populations of children, such as children with disabilities, have gradually received more and more attention in terms of the services and financial assistance they need. Most child care professionals have some knowledge about children who have very identifiable disabilities, and they have system support for identifying these children and finding an appropriate referral source to provide services.

Contained in this book is information concerning the problems that some school children live with day to day: divorce, loss of another, substance abuse, homelessness, abuse, depression, and suicide. In many instances there is no flowchart that shows the school system how to refer these children through some cascade of services. In fact, the problems seldom are discussed as a school's concern, except in isolated circumstances and by caring professionals who have become aware of a particular child's situation.

Unless they are diagnosed as disabled by the most stringent criteria, these children are not formally categorized with labels for which money has been earmarked to help cure. Yet they are in school, day after day, struggling with issues that would arouse the anxiety and challenge the sanity of even the strongest adults. Many of the children, along with their counselors, teachers, and social workers, receive minimal help in trying to find ways to cope with these tragedies

Issues Addressed in This Book

Homelessness

A major tragedy in our society today that is propelling youths into different types of crises is homelessness. Homeless youths are at greater risk for growing up in a single-parent home and suffering from loss, abuse, depression, and suicide.

Homelessness has become a major problem in the United States. Traditionally, the homeless in America consisted largely of alcoholic, middle-age men living on skid row in the big cities. In the 1970s a large number of younger, mentally ill men and women were deinstitutionalized with no place to go and no one to take care of them, so they joined the homeless. By the 1980s the demography of the homeless had changed sharply. Estimates of the number of homeless ranged from 250,000 to 2.5 million, with the fastest growing segment being families. In 1987 there were 5,020 families, including 12,303 children. By 1991 the estimate on the number of homeless was 3 million, with approximately one third being single mothers and young children. It also has been estimated that 20% of homeless people in shelters are children and adolescents (Alperstein, Rappaport, & Flanigan, 1988; Rescoria, Parker, & Stolley, 1991).

It has been documented that youths who are not only economically poor but also homeless have a greater number of health problems, psychiatric problems, and learning problems. These children and adolescents are more subject to a number of sad situations and endings: they have greater health problems; a higher number of preschoolers who test in the borderline to mentally retarded range and who are more seriously language delayed; an increased incidence of AIDS due primarily to drug use; a higher incidence of physical and sexual abuse by strangers on the streets; more neglect by one parent who cannot cope without a spouse; and a greater number of homeless youths involved in delinquency and gangs in an attempt to have a home of some kind (Alperstein, Rappaport, & Flanigan, 1988; Athey, 1991; Fox, Barnett, Davies, & Bird, 1990; Hersch, 1988; Robertson, 1986; Russell & Williams, 1988; Whitman, Accardo, Boyert, & Kendagor, 1990). Homelessness is having devastating effects on our youth.

Separation and Divorce

Divorce is a major concern confronting today's society. The number of divorces each year almost equals the number of marriages, and yet a large segment of the population in the United States does not consider this a problem. Modern attitudes toward divorce in this country are enigmatic. Divorce has become the focus of comedy shows for television. "No fault" divorce is common, and the legal papers to file can be purchased in many book and stationery stores—no lawyers, no fees, no hassles, no problem. People have divorce parties to celebrate the dissolution of the union of two people who once had an intimate relationship—in many cases, a relationship that produced children. Greeting card companies now offer so-called "cute" and "funny" cards to send to couples congratulating them on their divorce and encouraging a celebration. Even so, divorcing couples are flocking to therapists for help in coping with this stressful change in their lives, and couples with endangered marriages are overflowing counselors' offices. Some parents seek help for their children during this process, but they are relatively few. All things considered, it seems that divorce and separation is "funny" only to those on the outside. It is seldom a jovial matter to the couples or to their children. For whatever the reasons, many have lost sight of the importance and the impact separation and divorce have on the children.

It is sad indeed to observe a child telling a teacher that his or her parents are getting a divorce, only to get a response such as "Uh huh, where is your homework?" Often these children have no one to turn to except their peers, who might be in the same predicament. Peers can be very helpful to each other and can at least provide some comfort. They do not, however, always have the answers or solutions for many of the problems these children need to resolve. Informed professionals in the schools should be working closely with these youths.

The Loss of a Significant Person

When people talk about the loss of a significant person it is usually in the context of losing a parent through divorce or death. There are many types of loss that are significant: loss of parents, siblings, friends, classmates, teachers, and any person that has become important to a child.

A loss can come about in a variety of ways, not only through death. It also may happen through long-term or irrecoverable illnesses. This type of loss can be just as serious as, or perhaps more than, the total or complete absence of a loved one. Perhaps there is nothing more devastating to a child than to have had a parent, normal in all respects, and then lose him or her to mental illness. Some children are living with parents who are physically present but emotionally unavailable to them—parents suffering from mental illness who are sometimes there, sometimes withdrawn; sometimes the way they used to be, and sometimes an entirely different personality. It is, in fact, a living nightmare for the child, who expends great energy clinging to that parent, trying to "bring back" the person the parent once had been. After such tormenting experiences, the child's life will never be the same. Tremendous efforts are needed to assist these children in making the best possible adaptation and adjustment. The schools are in an excellent position to provide day-to-day assistance to these children. At the very least, they can provide a stability that the child does not have at home.

Much of the same can be said about situations in which parents have long-term physical illnesses. A major difference in this type of situation is that the opportunities for positive and satisfactory resolutions are greater. As long as the parent's mental faculties are intact, intervention can be very successful. The need for the schools to be aware of these situations is paramount. Without knowledge and understanding, they can hinder resolution and recovery by misinterpreting a child's behavior. With knowledge and understanding, they can be great facilitators for the child.

All of us must come to terms with death, but for most people this is an experience to be dealt with later in life. The usual sequence of events flows with the mature adult coping with the death of parents, then, in advanced years, accepting the inevitability of his or her own death. This is the natural process, but many experience these events in a different sequence and, consequently, suffer greater stress. The loss of a parent is not only a crisis of major proportions to a youth, it is also abnormal in the life process, creating a wide variety of compounding problems.

Too often, when a child in the family dies, attention turns entirely to the parents while the siblings are pushed into the background; their grief, fear, and anxieties are forgotten. For some reason, they are expected to go on as usual, stay out of the way, and not bother the adults around them. School may be the only place where some children can have their needs met during this time of family crisis. We are all confronted with death more often than we consciously realize. Virtually everyone has had a relative, friend, or neighbor who had to cope with the death of a significant person. Unless there is a death in the immediate family, it is fairly typical of most people to repress the whole matter. Yet death is dispersed throughout life on a regular basis. Nearly all seasoned professionals have either worked with or known a young person who died while still a student in school, a result of either a traumatic accident or a terminal illness. It is as upsetting to the children as it is to the adults. Again, the need for the school's attention and intervention in these matters is clear.

Today, there are children attending school who have terminal illnesses and are practically dying day by day. The ramifications of the effects on a classroom of children can be obvious. There are still those, however, who believe the best way to handle this is to go on as if nothing has changed. Although some schools are focusing on these situations through death education programs, there are many that still are ignoring the problem.

Child Abuse

The incidence figures in the current literature seem to indicate that child abuse is increasing. We really cannot be sure if there is more child abuse now than ever before or if the rising number of cases only reflects a public awareness of the problem and a professional involvement that previously was nonexistent. The early books and research, written mainly by physicians, are replete with case stories of the many and varied ways children have been physically tortured by adults. The discovery of a syndrome that allowed the identification of battered children was a tremendous breakthrough. Perhaps of equal importance today is the recognition of another type of abuse—emotional.

There are some who do not consider this new knowledge as important as the discovery of the battered-child syndrome because the emotionally abused child is not in a life-threatening situation. In the medical community, physical health always has taken precedence over mental health and emotional well-being. For those concerned with the mental health of children, the recognition of emotional abuse is as important a breakthrough as the recognition of physical abuse.

In many ways, emotional abuse can be more damaging in the psychological sense than physical abuse. Physically abused children can identify the source of their torment; can tell what has happened or is happening to them; know who causes the pain; and can tell precisely what hurts them. Emotional abuse is insidious torture, and in its own way it too destroys children. To speak of the emotional death of a child is not an exaggeration to those of us involved in the development of self-concept, self-esteem, and emotional health. Helping youth cope with emotional abuse is difficult work at best. Children in this predicament do not always know what is happening to them; they cannot describe in real concrete ways what damage is being done, how the pain is being inflicted, or even what exactly is making them feel so bad. Unlike physical abuse, the child cannot say, "He twisted my arm," "She pulled my hair out," or "I was burned, kicked, and locked out in the cold with nothing to eat." Instead, we are working with children who, on a daily basis, are being made to feel worthless, bad and unwanted and who, for the slightest transgressions, if any at all, are told by a parent that they "should never have been born," "should be dead," "will always be no good," or "are hopeless failures." These are the more obvious examples of emotional abuse. Some parents never verbalize these feelings about the child but manage to communicate these messages just as clearly through covert actions.

How important is it for professionals to know about the different forms of abuse? In order to cope with the confusing and noxious environment they live in, these children develop styles of behavior that are displeasing and disruptive to the schools. Without knowledge and the willingness to understand and help these children, the schools can become the final annihilating factor in a child's emotional death by administering more punishment for unpleasant and inappropriate behavior that the child cannot really help and adults do not really understand. It can be an even more serious matter. A case in point occurred in Wyoming, where two abused children ended up killing their father. We cannot help wondering how things would be today for those youngsters had someone in the schools been trained and knowledgeable about child abuse—if they had listened when the children asked for help!

For some reason, social agencies and judicial systems have more difficulty knowing exactly what to do about exploitation and incest than knowing what to do about child molestation and rape. There still are people, even educated people, who believe that some children provoke this behavior in adults and that those children are, in some way, just as responsible for the incidents as the adults involved. For example, in 1982 a Colorado judge in two separate incidents gave two young men who had molested two small girls lenient sentences, followed by early probation. Furthermore, stipulation for early probation such as psychotherapy was not even recommended, let alone ordered.

What constitutes sexual abuse of children? There is and has been much debate over this issue, and no definitive rulings or laws exist concerning limits on the use of children in photography, motion pictures, and plays. In September of 1980, a newspaper article described auditions that took place for the part of Lolita in the play by the same name. Actresses older than 13 were told they were "over the hill" for the part. Fifty little girls under the age of 13 were interviewed for the role of a child (Lolita), who is the sexual obsession of her 38-year-old stepfather.

Before the interviews began, the 50 girls, with their mothers, were warned that the play included scenes of "sexual intimacy" and that "anybody whose mother isn't interested in having you play that kind of thing shouldn't be involved." No one left the room. The mother of one child was quoted as saying, "Molly can handle it. But it's up to her. It's not up to me." The playwright said he was looking for a nymphet and defined a nymphet as "a young girl who can provoke the most abominable lust in a man, maybe without even knowing it." Many of the little girls had a different idea of a nymphet. One aspiring child actress thought that a nymphet is a girl who is very beautiful and loved by everyone.

From a research standpoint it is unclear how, in the long run, children who have been used for what is known as "kiddy porn" are affected emotionally and psychologically. It is known that some children involved in pornographic movies and magazines eventually have turned to prostitution.

To some it becomes a very confusing issue when parents give their consent, and debates ensue concerning the difference between art and pornography. Many would argue that *Lolita* is art; however, although this perhaps was not the playwright's intention, the play is about sexual abuse, and asking a child to act it out seems strikingly like more sexual abuse.

What is really at issue is how a child interprets these experiences. For professional groups, a position of "better safe than sorry" is appropriate; it could be some time before it becomes apparent that the child was seriously damaged emotionally by what, I think, amounts to sexual exploitation.

The sexual abuse of children is a problem that finally has been given great attention and has become real news and made shocking headlines. It is difficult to know how many of the children professionals work with every day are actually being sexually abused; it is a certainty that many have escaped our attention and have thus lost the opportunity to receive the help they so desperately needed. We should be able to ensure, now that there is so much awareness, that these children are not overlooked.

Satanic, ritualistic sexual abuse recently has been given attention but is still clouded in mystery.

Depression and Suicide

Children are any nation's resource and source of joy and hope. Not many people ever think of children as anything but happy, full of laughter, and free of all cares and responsibilities. Although we have been slow to recognize and acknowledge it, suicide and suicide attempts are not infrequent in childhood and adolescence. It should be noted that the rate of suicide among children is believed to be rising, and that among adolescents it is ranked as the second leading cause of death. It also is believed that the suicide statistics for young people are underestimated by as much as 30%. We do not have complete understanding of why such phenomena occur, especially with the young, who should have hope.

That suicide occurs among adolescents has been established and is well documented, but few believe it exists among small children. It does, and probably at a higher rate than we really know. Many freak deaths in small children are called accidents. They are not all accidents, by any means. The mental health community is certain of this but is hard pressed to produce concrete evidence for law officials. Young children do not leave suicide letters; they have not yet learned about them, and some children are so young they have not even learned how to write. Young children rarely talk about suicide the way older youths do; they have not yet learned how to talk about it. Cognitively, the ability to verbalize at a level to which an adult can relate has not developed yet either. Nevertheless, careful clinical histories overwhelmingly establish that child suicide exists.

The abuse of drugs and alcohol by children and adolescents, often a sign of depression, is viewed in two opposite ways by society. On one side there is great alarm and concern about substance abuse. On the other side there is an almost blasé attitude about the matter. Adults have used alcohol themselves, so they are not as concerned about adolescents using alcohol as they are about their using other drugs. Typical comments are that it is only a fad, it is not so different from many of the rebellious things other generations of adolescents have done, and it will go away eventually. Tragically, in many cases it is too late. Substance abuse and suicide among adolescents are interrelated.

SCOPE OF THIS BOOK

This book focuses on crisis situations that any child in our society could experience. These children are in real jeopardy if we cannot help them find the means to cope with their problems. Each chapter in this book addresses intense issues or events that have an immediate impact and could produce prolonged effects on children—issues or events that should be of interest to any professional concerned with the mental health of children. These topics are not usually included in a training curriculum in education, and yet they are problems that eventually confront all professionals who work in the schools.

Professionals who are going out to work in the schools cannot remain ignorant about these tragic life events. They already are more aware than ever before; at the very least they have as much information as the general public, which, at least is a beginning. The purpose of this book is to give the school professional more detail than the thumbnail sketch the media prepares for public consumption.

Professionals cannot beg off the responsibility because of ignorance or take the laissez-faire attitude that someone else will take care of these problems. In the "real world," relatively few of these children, for whatever reasons, ever get psychotherapy or some other highly specialized type of help. We can help these children. So, want it or not, their tragedies are the schools' tragedies too, and it becomes our responsibility to do something.

Whom Is This Book For?

As far back as 1970, the Joint Commission of the Mental Health of Children determined that all babies are born with seven rights:

1. to be wanted
2. to be born healthy
3. to live in a healthy environment
4. to satisfaction of basic needs
5. to continuous loving care
6. to acquiring intellectual and emotional skills enabling them to achieve their aspirations and cope in society
7. to receive care and treatment (pp. 3–4)

Over the decades we have fallen quite short in guaranteeing these rights to all children. Services are provided in a piecemeal fashion to very circumscribed populations. Divorce; loss and death; emotional, physical, and sexual abuse; and depression and suicide are the topics of this book. All of these have a common thread that links them together. Each of the crises is fraught with emotional pain and the anguish of alienation, rejection, isolation, and despair. The youths who have coped successfully with these stressful life crises have had the necessary ingredients that promote good mental health: understanding, support, empathy, and help. Those young persons are the ones who were fortunate to be in dynamic, facilitating school environments.

This book is really a challenge for all professionals in the schools to do more for more children than we have been doing. With each new request for more service, a scream of protest resounds: "How much more can we expect the schools to do?" Providing the needed services does not necessarily mean more time and more money; help can be provided with the resources that already exist just by prioritizing and reorganizing. It is a constant and consistent complaint of counselors, teachers, and other school personnel that a major portion of their time is spent on things that have nothing to do with their training and expertise. The busywork of rescheduling, filling out forms, shuffling papers, and all of the minutiae that highly trained and highly paid professionals are required to do could be put in the hands of clerks, so that the people who have the skills are free to provide the services and the help that children in crises so desperately need. Some intervention models can operate at no additional expense. Even if it does take more money, that is beside the point; aren't the children worth a little more—whatever it takes? Those involved in providing services know it is worth whatever it takes because they have seen the results of neglect.

This book is not written for one professional group more than another, because it is really designed for all people who deal with children in the school setting: counselors, regular teachers, special education teachers, social workers, school psychologists, administrators, nurses, other specialists, and professionals in private practice who consult with us. It is impossible to predict who might influence a child in a positive way, which person in a child's life could be selected as a confidant to the secret agonies being experienced. When your whole world is coming down around you, one helper usually is not enough.

This book is for people who want to work as a team in one of the child's most natural environments—the school. The last chapter focuses on how we can help and who is most likely to take on the task of caring for these children. Few adults can totally avoid involvement or completely ignore a child suffering psychological and emotional stress and pain. A system that tries to ignore, and succeeds, becomes an inhumane place where the adults function as sterile machines. That is not what we want for our children, and it is not what we want for ourselves.

Knowledge and Empathy

This book is not just a presentation of research investigations or a detached set of clinical case histories, serving only to bore the reader into a comatose state with a litany of studies. Most of all, its aim is to help prevent people from becoming so removed from these problems that they begin to categorize children into neat little niches and then forget them. It was written to make people aware of these childhood crises—to be more knowledgeable and better educated professionals. I also wanted something else: for people to feel for the children in these tragic situations. In order to bring the reader in touch with how these children feel and allow them to experience their worlds, each chapter opens with fictional vignettes. These very short stories come from my subconscious and have been stored away there for quite some time. They are based on some of my own experiences and on some of the experiences of children that I have worked with over the years. My own life has been affected in specific ways by some of the crises that are depicted. Because of the effect on my own life, those experiences have made me feel very close to the children in this book; I understand them. Knowledge is important, even critical, but so is empathy. I wanted to blend the two in this book because both knowledge and empathy are needed to be effective helpers for these children.

How true to life are these stories? Their validity was tested with over 200 junior and senior high school students in regular and special education classes, as well as with some of their teachers and counselors. This was not a research study, however; the intent was to discover if adults and youths could relate to the characters in the stories. They could, and other aspects were revealed in the process: (a) some of these youths were going through these experiences and had not told anybody until they read the stories; (b) many of these young people already have a lot of empathy; and (c) they have some very good ideas about how to help each other. What a resource they can be! That their responses were so right is partly why peer counseling is discussed in the last chapter.

I hesitated at first about letting them read the stories; the language is rough at times and so are some of the scenes. Both, however, are accurate portrayals of the way some youths respond and the way things happen in these situations. I don't condone the language; it is just the way things are and is not anything new to the children who read them. After reading the stories, some children identified themselves for the first time as having similar problems and now are getting help. That was an unexpected bonus!

Few people can get through life tragedy-free and completely emotionally unscathed. Odds being what they are, the chances are high that as you read you might hear yourself saying, "This is my family!" or "I've been through this. I've felt that way before!" If you are among the very few who have never been affected personally by any of the crises in this book, then you are truly fortunate. More than for anybody else, this book is for those totally inexperienced with these tragic aspects of life.

This book was not written to induce people to wallow in pity and sympathy. I do hope that it jolts you in such a way that you will, from now on, be aware and alert, sensitive and empathic. The book really was written in the hope that professionals will be better able to provide the psychological nutrients that help the children develop the coping mechanisms they need not just to survive but to have some of the same opportunities to develop healthily and happily and to live fuller and richer lives. It was created with the desire that future children will meet in the schools adults who can help them reduce their feelings of alienation, rejection, isolation, and despair and who can show them how to attain some expectation for a better life.

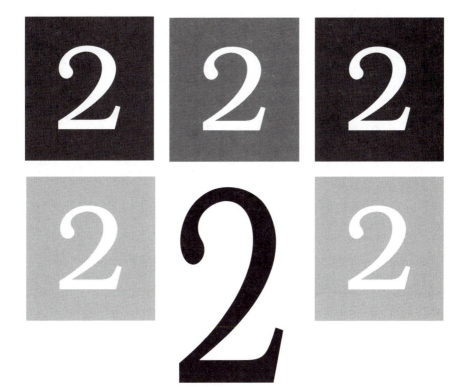

Children and Adolescents Coping with Separation and Divorce

LISA

"Living with Dad is a swell idea. Mom thought I'd be upset, so she said it was just for a while. 'Until I get on my feet, get a job, and find a place to live.' Marcie would stay with Mom. She's Mom's kid but not Dad's. Just me— I'm the only one that's Dad's kid. Marcie's dad is Bob. Mom and Bob are getting divorced, you know.

"I don't know why Kay and Wylene get so mixed up over that. I've explained it a million times but they just don't get it.

"Every now and then they ask me again, 'If Marcie is your sister, and her mom is your mom, and Bob is Marcie's dad, then isn't Bob your dad?'

"How many times do I have to tell them? Bob is my stepdad! Then they always ask, 'Is Marcie your stepsister?' And I have to tell them again, 'No, she's my real sister!'

"God, why is that so hard to understand? My mom is my real mom, and my sister is my real sister, and Bob is my stepdad, and I have my own real dad who lives someplace else.

"Then Wylene—she's so damn stupid—asks again if my real dad is Marcie's real dad. No, he's just my real dad, for the forty billionth time! They just don't get it, you see. Jeez! It makes me so mad! Why do they keep asking the same dumb questions?"

"Aren't you getting way off track with all this, Lisa? Changing the subject isn't going to change the mess you're in right now," Crawford said. "Only last year you were a pretty good student, now you're in this office at least once a week because of a complaint from somebody. And I haven't seen any evidence that you're trying to change. You're supposed to be in here now to work on the problems you're having in school. Instead, you come in and go off on tangents that have nothing to do with why you were sent down here in the first place."

"I didn't want to come to this damn office anyway! Why do I have to be in counseling? Shit! I wouldn't be here 'cept the principal said, like he's real hot shit or something, 'Go to Mr. Crawford's office!' I'm not crazy. I don't need any counseling! This sucks!"

"That's really nice language coming out of a pretty young girl's mouth. Spoils your looks."

"So! What's the big deal anyway? Mr. Shrink!"

Lisa dug down deep into the chair, glared at Crawford, looked at the floor and then out the window. Her jaw was clamped tight and her body was stiff. That's it, she thought. No more talking! They call you in and tell you they want to help. "I'm here to listen, to work on your problems," they say. Then when you try to talk they give you a bunch of BS. They don't want to listen, just want you to listen to them.

Crawford dropped his pencil on the desk. He was disgusted. You could tell by the way he wrapped his fingers around his forehead and pushed his chair back against the wall. He blew out cigarette smoke in a way that suggested that if he could he'd blow away the whole damn school and every kid in it.

"The big deal," he spit, "is that you've had five Saturday detentions in 10 weeks, you're failing most of your classes, you smart-mouth your teachers, you're tardy most of the time, you've lost books . . . ."

Crawford droned on, listing the school infractions. Then he started on Mrs. McKay's complaints. "Your mother says she doesn't know what to do with you. You're no different at home, won't do anything she asks. You leave at night and she doesn't know where you've gone, coming in at all hours. She knows you're hanging out with Torry and his friends. She doesn't want you to, and I've talked to you about that crowd. They've all been picked up for using dope, drinking, others for worse than that. Torry's been in juvenile detention. Is that what you want? You want to end up in juvenile detention?" Lisa turned and glared at Crawford. God, what a turkey butt question that is, she thought.

"No, I don't want to go to juvenile detention. Besides, I'm not doing anything wrong, just riding around with my friends. What's so bad about that? Anyway, it wasn't Torry's fault. They shouldn't have put him in juvenile detention. He wasn't doing anything. The cops just pick on Torry. Everybody picks on Torry because of the way he looks, dresses. He can't help that, can he? Do you think people ought to pick on people just for how they look? It isn't fair."

"We've been over this ground before, Lisa. You know Torry was trying to break into one of those game machines. We're talking responsibility here. You taking responsibility for your own behavior. We're supposed to be here talking about you, anyway, not Torry."

"You brought it up," the girl snapped. "And my mom, and all the school stuff. All this crap! That's all you ever want to talk about. I don't know why I have to come down here. It's all we ever talk about. 'You have to take responsibility for your own behavior, Lisa. People don't pick on you. It's what you do that makes people do what they do.' "

She was mocking Crawford now, mimicking his words, intonations, and gestures.

"Mom, anyway, hell, so what! I'm going to go live with Dad. It'll be a lot better. He won't bitch about all this stuff. I'm going to a different school soon, anyway. So why do we have to keep going over all this again and again? I'll be glad to get out of this shit hole!"

Crawford sat up and glared back at Lisa. "Those details haven't been worked out yet, as you know. You may not transfer. Your mother and father haven't decided you'll live with him. His job requires a lot of travel. So he isn't home much."

"So what! I can stay by myself. I'm 13, you know. Not exactly a baby!"

"My point exactly," snapped Crawford. "You are not a baby. It's time you started taking responsibility for your own behavior. Also, your dad is thinking of remarrying. All these plans are just tentative. It might not work out. Even if it did, what makes you think your behavior is going to change just by moving? You have to start right now, changing it yourself. You'll be in the same messes there that you're in here if you don't do something about it yourself, and now! Do you understand, Lisa?"

"Oh, sure, I understand." Lisa's tone was not belligerent anymore. She was feeling depressed now. Her stiffened position in the chair changed to a slump.

"You're wrong, anyway. You don't know my dad. You think he doesn't love me. Well, he does! He really wants me to live with him. It doesn't matter if he gets married again. He'd have me live with him anyway. Besides, Mom can't afford to keep both me and Marcie if she divorces Bob. I have to live with Dad. If Mom doesn't have a job and has no money, she can't afford to have kids around. So how can she keep Marcie? She can't afford to keep me. She just wants to get rid of me. Too much trouble, you know. Bob's always screaming about how much everything costs—food, how much I eat, my clothes, the stuff I need for school, everything! Marcie, now, gets whatever she wants, no screaming. I'll be glad to live with Dad. I'm glad they're getting a divorce. I hate them all! They just care about themselves. They're all happier if I'm not around, Mom and Bob and Marcie. A bunch of turkey butts!"

"Well, Lisa, we're back where we started."

Crawford was tiring of his conversation with Lisa. "You need to go on to your last class. I'll give you a pass because you're late, but I want you to know that I'm recommending another Saturday detention. I don't see that you're getting the point yet about your responsibilities. I hope you get the message after this next detention. I don't want to have to see you in my office again. Another time and you're getting awfully close to suspension for the year. I hope that doesn't happen, but it's entirely up to you. We're getting to the end of our rope here."

Crawford wrote the pass and gave it to Lisa. He didn't move from his chair, and Lisa let herself out of the office, in a hurry to leave but in no hurry to go to class.

Being in the hall was a relief. Everyone was in class and it was quiet. In the distance Lisa could hear the band practicing out on the football field. Lisa thought about Wylene and Kay, who would be out there now, practicing too. She gave more thought to the two girls. They were okay to hang around with sometimes. Go skating and stuff like that. Mom likes them. "Nice girls." They're square britches, really. They don't like doing some of the stuff Torry and the rest of us like. They don't like Torry and the others either. Nothing ever happens to them, no Saturday detentions or anything else. They both have real moms, real dads, real sisters and brothers. Everybody in the same house, no stepdads, no explaining who everybody is, no screaming, no divorce, no moving, no problems. Zits only, that's their big problem. BIG DEAL! BIG DAMN DEAL!

Lisa considered the class she was supposed to return to after leaving Crawford's office. Science and Bowman, God, how I hate it! She agonized over the thought of going to that class. They'll all look at me when I come in. They know where I've been, in the nut man's office, where all of us nuts go when we have a "problem." I don't have my homework and Bowman hates me and everybody will be doing something. I'll go in and sit down and Bowman will say, "Glad you finally decided to join us. What's the answer to blah blah blah?" knowing damn good and well I won't know what's going on. She likes to make me look like an ass in front of everyone. God, I hate her! A real turkey butt!"

Lisa's thoughts turned to Torry. It's been awful since he was kicked out of school. He's the only one that's really fun, that I can talk to. He's at the arcade now, I know it, having a good time, free. He doesn't have to listen to Crawford anymore or put up with all the other jerks. He would have graduated this year and really been free, except he is anyway. Says he's not going back. Maybe he'll go to California and check it out! Wants me to go too, really scary, though. If I tried and got caught, that's it. Mom said she'd turn me in to Juvenile as an incorrigible, whatever that is. Anyway, I guess it means

I'd be in reform school. Bitch! She'd put her own kid in jail. It's all Bob's fault. She wouldn't do it if he didn't want her to. He wants to get rid of me. I hate his guts! Hers too! They can have each other! What's the difference if I go to Bowman's class now. I already have detention. I'm already late. Don't have my work, so I'll just get in more trouble. Shove it!

It was sunny and warm outside, and the fresh air felt good to Lisa as she ran down the street toward the arcade. She had not felt so good in a long time. She ran as fast as she could for several blocks, until she was sure that no one from the school could see her anymore, then stopped to catch her breath. Lisa was feeling excited but relaxed, as if a ton had been lifted off her shoulders. She felt free and couldn't wait to see Torry at the arcade. Her mind was made up. No more Crawford. No more Bowman. No more principals. No more work. No more school. No more screaming and fighting and trying to decide where she should live. No more anybody telling her what a mess she was or what a mess she was in. No more detention.

No more crap! California. Check it out! Go for it! We have to go now! I'll tell Torry we have to go now so they won't be able to stop us. He said we'd be okay, can get jobs and do what we want. Torry loves me. He's the only one who loves me. He's the best, a real fox. He knows a lot of stuff. He'll take care of me. He has his own car. Oh, how excellent! Totally awesome!

....

Coping with Separation and Divorce

The story of Lisa illustrates the pain and confusion some children feel when a family disintegrates. She had already experienced this disintegration when her mother and her biological father divorced and is now under the stress of expecting another disruption as her mother and stepfather talk of divorce. Lisa has struggled to understand (and explain to others) her role in this new family. She is her mother's child but not her stepfather's. She has a half sister who is her mother's child and her stepfather's child. Where does Lisa fit in in this new family? The question constantly arises as to whether or not her sister is her "real" sister, and if so, who is Lisa in this family unit?

Lisa's story also illustrates the fears of some children about who will take care of them when there is a divorce and the extreme confusion when there are multiple marriages involving non-blood relatives. Lisa is like thousands (a conservative estimate) of children in the United States who feel alienated. She tried to reach out for help to her counselor by attempting to tell her story, but he was notably lacking in empathy and understanding. The counselor became obsessed with system rules, Lisa's infractions, and her seemingly total disregard for her school situation. His attention was focused exclusively on her surface behavior, since he could not see what was really bothering Lisa, causing her pain, and precipitating her behavior.

Runaway children are almost epidemic in the United States. Lisa will join them because they will listen and understand. She believes the boy in her life (Torry) will take care of her and give her the love she needs, and she desperately needs to feel like she belongs to somebody.

In 1970 the U.S. Census reported that one in every four marriages ends in divorce. This figure increased in 1977 to one in every three marriages. Nationally, divorce is on an upward swing that shows no sign of diminishing. It has, in fact, increased dramatically over the past 2 decades, to the level at which it is estimated that over 40% of new marriages will ultimately end in divorce. Although the birthrate in the United States is declining, the number of divorces in which children are involved is increasing (Chiriboga & Catron, 1991). Over 1 million children in the United States below age 18 are affected by the divorce of their parents. With such high figures, it is important for counselors, educators, psychologists, and the parents to understand the impact that divorce may have on children.

With this overwhelmingly large number of children affected by divorce in their families, the problem has assumed crisis proportions. Demo and Acock (1988) stated that divorce is one of the most serious crises in contemporary American life. Of the families they studied there were none in which at least one person was not feeling distress or exhibiting disruptive behavior. This was especially true during the first year following divorce.

Divorce is a disorganizing and reorganizing process, particularly when children are involved. This process often extends over several years. Divorce has the potential for growth and new integrations, but it is often rocky and tortuous, and many underestimate the problems and difficulties of such a transition. The central dilemma in divorce is the conflict of interest between the child's need for continuity to support development and the parents' decision to break up the family structure that has provided the child's main supports (Wallerstein & Kelly, 1976). It often is difficult to separate the effects of the divorce itself from those of the trauma preceding or following divorce.

Demo and Acock (1988) estimated that less than two thirds of American children live with both biological parents. They also estimated that the percentage of black youth who will live with only one parent for some period of time before the age of 18 is as high as 94%, and for white children the figure is 70%.

The Separation Period

Immediately upon the separation of their parents, children often become the object of their parents' most intense struggles. Dividing the material objects takes only a few weeks or months, but children can remain a focus for years. Statistics show that divorces with children involved are 10 times more likely to be followed by relitigation than divorces that do not involve children. Parents often use children to continue to control and frustrate each other (Derdeyn & Scott, 1984; Leahey, 1984).

Many studies consider the effects of divorce on children without any specific age delineation. Children of divorced parents are treated as if they all share the same common reactions. The most frequently cited symptoms are anxiety, denial, and guilt (Chiriboga & Catron, 1991; Henning & Oldham, 1977; Peterson, 1989). Others theorize that divorce has the potential for disrupting the flow of the natural developmental process in children because several years of disequilibrium might follow a divorce. A span of several years represents a significant proportion of a child's entire life experience; however, it is believed that the disruptive process can be reversed or modified with counseling (Beck, 1988; Chiriboga & Catron, 1991).

According to Scott and Senay (1973), separation has been identified as the period of greatest stress in the marital disruption process. To fully understand the consequences surrounding a divorce, we need to be aware of different factors and realize that divorce is not a short-lived event. It may be difficult to distinguish between the effects of the legal event of divorce and those of the prolonged trauma preceding and following it. For most children, the central event of the divorce process is the parental separation. This event evokes or greatly intensifies the predominant initial responses of the child.

Rarely does the post-divorce family structure stabilize within the first year following the parental separation. The prolonged disequilibrium of the family frequently is accompanied by a decrease in the emotional availability of the custodial parent. For the young child, this time span may occur during phases of development considered critical to later adjustment. Generally, the later a separation occurs, the less detrimental the effects on the children, both boys and girls (Dail, 1990; Reinhold, 1988).

Factors Contributing to the Ability to Cope

We cannot generalize about the effects of divorce on children. The present research suggests that children from divorced families cannot be treated as a homogeneous group. However, the impact of divorce on children and whether they can successfully cope with the stress depends on several factors that most researchers agree on: (a) the age and gender of the child when the divorce occurs; (b) how mature the child is; (c) the financial situation of the parents; (d) the conditions that led to the divorce; (e) how much discord existed before the divorce; (f) the type of relationship the child had with each parent and with siblings; (g) the child's own ability to adjust and handle stress; (h) whether the child has significant people available for emotional support; and (i) whether or not the parents have continual conflict after the divorce (Dlugokinski, 1977; Peterson, 1989; Reinhold, 1988; Zimiles & Lee, 1991).

Functions of the Family

To understand the effects of separation and divorce on children, there must be a focus on the family as a unit, stressing the significance of the role of the family in all aspects of child development. Marital dysfunction, the predicament of troubled families, and the influence of instability on its members are seen as being inseparable from the eventual effects of the breakdown of the family unit. The family is analogous to an individual with sequential stages of development and critical turning points. Similar to an individual, the nuclear unit of father, mother, and child has a natural history of its own.

Ackerman (1966) used the phrase "familial organism" to describe the family qualities of living process and functional unity. Life cycle stages trace the evolution of the family, beginning with the formation of the family system as distinct from the background families, the childbearing and rearing years, the children leaving home, the two-person family once again, and finally, the sole-survivor stage (Greene, 1965).

Numerous purposes and functions of the family exist as it continuously evolves. These functions, such as union and individuation, care of young, reciprocal need satisfaction, affection and unity bonding, and training for social participation, indicate the many facets of the "familial organism" (Ackerman, 1966).

The primary responsibility of the family is the socialization of its members. The parents are the main socializing agents of the siblings. The offspring reflect the psychological identity of the parental pair. As children, in a sense, shape parents to their own needs, unique personalities emerge.

Greene (1965) stated that a multiplicity of relationships exists within the family. There are subsystems of the marital pair, such as the parent–child set and the siblings set. The plurality of the possible interaction patterns is an illustration of the complexity of the unit. The emotional fate of the child is very strongly influenced by the stability and balance of the subsystems.

The essence of the family determines and becomes a part of the internal makeup of its members. The significance of the structure and the amount of energy involved in maintaining and balancing from within the family cannot be underestimated.

It is paradoxical that the work of parenting is not given similar status to other kinds of work requiring comparable time and skill. Lomas (1967) noted this lack of status as a part of the picture of "why families fail." The work of child raising is seen by society as traditional and somewhat mundane. It has an existential nature in that child rearing cannot be easily measured, marked, and presented to the world as an unambiguous achievement.

The question is raised whether the family has become alienated from society. More often than not, society is intolerant when faced with the alienated problem family. Assuming that society is more concerned with the apparent than the real, the problem family is coerced to conceal its unhappiness and lack of communication. Outwardly, it may maintain a public face of normality or even super-respectability. In turn, this secrecy is what makes it extremely difficult for society to come to the aid of the troubled family unit.

Lomas (1967) viewed the preservation of the family as not purely a private affair for a family member. A member's failure or refusal to preserve the family has immediate repercussions on others whose internal family is threatened. Essentially, the preservation of the family is equivalent to the preservation of self. A breakdown of the family may sometimes be experienced by the child as shattering the world to bits.

There is a powerful sense of self, and "family self," acting within the family structure. Disturbances within the structure, either of an individual nature or in relation to other family members, can lead to a dysfunctioning of the unit. Family psychopathology is commonly revealed when a family member or members are in need of outside help. Typically, there are underlying family problems that relate to the disturbance of an individual in therapy.

In an illustration of the interrelationship of family problems, Tharp (1965) listed the five functions of roles in marriage as follows: solidarity, sexuality, external relations, internal instrumentality, and division of responsibility. His assumption was that disturbed roles within the areas of the married-couple relationship result in a disturbed parent–child relationship within the same areas. As a therapist, he advocated treatment of the role function within the marriage as a corrective procedure.

Tharp's study centered on a 45-year-old physician, his wife, and his two sons, ages 10 and 13. Problems were diagnosed in the area of solidarity, in which a deficit led to an excess in the parent–child relationship. Similarly, a deficit in the sexuality function resulted in an intensified mother–elder son relationship. In the area of external relations, a competition resulted with respect to the younger child as to how he should represent the family when in school: the parents fought over whether he should be an achiever or more relaxed. The child was caught in between. A direct relationship was discovered between marital dysfunction within one of the five areas and the likelihood of parent–child disturbance within the same area. This study points out the complications facing the child in family disturbances. Although children may not be a causal factor, they are not immune to the results of family disturbance.

Boszormenyi-Nagy and Spark (1973) elaborated on the efforts of a child to maintain family structure or to reestablish relationships, with the subsequent effects on psychosocial development. Safeguarding loyal adherence to the family may lead to failure in outside social involvements in the categories of school phobia, learning failure, or delinquency. Real or alleged delinquent acts by a child may serve to bring the alienated parents together by diverting attention away from their mutual destructiveness. In Lisa's story, this may have been her intention. Children of constantly battling parents may feel hurt, rejected, overstimulated, or depressed; however, they will tend to feel obligated to save the parents and their marriage from the threat of destruction.

Regressive behavior on the part of the parents during disputes may be manifested by caretaking roles in the child. For example, a 7-year-old dialed the police during an attack made on his mother by his father. Sometimes a preadolescent child is seen reassuring both sides in the face of incompatibility and divorce. In some cases parental strife affects the emotional growth of children, who may halt their efforts toward independence if it appears detrimental in their eyes to the family structure. Some children act as a cementing agent. Three- and 4-year-olds have, in the presence of strangers, made efforts to hide the problems of their parents. This indicates the depth of the societal impact on maintaining an apparently cohesive family appearance (Boszormenyi-Nagy & Spark, 1973).

There are indications that less harm results from the regressive or infantile behavior of parents when there is mutual reliance among siblings. That is, in multiple-sibling families, a development of basic trust may result from the adoption of reciprocal parenting functions among siblings. This role exchanging is common in lower-class ghetto settings, where a 3-year-old, for example, may be found warming milk for a baby if the mother is drunk. Unfortunately, the crippling effects on the child of premature adult functioning are uncertain.

As pointed out, children often neglect their own interests, drives toward independence, completion of schoolwork, and so forth, when faced with feelings of overresponsibility. Owing to their deep loyalty to the family unit and their strong emotional needs, children often are willing to sacrifice themselves and accept inappropriate roles.

Various roles have been observed to be assigned to children in cases of family breakdown (Boszormenyi-Nagy & Spark, 1973). One child may be assigned the role of the "well sibling." This child may appear overtly good, quiet, and conforming in the eyes of the parents and therefore assumes the role of parenting. The "scapegoat" role is commonly observed in the behavior of a delinquent child. In this case, a child may be using a social institution as a parental substitute. Owing to lack of parental control, the child relies on help from such other authorities as schools, social agencies, and legal authorities to contain self-destructive behavior (Lisa?). In effect, they may be exemplifying inverse loyalty to the family by indirectly bringing order and assistance to a chaotic home life. It is interesting to note that Erikson (1968) referred to this as a negative identity for a child, which he said may be preferable to that of being ignored, detached, and a nonobject in a family. In effect, the unmanageable child who adopts a "bad" role assignment is acting out reactions to family tensions away from the home, and by so doing rescues himself or herself from a nonexistence.

In delegating roles to children, distressed parents often tend to view their offspring as objects. The "pet" child typically is treated as an object whose purpose is one of loyally reflecting affection and acceptance, but the needs of this child may be entirely overlooked. Additional object roles include family referees who mediate for the enemies in conflict. These family referees are captives who are shut out from the gratification of their needs and become sacrificial objects and victims of abuse (Boszormenyi-Nagy & Spark, 1973).

In summary, when parents experience total frustration within the marital relationship, they tend to vent or redirect their anxieties toward a new resource, most often the children. Children become parent-like substitutes, and depression is often the underlying family affect. Learning and behavior difficulties, psychosomatic illness, accident proneness, and suicide are common reactions of children in this situation.

A complex dilemma is operating when children repress and deny their own needs, postponing growth and development in a loyal attempt to meet the parents' needs. Yet these efforts are met with ambivalent responses since they cannot possibly undo underlying causal situations.

As the home situation becomes more and more drastic, separation and divorce become an actuality. According to Kliman (1968), a great deal of preventive work needs to be accomplished well in advance of the separation. This can be done by explaining the reasons for separation to each child according to each child's ability to understand. This allows children to vent their resentments beforehand.

THE PYSCHOLOGICAL IMPACT OF DIVORCE

In general it is believed that, in divorce, anxiety is a necessary condition to stimulate those involved to plan for the future rather than dwell on the past or become immobilized by the present distress (Jauch, 1977). Depression and anxiety are closely linked; when anxiety is so excessive that it is intolerable, depression becomes the coping mechanism for blunting anxious feelings (Dlugokinski, 1977).

Another generalization is that children react with guilt feelings, thinking they are in some way responsible for the problems of the parents. They view the absence of one parent as punishment for their misdeeds. Even though these generalizations are partly true of all children, specific age groups show markedly different reactions to divorce and separation.

Effects on the Preschool-Age Child

According to a number of investigators, for the majority of children in this group, divorce has a significant impact and represents a major crisis. It has been found that there can be acute behavioral changes that present real management problems in 62% of the children. Some specific, initial behavioral reactions are cited: shock, depression, and regressive phenomena, such as bed wetting. Soiling, enuresis, and eating and sleeping problems also are mentioned as common behavioral reactions. In addition, anxiety and confusion are common to children of divorced parents, usually because the parents do not fully explain what is happening, and the child's understanding is incomplete. With an incomplete understanding of the situation, the child may feel responsible for the breakup, especially if being "good" was related to being loved by the parents. It is generally accepted that divorce causes feelings of guilt in the child (Beck, 1988; Gannett, 1986; Peterson, 1989; Roy & Fuqua, 1983; Wallerstein, 1983).

Another way the young child may try to cope with the difficult circumstances is to deny the whole situation, living as though the parent has not left. At the same time, the child also may be fearing the loss of the custodial parent. It has been shown that the absence of the parent of the same sex is likely to be most disruptive in these years (Sherman & Lepak, 1986). Apparently, cognitive disruption is the most severe and social developmental disruption appears to be greatest if the father leaves during the preschool years; however, the impact depends largely on the emotional stability and love of the mother. Most researchers find that negative behaviors are greatly reduced 2 years following the divorce (Biller, 1971; Ellison, 1983; Kalter & Rembar, 1981; Marino & McCowan, 1976; Peterson, 1989; Reinhold, 1988).

Since the divorce rate is highest in the first few years of marriage, children of newly divorced parents tend to be predominantly the younger ones. Preschool children who are struggling to comprehend the cause of the separation or divorce frequently assume that they had a role in precipitating the event (Ellison, 1983; Kalter & Rembar, 1981; Peterson, 1989). They quickly learn that when they are bad they are punished. To young children, divorce may seem like a retribution for their wrongdoings of the past. Children with guilt feelings may consciously or unconsciously seek out punishment for themselves by manifesting unacceptable behavior in school. To alleviate guilt feelings, children need to hear from their parents and teachers that nothing they said, did, or thought had anything to do with the divorce (Grollman & Grollman, 1977; Morgan, 1984).

Effects on the Elementary-Age Child

The most commonly cited behaviors and concerns of a child of this age include guilt, anxiety, fantasies, and social problems with peers. It is believed that guilt comes from the child having at some time wished the parent gone and that excessive anxiety comes from trying to decide which parent to live with and then fearing rejection by the parent not chosen. Children also worry about who will take care of them if the custodial parent becomes sick. It appears that children of divorced parents create numerous unrealistic fantasies about the parent who has left (Bayrakal & Kope, 1990; Chiriboga & Catron, 1991; Henning & Oldham, 1977; Leahey, 1984; Parish, 1981; Peterson, 1989).

The responses of children in this age group to divorce are distinctly different from those of preschoolers. Seven- to 10-year-olds show developmental differences in perceptual, cognitive, affective, and defensive strategies. Within this age group, several characteristics are common.

Sadness and grieving. Unlike the preschool child, who makes extensive use of denial through fantasy, 7- to 10-year-olds are aware of suffering and manifest pervasive sadness. The intensity of the child's distress does not seem to be associated with the amount of turmoil generated by the parents. Unlike adolescents or adults in mourning, the ego structure of children this age is such that there is less ability to alternate denial with suffering in order to lessen the painful experience over time (Amato, 1987).

The majority of these children express their sorrow directly in counseling interviews. Crying and sobbing are not uncommon, and many children, if not in tears, are on the brink of crying when discussing the divorce with another adult (Bayrakal & Kope, 1990).

Fear of abandonment. Most 7- to 10-year-olds are frightened about their current, unstable family situation and what it means for the future (Milne, Myers, Rosenthal, & Ginsburg, 1986). For most children in this age group, the dissolution of the family makes them worry that their whole world may topple down. Some of these children begin to fear that the custodial parent also will desert them. As a result, they become overly dependent on the remaining parent and unwilling to attend school, often developing psychosomatic illness and school phobia if pressured. One of the most difficult problems for this age group is the inability to understand divorce because of parental secrecy. When parents avoid talking about the subject of their divorce, the children's fears frequently become magnified. Reality is replaced with fantasy and psychological defenses. Further problems develop when the child's fears and anxieties about the divorce are not resolved. Some of the main problems these children encounter are: (a) feeling alone and cheated; (b) hoping the parents remarry; (c) missing their fathers or mothers; (d) blaming their mothers or fathers; and (e) feeling torn between parents (Dail, 1990; Fine, 1986).

Effects on the Adolescent

Several factors have been established as affecting the impact of divorce on an adolescent: (a) dynamics of family relationships prior to divorce, specifically, the degree of conflict pre-existing; (b) the nature of the marital breakup; (c) the relationship of the parents after the divorce; (d) the developmental stage of the youths at the time of divorce; and (e) the strength of personality and coping skills of the adolescent. While younger children experience problems in peer relations, adolescents tend to be more active in dating and sexual relations (Beck, 1988; Demo & Acock, 1988; Fry & Trifiletti, 1983; Kurdek & Sinclair, 1988; Montare & Boone, 1980; Smith, 1990; Steinberg, 1987; Zussman, 1980).

Anger, hostility, and depression are mentioned as common reactions to divorce because some adolescents feel alienated from one or both parental role models, which causes them to push away from the parents. These reactions have resulted in isolation, depression, or running away. Other reactions seen are grief, shame, resentment, phobias, anorexia, and sleeping problems, all accompanied by difficulties with academic schoolwork (Beck, 1988; Roy & Fuqua, 1983). Adolescents in mother-only homes or in conflict-ridden families are more prone to commit delinquent acts such as lying, stealing, dropping out, joining gangs, using drugs, and becoming sexually promiscuous (Brendtro, Brokenleg, & Bockern, 1990; Demo & Acock, 1988; Gannett, 1986; Reinhold, 1988; Zimiles & Lee,

1991). Overall, adolescents are not affected as much by the intactness of a family as by parental discord.

Various other studies, however, indicate a greater incidence of delinquency in children from broken homes than in children from intact families. It is not clear, however, whether divorce is the major contributing factor or whether poverty and lower socioeconomic status are the major contributing factors to delinquent behavior (Demo & Acock, 1988; Gannett, 1986). Nevertheless, we must take into account that in most cases of divorce there is a loss of income and a lowered standard of living. Also, if we consider that the remaining parent, who must work, often has to leave the youth alone, then delinquency as one outcome of divorce is not an illogical effect (Dail, 1990; Reinhold, 1988; Steinberg, 1987).

Single-Parent Home, Mother Only

Real attention to the role of the father in child development takes place only after the father is gone. In terms of academic achievement, Blanchard and Biller (1971) studied third-grade boys with respect to father absence before age 5, father absence after age 5, low father availability, and high father availability. In this study, father absence was largely due to separation and divorce. Academic achievement was rated and indicated that the academic performance of the group with high father availability was very superior to the other groups. The group with early father absence and low father availability functioned below grade level. The groups with high father availability performed consistently above grade level.

So, it may be speculated that highly available fathers afford their sons models of motivation and achievement. In a rare study (Santrock, 1972) that included girls, it was found that girls with an absent father scored lower on achievement tests than did girls with fathers present. Both boys and girls between the ages of birth and 5 years of age seemed to suffer more than children between the ages of 6 and 11, and, boys seemed to be more negatively influenced by a father's absence than girls. However, remarriage of the mother within 5 years of a divorce seems to have a positive influence on children of both genders and all ages (Chiriboga & Catron, 1991; Colletta, 1979; Levy-Shiff, 1982; Reinhold, 1988).

Single-Parent Home, Father Only

Until more recently, children of divorced couples were nearly always placed with the mother; therefore, the focus of past studies has been on paternal absence. One study (Santrock & Warshak, 1979) compared father custody to mother custody in terms of the children's behavior and the support systems of each parent. Boys and girls in both situations were studied, and results showed that girls suffered more adverse effects no matter which parent had custody. Another aspect of this study examined the support system of single fathers who were parents and found that they used relatives, day care, and friends twice as much as mothers who were single parents, and that children who were living with their fathers had significantly more contact with their mothers than children who were living with their mothers had with their fathers. The results of the Santrock and Warshak study (1979) showed that the children who had contact with other adult caretakers were the ones with the more positive emotional and behavioral reactions. Children who had negative reactions were the ones whose parents (father or mother) had fewer support systems, resulting in the children spending less time with other adult caretakers.

Two Mommies, Two Daddies

An estimated 1 out of 10 people in the United States is gay or lesbian. There are approximately 1.5 million lesbian mothers, most of whom had previously been in a heterosexual relationship, who now reside in a family unit with their children (Hoeffer, 1981). The goal for school personnel must be to respond to these parents and their children with the same respect they show other children's families (Clay, 1991). In a time when AIDS has forced schools to tackle such controversial subjects as sexual behavior, homosexuality remains a sensitive and, for the most part, taboo subject. The New York City public school system has in the curriculum a section on homosexuality that is being strongly fought by some parent groups.

Students who have gay or lesbian parents need some special attention. The message that society puts out is that their parents are outcasts. In church, homosexuality may be described as a sin. Some of their parents may have been fired from their jobs for being gay. The children learn that their parents cannot serve in the U.S. Armed Forces unless their sexual orientation is hidden. Although under the Clinton administration in Washington, D.C., this might change, it is, nevertheless, out in front of the children with a great deal of negative criticism. The typical high school can be a very hostile place, and hostility can be found among some teachers and other school personnel (Stover, 1992).

The main question that society has about gay and lesbian parents is what kind of effect the parent's sexuality has on the children. The available research indicates that the parents' sexual and affectional orientation, in itself, has no effect (Clay, 1991; Fox, 1991; Hare & Koepke, 1990; Wyers, 1987). There is no apparent relationship between a parent's sexual and affectional orientation and the sexual identity of the child. Gay and lesbian parents note that second-generation homosexuality is rare and that the parents of most homosexual adults are heterosexual (Clay, 1991; Stover, 1992). There is no evidence of confusion in gender or sexual identity for the child as a result of having one or two gay parents. Studies also show that the overall level of emotional adjustment of children of lesbians is the same as that of children of heterosexual mothers (Clay, 1990; Devlin & Cowan, 1985; Levy, 1992; Powell, 1987). In general, if the child's parents are well-adjusted and open about their homosexuality, there is a good chance the child will be well adjusted.

Not only is there no real evidence of negative outcomes, but a number of positive effects that a child raised by lesbian or gay parents may experience have been noted including: an increased appreciation of cultural diversity; greater ease in being different; more tolerant, accepting, and nonjudgmental views; greater sensitivity to social justice; strength, sensitivity, compassion, independence, and maturity beyond their years; a deep parent–child relationship; and very close family units (Clay, 1991; Hare & Koepke, 1990). Children of lesbian and gay parents are, however, at risk for experiencing greater rejection, isolation, and harassment in their communities. There are a number of things teachers can do to help these children:

- Assist other school personnel in the awareness that gay and lesbian parents exist and need the same respect shown to other parents.
- Use contemporary terminology (e.g., gay/lesbian) the same as would be done for other minorities (e.g., Native American).
- Educate the class about family diversity to ensure a healthy self-identity.
- Mention gay and lesbian family groups in a positive way.
- Alert the gay or lesbian parents if their children are harassed for being from a different kind of family and help the parents develop strategies for preparing their children to cope with harassment.
- Respect the wishes of some parents to maintain secrecy.

- Offer extra encouragement to attend school and classroom social events to those who need it.

- Examine your own values for bias and negative stereotypes that you might project onto the child.

- Normalize the child's experience by pointing out that a family is two or more people who love and take care of each other. When children are ridiculed or questioned about having two mommies or two daddies, use simple statements such as: some kids live with a mother and a father, some with just their mother or just their father, some don't live with a mother or a father but have others who take care of them and love them, and some have two moms or two dads. Families can be different.

Summary of Gender Differences

For some young boys, the loss of the father causes an acute and violent disruption of the process of masculine identification. More dramatic changes have been demonstrated by preschool boys, who seemed extremely vulnerable to gross disruptions of identifications already in progress.

It has been found that the sex-role development of boys whose fathers are present is influenced by the father-son relationship, but for father-absent boys the mother-son relationship assumes critical importance in sex-role development. The mothers of father-absent boys have the potential for either encouraging or discouraging a boy's masculine development. In general, however, there seems to be no significant difference between father-present and father-absent boys in overt masculinity (Biller, 1969; Crumbley & Blumenthal, 1973; Parish, 1981).

In an earlier study, Biller and Borstelmann (1967) believed that there were three aspects of sex-role development: (1) sex-role orientation, which is the perception and evaluation of the masculinity or femininity of the self; (2) sex-role preference, which is the individual's preferential set towards symbols and representations that are socially defined; and (3) sex-role adoption, which is how masculine or feminine the individual's behavior seems to others.

If this line of reasoning is followed regarding masculinity and sex-roles, then although a father-absent boy may have a strong motivation and desire to be with a father figure and to be masculine, such motivation may not be sufficient to promote a masculine orientation or adoption in the absence of a masculine model. When a boy's father is absent in his preschool years, the boy's opportunities to interact with and imitate males in positions of competence and power usually will be severely limited.

The essential task of adolescents is the development of an identity. It is generally understood that identity is established through identification with the parent of the same sex. The main problem seen in boys whose fathers are absent is the manifestation of "excessive masculine" traits, which frequently are expressed through delinquent behavior.

The main problem seen in adolescent girls whose fathers are absent is an inability to respond appropriately in heterosexual relationships. Girls, it appears, either show sexual shyness and anxiety around males or engage in excessive sexual behavior. Other behaviors observed include seeking proximity to and attention from males, early heterosexual behavior, and exaggerated responsiveness and openness to males (Barclay & Cusumano, 1967; Biller & Bahm, 1971; Erikson, 1968; Hetherington & Deur, 1971; Marino & McCowan, 1976; Parish, 1981).

Surprisingly, the results of one study showed that reactions to divorce did not differ significantly between boys and girls (Reinhard, 1977). In this study, when there were negative reactions, the same behavior problems were observed in both sexes. There was no explanation for why this study found results that were different from those in all other studies. Perhaps the study was flawed in some way. On the other hand, it could be that Reinhard had no preconceived notions of gender differences and therefore did not look for artificial ways to distinguish males and females.

ADOPTION AND DIVORCE COMPLICATIONS

Adoption has provided an effective procedure for society to care for children who, for one reason or another, are separated from their biological parents. However, it is increasingly clear that adoptees are more vulnerable than the population at large to the development of identity problems in late adolescence and young adulthood. Divorce occurs not only between biological parents but also between couples who have adopted. This creates some very special types of problems for the adopted children (Bass, 1975; Gallagher, 1971; Grow &

Shapiro, 1975; Katz, 1974; MacIntyre, 1976; Neilson, 1972, 1976; Sorosky, Baran, & Pannor, 1975).

A healthy personality develops when it is supported by continuity between an individual's past experiences and future possibilities. This is a difficult enough process for someone raised by biological parents and even more complex for the adoptee, whose genetic and historical ancestry often is unknown. Adopted children, particularly adolescents, find themselves in an even more precarious position when divorce occurs. The question of "Who am I?" gains momentum when the youth approaches adolescence. This is the time when the teenager becomes intensely and personally concerned with the riddle of life, its beginning and its ending, and its genetic significance (Rogers, 1969; Sorosky et al., 1975).

A high percentage of parents of adopted children seek psychiatric treatment for their children. The research confirms a general condition labeled the "adoption syndrome," which is diffuse in its symptoms but has enough discernible patterns to be identified (Cunningham, Remi, Loftus, & Edwards, 1975; Goodman, Silberstein, & Mandell, 1963; Schecter, 1960; Tec & Gordon, 1967). The following sections describe the most common characteristics of the adoption syndrome. As these factors are discussed the reader should keep in mind what already has been discussed about divorce with the understanding that adopted children under stress of divorce additionally experience these same difficulties.

Disturbances in Early Relationships

The first aspect of this factor is the adopting parents' attitude toward parenting. Emotional disturbances emerge among adopted children when the adoptive parents find it very difficult to express their own feelings about the facts of adoption. Parental difficulties in discussing adoption are related to the parents' fears about their adequacy as parents, to their feelings about their own infertility, and to their feelings about the illegitimacy of the child whom they adopted (McWhinnie, 1967).

The second, and more difficult to resolve, factor is the degree of identification that occurs with children who are not adopted within days of their birth. This critical situation is influenced by the age at adoption and the extent of early maternal deprivation. Children who are adopted after 2 years of age often have experienced hurt and are not aware that their feelings are valid and appropriate. Frequently they become inhibited in normal expressions of pain and anger for fear that the adoptive parents will abandon them or use extreme punishment (Neilson, 1972).

Clearly, then, in the case of a child who has been adopted and whose adopting parents subsequently divorce, these problems become compounded. The parents' feelings of inadequacy solidify, and angry words emerge expressing the need for a partner who can give them a child of their own. The child may become the target of anger and a scapegoat for the divorce, especially if the child has been a problem because of his or her emotional disturbances.

Adopted children usually feel even more guilt over the divorce than do natural children of divorced couples. They become more withdrawn and more fearful. Certainly, the common fear of adopted children—that they will be abandoned or severely punished—is a nightmare come true when the parents do divorce. Not once but twice now, the child has been left by a parent. This experience exacerbates existing feelings of unworthiness (Morgan, 1984).

Unresolved Oedipal Complex

According to psychoanalytic theory, the oedipal stage of psychosocial development eventually leads to emancipation of the adolescent, the resolution of incestuous strivings, the final identification with the parent of the same sex, and the establishment of a stable, growth-productive relationship with the parent of the opposite sex (A. Freud, 1956; Sorosky et al., 1975). When a disturbance occurs during this stage of development, ambivalence lingers beyond the normal termination of this complex. This oedipal period is a time when the child experiences many ambivalent feelings about the parents. Normally during this stage children fantasize a great deal and, when frustrated, imagine better parents who would cherish and love them much more (Schecter, 1960).

It has been suggested that telling children about adoption between the ages of 3 and 6 could affect negatively the outcome of the identification process. When this happens, there are significant occurrences of overt aggression and sexual acting-out behavior, most often directed toward the mother (Offord, Apponte, & Cross, 1969; Schecter, Carlson, Simmons, & Work, 1964; Tec & Gordon, 1967).

If divorce occurs during this developmental stage of the adopted child and if the child knows of the adoption, aggression becomes more intense, fantasies of better parents are stronger, and sexual acting-out behavior is more frequent and more exaggerated (Morgan, 1984).

Fantasies of the Lost, Perfect Parents

Years ago S. Freud (1950) noted that part of a child's normal development is the questioning of natural parentage. Almost all children approach their parents with the question, "Am I adopted?" Freud theorized that this fantasy is abandoned when a child resolves the dilemma of feeling love and hate for the parents.

Adopted children deal with another set of facts—namely, that they do have two sets of parents. This often leads to attributing qualities of good and bad to one or the other set of parents. It is not uncommon to hear adopted children respond to a parent who has just corrected or denied them something they want by saying, "When I find my real mother and real father, I'm going to tell them how mean you are to me." Adopted children who are struggling with this conflict often identify with an imaginary set of parents and demonstrate this by acting in a way that conflicts with the adoptive parents' value system (Offord et al., 1969).

Some emotionally disturbed children perceive their adoptive parents as inadequate and fantasize their natural parents as better qualified to parent. Frequently, these children transfer feelings from their adoptive parents to other significant adults, such as teachers or counselors (Eiduson & Livermore, 1975).

When divorce takes place, adopted children more readily fantasize that their real parents—out there somewhere—are certainly better qualified to be their parents. In a sense, this child is lost among strangers: the biological parents are nowhere to be found, the adoptive parents are separated, and perhaps a new step-adoptive parent enters the picture. In addition, consider the confusion and almost total disorientation if the one original adoptive parent and the new step-adoptive parent decide to divorce. Many times teachers do become parent substitutes. These teachers are viewed by the child as more stable individuals, particularly if they are teachers who have been at the same school for some time. The young child, especially, fantasizes the teacher as the long-lost natural parent.

Need for a Genetic History

As adopted children reach adolescence, their bewilderment concerning their own genetic inheritance and history intensifies as sex and parenthood become part of reality. Children who had never known a parent who had died but who know of the parent through loving and cherished memories passed on by another family member have no problems putting their image and identity into the background. The parent who is alive but not present, who is resented and perhaps feared by the substitute parents, is ever-present in the adolescent's inner life. Apparently, it is much more difficult in adolescence to become liberated from a hidden parent than to become liberated from one who is present (Rogers, 1969). Many adopted youths start roaming around in search of their real parents. When adopted parents divorce, this tendency to go looking for the natural parents is heightened. Most often this is reported as running away, without the understanding that the child is in search and not necessarily in flight (Schecter, 1960; Sorosky et al., 1975).

Adoption Syndrome Causes

The literature on adoption provides many possible causes of disturbance in adoptees. The research emphasizes parent–child relationships, along with genetic and age factors. Following are some of the reasons for emotional disturbance in adopted children, even excluding the compounding problem of divorce.

1. Friction and anger exist between parents for failure to have children of their own.
2. Adoptive parents are subject to extensive scrutiny by agencies and others. They become unable to establish realistic limits for their adopted children.
3. The adopted child, particularly during adolescence, may identify with the "bad" biological parent.
4. Genetic factors may have some influence on the development of disturbance and certain personality types.
5. If the parents view the child as "conceived in sin," this view may exacerbate any tendencies the parents might have to project their own "sinfulness" onto the child.
6. Children adopted at later ages may have experienced varying degrees of abuse and neglect.
7. Adoptive parents may become jealous and feel excluded.
8. Adoptive parents may transfer onto the child any negative and disapproving feelings they may have about the biological parents.
9. The adoptive parents may have fears about the child's inherited traits.

10. Some adoptive parents insist the child show great gratitude, which causes feelings of resentment and rebellion in the child.

11. The extended family can make the child feel like an outsider.

The foregoing reasons for emotional disturbance in children are derived from a number of sources (Bass, 1975; Cary, Lipton, & Myers, 1975; Cunningham et al., 1975; Derdeyn & Scott, 1984; Leahey, 1984; McWhinnie, 1967; Offord et al., 1969; Simon & Senturia, 1966; Tizard & Rees, 1975; Work & Anderson, 1971). Although some basic patterns appear to occur frequently among emotionally disturbed adoptees, it should be stressed that more research is needed, especially among the non-emotionally disturbed adoptees and their adoptive parents. Perhaps the normal adoptee would help provide answers to the problems of adoptees who do not adjust well.

Little attention has been given to adopted children from homes in which divorce occurs. Obviously, the symptoms of adopted children and the symptoms of adopted children from divorced families would be similar but with the latter being much more extreme. In fact, adopted children of divorce face such a complex situation that it warrants a great deal of research, which to date has not been done.

A case study is used here to illustrate the extreme pain and disorientation of a child in cases where the child is adopted, when adoptive parents have divorced and remarried, when the stepparent adopts the child, and when the original adoptive parent and the step-adoptive parent then divorce. This is an actual case, disguised in some ways; however, the facts are not distorted and the disguising of characters does not change the overall picture of this youth who has experienced an extremely painful and confusing existence.

Robin: A Case Study

Robin was adopted and taken home within days of his birth. Both adoptive parents are highly educated professionals in the upper-middle-class income bracket. When Robin was 5, the adoptive parents divorced and Robin lived in the home of his adoptive father and new stepmother. When he was 6, the adoptive father and new stepmother adopted Robin; however, the

Continued

original adoptive mother still had visitation privileges, and Robin frequently spent holidays and part of the summer with his first adoptive mother. When Robin was 9, the original adoptive father and the second adoptive mother divorced. This time Robin's adoptive father did not take custody and the child lived with his second adoptive mother. The second adoptive mother remarried when Robin was 10. The child now had a stepfather. This man did not adopt Robin, and as before the child still spent some time with his first adoptive mother and on occasion would have visitations with his first adoptive father.

When Robin was 12 years old, his second adoptive mother divorced his stepfather, and Robin returned to the home of his first adoptive father, who had married for the third time. Robin now had a stepmother; she did not adopt the child. At this point, Robin has had two adoptive mothers and one stepmother. He also has had three fathers: the original adoptive father, the husband of the second adoptive mother, and the husband of the original adoptive mother, whom he visits on holidays and during the summer.

A history of school difficulties followed Robin as he entered junior high school. The files from elementary school contained teachers' records of chronic misbehavior, excessive absences, and fluctuating grades that ranged from above average to failure. In junior high school he was referred to special education for the same learning and behavior problems noted in elementary school. Robin was placed in a resource room on a half-day basis. His behavior in the special education placement was satisfactory. His teacher (a female) recorded that Robin was pleasant and friendly and made an effort to do his work. However, in his regular classes he would not work, intimidated other students with aggressive behavior, and got into violent conflicts with teachers (primarily male). The assistant principal (a male) decided to take on Robin as a special case. His intent was to become a surrogate father image to Robin; however, in just 2 weeks the assistant principal found himself in constant power struggles with the boy. Robin's resource teacher noted that the assistant principal's style of interaction with the boy had become what could almost be called abusive. This was attributed to the man's feelings of frustration because he had chosen the boy for special time and effort, with unsuccessful results.

Continued

The assistant principal would not give up his involvement with Robin, and he became tougher and more resolved in his efforts to change the boy. Within a month, Robin's absences became more frequent, and when he did come to school he often left as soon as his resource period ended. His adoptive father came for conferences whenever they were requested but appeared to be detached from the situation. During one conference, the father stated in Robin's presence that he had attempted to get the boy's first adoptive mother to take custody of the boy. She had refused because it would interfere too much with her work.

Robin's behavior continued to deteriorate and most of his grades were failure marks. He was in constant trouble at school for fighting, truancy, rude behavior to teachers, tardiness, and neglect of school assignments. A recommendation for therapy was made by the school, and his father sent him to a psychologist. Therapy started just before Christmas but was interrupted during the holiday break when Robin left to spend the vacation with his first adoptive mother.

Robin returned for the first day of school after the Christmas break and was then absent for the following several days. The school finally was notified that, during his absence, Robin had stolen a motorbike and disappeared for 2 days before the police found him. A special meeting was called at the school to arrange another school placement. Robin was placed in another school that had an all-day special class for emotionally disturbed youths. The teacher of this class was male and the composition of the class was all boys. Within 2 weeks, Robin was reported truant; following this, his father reported him missing. Robin left no notes for his father or anyone at school. He took a few of his belongings and ran away. Robin has never been found.

Here is a case in which early intervention in the form of therapy might have helped Robin, but the real tragedy is the school's failure to recognize the boy's needs and to understand his behavior. The assistant principal started with good intentions and might have been able to make a difference in Robin's life. Instead, he found the boy's behavior too threatening and allowed his own ego to control his interactions with the child. Clearly, the man did not understand Robin's conflict and,

Continued

instead of helping, exacerbated the situation by getting into masculine power struggles with the boy.

REACTIONS IN THE SCHOOL SETTING

Pecot (1970) described many of the possible reactions that teachers may see in children whose parents are going through a divorce. If the child has a fear of being abandoned by the remaining parent, the child may be unwilling to leave the parent to attend school. If the child does attend school but internalizes fears of abandonment, then total preoccupation with the possible loss of the remaining parent can result in reduced motivation and loss of interest altogether in school activities. Defense mechanisms such as withdrawal or daydreaming may be used as a method of protection from inner anxieties and insecurities.

A child may attempt to meet dependency needs through his relationship with the teacher, who may become a substitute parent for the child. If the child then becomes overly dependent on a particular teacher, she or he could have difficulty adjusting to a different teacher at the start of the new school year and may be unable to give up the previous close relationship.

The fear of abandonment may raise feelings of hostility in the child toward the parent who left, or even toward the remaining parent, peers, teachers, or other people with whom the child comes in contact. Symptoms of emotional problems seen in school, such as the ones already discussed, may seem bizarre, inconsistent, and confusing to teachers when these children are observed in school without an understanding of their family situation. Many investigations into the effects of divorce on children have found an increase in aggression and acting-out behavior in school (Ellison, 1983; Felner, Strolberg, & Cowen, 1975; Kelly & Wallerstein, 1977; McGord, 1962; Montare & Boone, 1980; Pecot, 1970; Ryker, 1971; Silvern & Yawkey, 1974; Tuckman & Regan, 1966).

The impact of two types of crisis-producing experiences, parental death and divorce, were studied by Felner and associates (1975). The children in the primary grades had been identified through a program for early detection and prevention of school maladaptation. They had been referred by their teachers for behavioral and educational problems, such as acting out or withdrawal, and when evaluated were found to be experiencing greater maladjustment problems. They showed excessive restlessness, obstinate behavior, acting out, disruption of class, and impulsiveness. When children of divorced parents were compared to children experiencing a parent's death, it was found that the children of divorced parents showed elevated acting-out and aggressive patterns, whereas children who experienced a parental death manifested heightened shyness, timidity, and withdrawal. One way this behavior in children of divorced parents has been explained is that it is a reflection of the parents' conflict, and the final act of separation exaggerates such behavior (Birtchnell, 1969).

Children of divorced parents were interviewed by therapists 1 year following the initial separation of their parents. The wide spectrum of responses in children of school age had diminished in intensity, and the intense pain and suffering they had experienced initially had disappeared. In its place, however, was a sad, resigned attitude about the divorce—in contrast to the attitude of much younger children (5-year-olds), who still fantasized about their fathers' return. Older children, realistically although reluctantly, accepted the divorce as final (Kalter & Rembar, 1981; Kelly & Wallerstein, 1977; Leahey, 1984; Parish, 1981).

Strong wishes for parental reconciliation persist in about one third of the boys. This is most often in the context of a continued wish for more contact with the father. Loyalty conflicts are less of an issue 1 year later, even for children whose parents continue to press for allegiance.

Open anger toward the father does not seem to be characteristic of younger children, although for some the capacity to express anger toward the mother increases. Younger children differ from adolescents in that they continue to sustain the appearance and fantasy of a satisfying relationship with their fathers, even when the father is openly rejecting. Adolescents and older children of school age respond to rejection by becoming angry and rejecting the father themselves.

It appears that after 1 year of parental separation, about one half of the children of school age either improve in their general level of psychological functioning or maintain their previous developmental strides. A small percentage seem to maintain the negative reaction that is seen initially. Some children do become significantly worse and deteriorate psychologically (Kurdek, 1981; Leahey, 1984).

It has been documented in several studies that children who are older have a greater ability to master their conflicting feelings about their parents' divorce because they use defenses of denial, courage, increased social activity, and avoidance of home, and because they seek more support from others. In many children there is a noticeable decline in both school performance and the ability to relate to peers. Again, Lisa illustrates these symptoms. Most researchers agree that demanding and aggressive behavior increases in older children of divorced parents because of the lack of disciplinary experience from most mothers. This is a broad generalization, however, that may or may not be true and has not been proved. In terms of low academic achievement, it is thought that the child's education becomes a low priority of the family in the midst of a divorce, with the result that the child receives little attention and recognition for academic achievement (Kalter & Rembar, 1981; Kurdek, 1981; McGord, 1962; Parish, 1981; Pecot, 1970; Tuckman & Regan, 1966). It may also be that the intense emotional upheaval experienced by the child inhibits his or her ability to attend well in school. After all, the cognitive and affective domains are inextricably intertwined.

Older children of school age sense that their custodial parents have become so preoccupied with their own lives and futures that it is as if they emotionally have moved away. This sensed loss of loved ones causes children to feel depressed and lonely, with the result that they overreact to criticisms from other adults such as teachers. Consequently, children may hesitate to participate in class, and efforts to encourage them to participate only threaten some children despite the teachers' genuine desire to be helpful.

Children who decide that they are unlovable or personally unacceptable may transfer some of those feelings to interpersonal relationships with peers as well as adults. They begin to doubt their self-worth, and this combination of a breakdown in self-esteem and a fear of further rejection becomes extremely anxiety-producing. Children who are able to overcome their immediate reactions of fear, shame, and worry are able to become content with their new family, friends, and even stepparents, and they eventually return to their prior levels of academic performance.

MITIGATING NEGATIVE RESULTS AND POTENTIAL POSITIVE OUTCOMES OF DIVORCE

The long-term development of a child need not be affected if the parents maintain a loving and stable relationship with the child and provide positive role modeling. It has been demonstrated that there should be few immediate emotional repercussions if the parents are mature and show concern for each other and the children. Divorce can be a direct cause of emotional disorders, depending on how the adults handle the situation (Birtchnell, 1969; Derdeyn & Scott, 1984; Dominic & Schlesinger, 1980; Hetherington et al., 1979; Kelly & Wallerstein, 1977; Leahey, 1984; Sorosky, 1977; Sugar, 1970; Wallerstein, 1983).

It appears that a good relationship between noncustodial parents and children can transcend the angers and instabilities of the family dissolution. It has been documented that most adolescents wish the parents had not divorced, but the majority feel that the divorce did not lead to rejection by one or both parents, to angry feelings on their part, or to rejection from peers. Nor did most feel that they had to fill an intermediary position or that there was competition between parents.

Some children feel that they benefited from the divorce. Some positive reactions noted are that they feel more mature than their peers and are more sensitive to the feelings of others (Cantor, 1979; Derdeyn & Scott, 1984; Kurdek, 1981; Leahey, 1984; Reinhard, 1977; Rosen, 1977; Wallerstein, 1983).

A number of researchers express the idea that a broken home may be better for the constructive development of the children than one filled with conflict and unhappiness (Grollman & Grollman, 1977; Leahey, 1984; Reinhard, 1977; Rosen, 1977; Sorosky, 1977). Many parents report that they believe they are better at parenting alone than trying to parent amid conflict and strife. In addition, a number of mothers feel that with their new identity as a working or professional woman they are, in general, better-adjusted people and therefore better mothers, and that the quality of time spent with their children is more important than the quantity of time. Since they feel that they are much happier human beings, the quality of the parent–child relationship seems to be greatly improved (Chang & Deinard, 1982; Leahey, 1984; Santrock & Warshak, 1979; Wallerstein & Kelly, 1976).

There is definitely a new kind of parenting evolving in our society, in which the custodial relationship has as its counterpoint parents who are neither absent nor fully present but who maintain a significant presence in the lives of their children. The effect of these new divorce family relationships on the development of children needs further study. A theory that explains the psychology of the part-time parent–child relationship needs to be developed to a much fuller degree.

CONCLUSIONS

The legal event of divorce is not the central factor in determining the outcome for the child; rather, it is the entire divorce process or chain of events set in motion by the initial separation. The assimilation of divorce-related changes is a process that can last several years.

While figures for the incidence of divorce are soaring, there is still conflicting information about the effects on the children. The research available to date is not thorough enough to support conclusions with a high degree of certainty. Too many of the studies are based on opinion and assumption, and they are not always backed by sound research. Another problem is that many studies concern referred adults and children—people who have come to someone with a problem—and we have no real way of knowing whether the problem was caused by the divorce or something else or whether it predated even the marriage. This dilemma gives a distorted picture that may not be typical of the entire population of divorced people.

There are strong indications by many writers that divorce is a traumatic experience for many children but that the degree of trauma depends on many factors that vary in each individual's experience. Factors that need to be considered in determining the impact for each child include the amount of conflict before and after the divorce, the age and developmental stage of the child, the gender of the child, the adjustment of the custodial parent, and the economic situation of the family following the divorce.

Certain behavioral reactions seem to be prevalent in particular age groups. Children of preschool age often are confused by a lack of understanding of what has actually occurred. They often react with regressive behavior or may try to deny the whole thing; however, negative behaviors usually disappear within 2 years. Identification problems seem to occur frequently for a child of this age, especially for boys when the father is absent.

The available evidence indicates that for children of school age divorce is a particularly difficult experience because they cannot use denial as well as younger children and, at the same time, have not developed the coping skills that older youths have developed. Problems of guilt, anxiety, and fear of abandonment are common for a child of this age.

In adolescents there may be anger, hostility, depression, academic problems, and sometimes delinquent behavior. Serious problems occur for some adolescents, including a fear of abandonment or rejection, an intensity in adolescent conflicts, and a fear of personal commitments that may result in their own marital failure.

Evidently, boys have greater problems due to divorce than girls, mainly because the typical situation involves custody by the mother and the absence of the father, resulting in the boy's loss of a male model. Girls, however, may have difficulty relating to boys during their adolescence if the father is absent from the home. And yet a number of studies concerning adolescents indicate that there are limited negative effects from divorce.

Most studies assume that a stressful marriage precipitated the divorce. We are more aware now that this is not necessarily the case. In our present society, general acceptance and liberalized divorce laws make divorce much easier. Value differences, unrealistic expectations, "mid-life crises," and a number of other factors can interact to create situations in which people feel the need to divorce.

If great stress and conflict exist in the home, a divorce may be the best solution for the continuing development of the child. However, the assumption cannot be made that the child's family life will necessarily be better after a divorce. There will be new pressures and problems for the single parent and the child to cope with, and most likely greater financial difficulties will exist.

Adopted children whose parents are divorcing (a much-neglected area in the literature) seem to have an even more difficult time coping with their situation. They need to cope with the usual problems of adoptees and the usual problems of divorced children, but the two unique sets of problems are there in combination, each set exacerbating the other.

The feelings of the children surrounding the divorce experience need to be brought out into the open and discussed, enabling the children to move beyond the strife and stress much more rapidly. Most children need some help in dealing constructively with their feelings. Professionals in the schools must become more knowledgeable of the issues involved so that they can provide appropriate help where needed rather than add to an already painful and difficult situation, thereby compounding the problems facing the children. Although it is undoubtedly impossible for us, as professionals, to prevent some initial conflict and suffering, our challenge is to minimize wherever possible reactions that result in long-term and long-range effects. From conflict can come change, and that may lead to positive outcomes.

Adjustment to divorce is possible, but it takes time. With the high incidence of divorce, new means of support are necessary. Substitute adult models are needed, along with support from relatives and friends. Counseling may be necessary or at least beneficial;

counseling and support groups are available for adults but still noticeably lacking for children. Innovative new ways are needed to help the children beyond divorce. At the very least, some of that innovation can take place in the schools. As a small example, teachers can modify their language to include different types of families (e.g., the single-parent family). Textbooks need to be revised to make the same accommodations. Counselors can advise other professionals in the school of a child's family status so that insensitive remarks are not made (e.g., "Be sure both your parents come; I want to talk to your father about this").

Most children of divorced parents report that they wish someone at school had asked how they felt about the divorce and discussed it with them, as well as given them something to read on the subject (Hammond, 1979). This seems a small thing to ask from school professionals but, as seen in Lisa's story, we are not really there yet. Some people are working on these issues now in the hope that future children will be able to find more help and information than those presently going through the experience.

Teachers and counselors note a significant response or change in behavior in school in more than half of the children whose parents have divorced. Many investigations into the effects of divorce on children have found an increase in aggression and acting-out behavior, and lower academic functioning. Although researchers have found severe emotional problems in children of divorced parents, it is important to know that the children most affected were the ones who were the least well adjusted prior to the divorce. Often there are behavior changes at school but not necessarily at home. The research shows that the natural development of the school-age child and adolescent becomes less dependent on the functioning of the custodial parent than it does for the preschool child. This provides evidence that school often becomes a source of support and gratification, especially if the child can substitute people in the schools as important adult figures (Chiriboga & Catron, 1991; Colletta, 1979; Dail, 1990; Demo & Acock, 1988; Kalter & Rembar, 1981; Kurdek, 1981; Morgan, 1985; Roy & Fuqua, 1983; Zimiles & Lee, 1991). New ways are needed to help children beyond divorce, and this can take place in the classroom. Teachers can modify their language to include different types of families (e.g., the single-parent family; the gay or lesbian family) and to take care to be accepting of nontraditional families. Forms should be developed that ask for "Parents' Names" rather than "Mother's Name/Father's Name." Textbooks must be selected that make the same accommodations. There also are books available for children who have gay or lesbian parents that can be found in most large bookstores. Some libraries are now carrying these books; however, because the issue is still negatively charged to some people, there are communities that want these books removed and burned.

The Loss of a Significant Person

Geneva

"Why aren't they home yet? It's 'bout 4 o'clock. Pappy said he was jest goin' to get her and bring her home—it's been hours. She's been in the hospital long enough. Why is it takin' so long?"

Geneva was almost pleading with her grandmother to make her mother appear. She was feeling sad, lonely, and scared again, the way she did when her mother first left for the hospital.

"Be patient, darlin'. They have things they hast to do before the hospital will let your mamma come home. Lots of business to take care of—talk to the doctors, pay the bills, and such. I'm sure your mamma is getting all prettied up before she comes home to see you. You know how your mamma takes pride in lookin' pretty for her family. I know she is anxious to see her baby—just as anxious as you are, honey, but she wants you to see her lookin' real pretty. She's probably fussing in front of the mirror—just so you'll see her at her very best.

"When she gets home, now, you mustn't bother your mamma too much—she'll need to rest and relax. Mamma's not completely well yet, you know. Doctors said this is just a trial—needs to see if she can get along okay at home. She had a bad accident—fallin' down those stairs and hittin' her head so hard. Mamma won't be up to any nonsense either, Genny. It would make her very sad to hear how things been going in school. She wants to be proud of you, baby. So you going to have to be a real good girl—do your work, no more bad grades, and no more complaints from the teachers 'bout not behaving in school—daydreaming and doing just the opposite of what your teachers say. Be good like you were before Mamma went to the hospital. I don't know why you've been behavin' like this when your mamma's been so sick. We have to be strong together for her. You needs to be a big, strong girl. Why don't you go brush your hair so Mamma will see you lookin' real pretty like her?"

Geneva thought about what her grandmother had just said and remembered how she always thought her mamma was the most beautiful lady in the whole world—with just a hint of red to her hair, green eyes, freckles, and beautiful skin. She wished she looked more like her mamma—with lighter skin. Her pappy used to say Mamma's skin looked like the color of coffee with cream in it. Geneva wished she was not so dark and that her hair was more like her mamma's, not like Pappy and Grandma Bertha—skin so dark and hair so black and kinky.

She wondered what Mamma would bring her when she got home. Her mamma always remembered to bring her some little thing when she went away to go visiting or even when she just went shopping without Genny. She thought about how sweet her mamma was. Her voice was like music, always soft and happy. She would come back from some place and act like it had been years since she had seen her daughter—even when it had only been a few hours or so. She would give Genny big hugs and kisses and some memento—a pretty flower, a bag of candy, once a beautiful little pin for her dress. Genny's mamma would help her with her homework; they would joke and laugh and sing and dance together. Ella would tell her daughter how beautiful she was—she did not have to look like Mamma; she was beautiful in her own way—and a lot like her pappy. Ella thought Pappy was the most handsome man—very tall, dark and strong looking. Her mamma said her hair was beautiful like Pappy's, jet black—they looked like African royalty. Genny should be proud. She always knew how to make Genny feel good—like she was the most important person in her mother's world. She would tell her daughter she could become anything in the whole world she wanted—a doctor, a movie star, a singer, whatever she wanted.

"Oh, Mamma, how I've missed you!"

Those words slipped out of Genny's mouth as she heard the key turn the lock on the front door.

"They're home! Grandma Bertha, they're home! Mamma's home!"

Genny ran from the kitchen to greet her mother at the door. She would hug her tight. She would hear Mamma's sweet voice again and feel her soft hands hold her face and caress and stroke her hair. Everything would be good again. She would be so good for Mamma—do well in school like Mamma wants, wouldn't be so forgetful. All she had been able to think of was Mamma. School wasn't too important with Mamma gone. She thought about her all the time and just couldn't pay attention to her studies. But now it would be just like before. Everything would be all right again.

"Oh, Mamma, my beautiful mamma! I'm so glad you're home!" Genny cried out as the door opened.

Pappy came in alone. Something was terribly wrong. Pappy looked like an old man—ashen, not black and tall and strong like an African king. His eyes passed over Genny in search of his mother, Grandma Bertha.

"Where's Mamma? Why isn't she with you? Why didn't you bring her back from the hospital? Is she in the car? When is she coming home? Pappy, where's Mamma?"

Grandma Bertha came out of the kitchen, looked at her son, and knew the worst had happened.

"Come to Grandma, Genny baby. Your mamma won't be comin' home, baby. Mamma's with Jesus. She's well and happy now, not sick anymore. Mamma went to a much better place. Remember church and the preacher talkin' 'bout heaven? Mamma's gone to heaven. She's an angel now, sweet baby. Here, here, let Grandma hold you. We'll go make some hot chocolate. Pappy needs to be alone for a bit. Grandma's gonna take care of you, dar-lin'. You don't have to worry."

"I want Mamma here—not with Jesus! Why can't Mamma be here, not in heaven! I want to see Mamma! Oh, Mamma! Oh, Mamma, come home! Please come home! I miss you, Mamma. Mamma, Mamma, Mamma."

....

Geneva's story is obvious. The purpose is to get us in touch with the child's feelings: feelings of loneliness, missing her mother, anxiety, and finally the terror of realizing that this dear loved one will never return. The story also illustrates one common way families will deal with a young child whose parent dies. It is not meant to be a negative example. On the contrary, the grandmother is sweet, caring, and sensitive to the child. She uses their religion to comfort Geneva, which in this family is quite appropriate.

The father's reaction is typical and also is not intended to imply he is a bad or uncaring father. He is simply human, overcome for the time being with his own grief. It is fortunate, actually, that at this moment in time Geneva has her grandmother, who has a belief system that provides help and comfort.

Although the continued absence of one or both parents through separation and divorce is considered a loss, the material in this chapter is separated because the content focuses on losses considered to create greater or more severe family disturbances that could impact a child over a lifetime. The content covers different types of losses that a child might experience: (a) the loss of a parent through death and through mental illness, (b) the loss of a sibling, and (c) the loss of a friend or classmate.

The literature pertaining to the effects that the death of a parent has on a child is bountiful; however, the research on the effects of the death of a sibling is more limited, and research that focuses on the effects on a child when a friend or a classmate (acquaintance) dies is almost nil. In this society, our attitudes about what children should be or are capable of being concerned with are extremely narrow. It is uncertain whether the adult position of avoiding the topic of death around children is because they do not understand children and think children are incapable of understanding; because they wish to protect children from pain and unhappiness; because the subject of death, the death of anyone, which is even frightening to some adults, would be much too terrifying for a child; or because of any combination of these reasons.

The first part of this chapter focuses mainly on the death of a parent; however, there is another way a child can experience the loss of a parent—namely, through long-term or lifelong mental illness. The loss of a parent through mental illness is an area that has not received much attention in the literature. The focus of most of this type of research has been to investigate whether offspring of mentally ill parents are themselves mentally ill. In other words, the effort of most researchers is to attempt to prove some type of inheritable factor in mental illness. Few researchers have just looked at what a child goes through when a parent has a mental breakdown and when the process of the mental illness takes a long-term or lifelong course. There is less emphasis on the possibility that emotional problems in children are a result of living in an environment with a parent who is unpredictable, incoherent, and emotionally unavailable. The vignette and case information will, it is hoped, at least give some insights into how children are affected and how some react to such situations.

In terms of losses, the first focus of this chapter is on the loss of a parent through death and the second on loss of a parent through mental illness. Finally, we examine the effects of the loss of siblings, friends, and classmates.

To start this chapter it is necessary to look at how and what children think about death in general.

ATTITUDES ABOUT DEATH

As professionals in the schools, we see our major role as that of preparing young people for life. Since every person who is born also must die, it is reasonable to consider that the continuation of our role is to instruct children that death is an integral part of the life cycle. In the United States today, many parents talk openly with their children about sexuality, childbirth, and biological processes attending the beginning of life, but these same parents have difficulty discussing the end of the life cycle. Death is dispersed throughout our lives on a daily basis and yet death is not part of the curriculum in our schools.

It may sound strange to speak of death as part of the school curriculum; however, long ago the McGuffey Fifth Eclectic Reader included many poems referring to death and dying and was one of the books commonly used to educate children in the early part of this century. Children then were more aware that death is the natural end to life (Fredlund, 1977).

During the first 2 decades of this century, most deaths occurred in the home, as did almost all births. Children in the home were exposed to conversations about death and illness and, in fact, even helped to care for the dying and terminally ill members of their families. Since medical technology was not as advanced as it is now, many children died of communicable diseases, and mothers frequently died in childbirth. As our society became more sophisticated, real experiences with death were taken out of the home. The ill and dying are now removed to hospitals or institutions. Medical technology has advanced to the point where we can now prevent most of the childhood diseases that formerly ended life at an early age, and rarely anymore do women die in childbirth. As a consequence, death and dying have become hushed-up topics not to be discussed, especially in front of children.

Our children are protected by adults from unpleasant situations, and most mothers try not to mention to their children that a friend or relative has a serious terminal illness. For the most part, children are exposed to death as something violent that happens on television or in the movies. It really is not uncommon for parents to allow children to watch the most violent and grisly show and then tell them it is only a story and the people did not really die. Consequently, many children grow to believe that death is rarely an occurrence in real life (Palombo, 1981).

Since the late 1960s, our culture has been placing more emphasis on people's feelings about life and death. As a result of the work of Elisabeth Kübler-Ross, physicians, counselors, psychologists, nurses, clergymen, and teachers have opened up the forbidden topic of death. Now people are beginning to realize that by denying that death exists, we are denying a part of the life cycle (Delisle & McNamee, 1981; Kübler-Ross, 1969).

At times children are faced with situations that may traumatically influence their lives. The death of a significant other is considered a crisis that affects a child emotionally in home and school life.

How a child reacts to the death of a significant other largely could be determined by the concept of death that is prevalent at that time.

Child's Conceptualization of Death

Research reveals that a child's acquisition of a concept of death proceeds through developmental levels, with certain identifiable beliefs occurring at different age levels. Certain factors were found, however, that need to be considered when talking about a concept of death and its development. One factor involves the question of what a mature or ideal conception of death is; it cannot be assumed that there is an obvious developmental goal.

Other general factors that need to be considered when looking at the development of a child's death concept is that the concept is very complex and not always an obvious result of certain variables. Concepts of death change, even at the adult level, when supposedly a concept has been formulated. Concepts of death are influenced by the situational context, leading to possibly different actions or behavior.

In gathering information about the concept of death, there are difficulties as well in assessing or determining these concepts. The methods of acquiring this information are inexact and vary from one report to another. Gathering information directly from children has difficulties inherent in the subject itself. That is, does a fear of death possibly color what a child is willing to report? At what age can a child verbalize feelings or beliefs? In interviews with adults, does the retrospective view give reliable information? Case studies that center on adults suffering from pathological behavior may find that the death of a significant person occurred in their lives and that this caused certain morbid reactions. In these cases, how many other events—situational, personal, and psychological—are operating that affect responses?

This is a complex issue, but general information has been obtained on what children think of death and how it can affect them, as well as what behaviors we as professionals can attempt to anticipate and help alleviate.

Concepts at Different Ages

Usually an understanding of death follows an orderly sequence from total unawareness to a logical consideration of death (Delisle & McNamee, 1981; Fredlund, 1977). Kastenbaum and Aisenberg

(1972) studied the work of Nagy, who in 1948 was one of the first psychologists to deal with children and the development of the concept of death. Nagy identified discrete states of thought that occurred in a particular sequence. Since that time others have studied how children think about death, and Nagy's states or stages have not really changed, although they have been embellished (Kastenbaum & Aisenberg, 1972). Rather than being a discussion of states, the information that follows is a compilation of understandings of how children in different age groups conceptualize death.

From birth to age 2 it is believed that the child has no concept of death; he or she may experience grief due to separation but has no realization of finality (Fredlund, 1977). Some still question whether the very young child (from birth to age 2) has a concept of death; it would appear from most studies that until age 2 the child does not. On the other hand, Kastenbaum and Aisenberg (1972) took the position that much experience and behavior relevant to death takes place during infancy and early childhood. They believed that the child may not have high-level thought operations but that death-related perceptions can exist and may be important predecessors to subsequent concepts. It is very difficult to discover how a child's ideas of death develop or what meaning a child attaches to death at a very early age. However, as children reach the ages of 2, 3, and 4, they often are able to verbalize enough about death that certain unifying traits of thought can be observed and seen to change in a rather predictable manner.

Three- to 5-year-olds generally deny death as a regular and final process; they see death as being like sleep—you are dead and then you come alive again. It is not uncommon for children to bury a pet or a dead bird they have found and later return to the grave site to see if it has come to life. At these ages there is a close relationship between death and departure, or separation. At this level, death is seen as a nonpermanent state that possesses characteristics similar to life, with no concept of universality or physiological cessation. Children may ask, "Where did he go? When will he come back?" In general, they see death as something that happens to older people, not to children, and particularly not to themselves (Delisle & McNamee, 1981; Palombo, 1981; Valente, Saunders, & Street, 1988).

A developmental sequence can be noted in what children see as the cause of death. Beauchamp (1974) found that 5-year-olds differed significantly from 3-year-olds in their perceptions of the causes of death. The 3-year-olds suggested such causes as naughtiness, anger, and wishful thinking. In retrospect, an adult recalled that as a young child her horse had stepped on her foot and she had become very angry and had wished the animal dead. When the horse died, this woman remembers believing for years that she had caused it to happen by wishing the horse dead. (She also felt guilty about the incident during those years.)

Five-year-olds, who viewed death as universal and irreversible, suggested realistic causes of death. Swain (1976) found that 5- to 7-year-olds were equivalent to 2- to 4-year-olds in their emphasis on the accidental and punishing nature of death. Others found that 4- to 9-year-olds considered death primarily to be caused by violence, hostility, illness, and accidents (Meyer, 1975; Steiner, 1966).

Between the ages of 5 and 9, children can accept the idea that someone has died, but they may not accept it as something that must happen to everyone, particularly to themselves. Some studies found that children in this middle group did see death as inevitable, although not personally relevant or applicable. Children tend to personify death in two ways: death is a person who makes people die, or death is a dead person. Children associate death with violence; it can happen to anyone but it happens mostly to the elderly. Around age 9, they become very morbid and frightened about death and begin to ask such questions as, "Mommy, will you die?" (Beauchamp, 1974; Hansen, 1973; Swain, 1976).

During the ages of 9 to 12, children recognize death as an inevitable experience that will happen even to the self. It can happen at any age; no one is immune. They have made the transition in both mental development and emotional security and can express an understanding of death as final and inevitable. However, this is still a very anxious period, and children sometimes deal with their anxiety through the façade of joking (Palombo, 1981; Swain, 1976).

In adolescence, youths become defiant about death. They feel immunity and almost dare death to happen to them. This explains in part why teenagers do some of the outrageous things they do, like playing "chicken" (racing two cars head-on at each other—the first to veer off is chicken) and attempting feats of bravery or skill in areas in which they have no experience or expertise. Apparently, by the mid-teens there is a key change, when the concepts expressed appear to become more abstract and, at the same time, more personally real (Swain, 1976).

Others have looked at the development of the concept of death and found that with children there is a progression of stages of thought, with some variability in the age at which a stage is reached. The greatest change appears to take place about the time when children enter school and begin demonstrating concepts that are similar to those held by other children, exhibiting less thinking along the lines of magic and a greater reliance on biological and social reality (Beauchamp, 1974; Hansen, 1973; Steiner, 1966; Swain, 1976).

Studies examining the development of the concept of death have found that age is the significant variable in this process of development. Socioeconomic level, sex, level of parenting education, degree of religious influence, ethnic origin, and even a death in the family and discussion of death in families were not significant variables in the developmental stages of a child's thinking about death (Beachump, 1974; Fallon, 1976; McIntire, Angel, & Strumpler, 1972; Melear, 1972; Mosley, 1974; Palombo, 1981; Peck, 1966; Swain, 1976).

In general, it can be seen that the causes of death take on qualities of magic, fantasy, and violence among young children who have not reached the developmental stage of seeing death as final, universal, and inevitable. As this concept develops, the perceived causes of death become more realistic. It may also be that the added experience with the causes of death provides help for the child in developing more advanced concepts of death.

Another aspect of children's concepts of death, and one that can affect their responses to the loss of a loved one, is their level of fear and anxiety. It should be noted, however, that fear of death and fear of the act of dying can be distinct issues. The fear of the act of dying is mainly associated with a particular way of dying. The fear of death (nonexistence, meaninglessness of life) is, for children, the basic dread of separation (Mitchell, 1967; Terestman, 1980).

Some studies of the development of the concept of death found that fear of death decreased as the child's concept of death matured (Anthony, 1972; Beauchamp, 1974). Other authors, however, differed with this idea and found that anxiety about death appeared more often in those who considered death to be final and universal (Alexander & Alderstein, 1958; Delisle & McNamee, 1981; Fallon, 1976; Melear, 1972; Terestman, 1980). Another factor that also may cause oscillations in anxiety and fear of death is the development of the religious theme of immortality and the age at which this belief is professed or studied and considered (Palombo, 1981).

LOSS OF A PARENT THROUGH DEATH

A child's reactions are somewhat different when a parent dies than when a sibling dies. This section will be concerned with the emotional responses to the death of a parent or a parent figure.

When a parent dies, external events impinge on the child's personality in three main ways. First, the child must deal with the reality of the death itself. Second, he or she must adapt to the resulting changes in the family. Finally, the child must contend with the perpetual absence of the lost loved one (Felner, Ginter, Boike, & Cowan, 1981; Moriarty, 1967; Raphael, Cubis, Dunne, Lewin, & Kelly, 1990; Tennant, Bebbington, & Hurry, 1980; Van Eerdewegh, Bieri, Parrilla, & Clayton, 1982).

Some responses include guilt, regression to an earlier stage of development, denial, bodily distress, hostile reactions to the deceased, hostile reactions to others, replacement attempts, assumption of mannerisms of the deceased, idealization, eating disorders, enuresis, discipline problems, sleep disturbances, learning difficulties, aggression, withdrawal, anxiety, and panic (Anthony, 1972; Elizur & Kaffman, 1983; Grollman, 1974; Kastenbaum & Aisenberg, 1972; Long, 1983; Moriarty, 1967; Solkoff, 1981; Van Eerdewegh et al., 1982).

The reaction of guilt is probably experienced at all ages from childhood through adulthood, but it can be very preoccupying and devastating to the young child. In the minds of young children, bad things happen because they are naughty, and therefore, they must have done something to make the parent desert them. They may feel guilty because they had hostile feelings toward the dead person and consequently feel responsible for the person's death. Because very young children believe in magic and fantasy, it is likely that they may latch onto unrealistic reasons for the death and feel unreasonable guilt with associated anxiety (Elizur & Kaffman, 1983; Solkoff, 1981).

When the child regresses to an earlier stage of development, the communication could be "I am still a baby and need you, so you shouldn't leave me." The denial reaction may be expressed openly, but it also can take the form of silence or the appearance of being unaffected (If I go on as usual then it isn't so). In bodily distress reactions, anxiety appears in the form of physical or emotional symptoms, such as tightness of the throat and loss of appetite.

Children may exhibit hostile reactions to both the deceased and others. They show anger because they feel unjustly deserted by the deceased and often turn their anger toward the doctor or toward God in an attempt to deal with guilt.

Children often idealize the dead parent in order to quell their own unhappy thoughts. Usually the characteristics they attribute to the dead parent are most unrealistic. This is not an entirely negative reaction, however, since identification is an unconscious process that can be constructive. The development of certain identifications that become independent of the person's death, such as the acquisition of hobbies or interests that were characteristic of the deceased, should be encouraged and overtly recognized as a sign of a child's love for the dead parent.

Literally trying to take the place of the dead person is recognized as harmful and something that should be discouraged. Youths may show anxiety in the process of unrealistic identification, taking on the symptoms that the dead person showed during the illness. This happens when some children become panicked about who will provide food and care.

These are only some of the possible reactions to the death of a parent. They may not all occur and they may occur at different levels of intensity in some children. Outward symptoms that also might appear are unsociability, obvious despondence, apparent lack of concern, lack of attention or interest in class, and a degree of forgetfulness about ordinary concerns (Elizur & Kaffman, 1983; Long, 1983; Van Eerdewegh et al., 1982).

Since the responses can vary in intensity, it is more important to attend to the variety and degree of the responses and their persistence, which are more indicative of a pathological reaction. How traumatic the death of a parent can be for a child is inconclusive in the literature. The extent of the trauma also depends on whether you read psychiatric or sociological literature, and even between these there is disagreement. Within the disciplines, the opinions on extent of impact can run the gamut from the extremely pessimistic to the optimistic (Bendiksen & Fulton, 1976; Birtchnell, 1969; Tennant et al., 1980).

The important roles separation and separation anxiety play in the development of the concept of death and the fear of death makes it likely that these factors are at work when a parent actually dies. The process of achieving independence in psychosexual development involves a whole series of separations in normal upbringing, and the way in which these earlier separations have been accomplished affects the resolution of separation trauma produced by parental death (Crase & Crase, 1989; Solkoff, 1981).

The normal process of acquiring sexual identification may be impaired by a parent's death in the same ways suggested in the literature on divorce (S. Freud, 1950). The effects of a death on the family equilibrium might be indicated by a difficult or imperfectly accomplished breaking away from the family. It is not unusual for sibling rivalry to become very intense and very disruptive. Extreme family turmoil and delinquency have been cited as some of the results of the death of a parent, especially when the parent who died was the controlling person in the family (Kliman, 1968; Shoor & Speed, 1963; Solkoff, 1981; Van Eerdewegh et al., 1982).

The age at which the death of the parent takes place and the sex of the deceased parent can be related to pathological behaviors or reactions in the child. In the early years, the most severe type of bereavement is loss of the mother. Apparently, maternal loss before the age of 8 can become a sensitizing factor in the development of psychoneurotic illness. In addition, unless mother loss is dealt with by adequate mother substitution, it can lead to pathological changes in personality development. A reaction noted in some boys is that, in later life, they may feel that all women have a tendency to hurt men and abandon them, with the result that they do not develop lasting, loving relationships (Grollman, 1974; Mitchell, 1967; Pattison, 1976, 1977; Solkoff, 1981).

Regarding paternal loss, Pattison (1977) found that, in the case of a boy, the loss of a father is significant because of the loss of a male person to imitate, someone with whom he could learn to temper his feelings of love and aggression. There appears to be more delinquency as a result of paternal loss (as in divorce), particularly if the death occurs between the ages of 5 and 14 (Elizur & Kaffman, 1983; Kliman, 1968; Mitchell, 1967).

Evidence is increasing that father deprivation may cause personality disturbances in a society that is based on the nuclear family, as opposed to the extended family of the past (Mitchell, 1967). Much more work along these lines needs to be done, especially in the context of our society, which is showing an increase in broken homes. Also, cultural differences need a great deal of attention, since there are minority groups in the United States in which the extended family is still very much intact and very powerful (Crase & Crase, 1989; Handford, Mattison, Humphrey, & McLaughlin, 1986; Raphael et al., 1990).

One important study (Long, 1983) does address the issue of cultural differences and the extended family with one group of Native American children. This study, well worth reading, points to the need for more research of this type. Basically, this study found that because the extended family concept is still intact among the Crow Indians, their children actually suffer traumatic, multiple family losses more frequently than does the population at large. These children are rarely abandoned, sent to foster care, or adopted by strangers; nevertheless, they suffer from the same symptoms of emotional disturbance that have already been mentioned.

Although there does not appear to be conclusive information on the ages at which the death of a parent becomes most significant, it is assumed that the most vulnerable are very young children (because of separation problems) and pre-adolescents (because of sexual identification problems). Several studies show that separation by death is not especially predictive of mental disorders later in life. It is noted that childhood bereavement is a serious personal crisis that can have serious consequences; however, there appears to be a normalizing effect over time. In a number of cases there are indications that separation by divorce can be more traumatic than separation by death (Anthony, 1972; Bendiksen & Fulton, 1976; Birtchnell, 1969; Furman, 1974; Grayson, 1967; Kliman, 1968; Tennant et al., 1980).

Not only is there disagreement about how traumatic the death of a significant figure can be for a child, there is even some evidence that the response can be favorable for some. Hofling and Joy (1974) found in some cases that if there was a neurotic relationship of considerable adversity or a situation fraught with guilt for various reasons, the individual could respond with improved mental health. This research was done with adults, however, and may not be directly applicable to children. In all cases, the age of the child and the relationship with the parent at the time of the death appear to be the most significant factors. To date, there is little research indicating any real positive effects on children when a significant figure dies or is lost to the child in some other way (Orbach, Gross, Glaubman, & Berman, 1985).

Children also may suffer parental loss through abandonment. How this affects children was shown in the previous chapter in the section on adoption and is addressed also in the next chapter on child abuse.

Danny

THE MARTIANS ARE COMING! THE MARTIANS ARE COMING! MARTIAN ATTACK! SMALL PEOPLE FALL FROM THE SKY! KIDS ARE DYING EVERY-WHERE! Danny put down his pencil; the drawing was complete. It was supposed to be like the pictures and headlines for the front page of a newspaper. He got up from the table and casually dropped the picture in his aunt's lap. He didn't really seem pleased with the drawing, and he didn't wait around to see what Aunt Carol thought of the picture. Without a word, he grabbed his jacket and went out the door.

Carol could see him from the kitchen window. He jumped on his bike and pedaled up the street like demons were on his tail; he was out of sight in less than a minute.

There had been so much confusion in the house that Carol had not had a minute to attend to Danny. Usually she took great interest in her nephew's drawings—sat with him while he drew and commented on how good the pictures were. Carol thought that Danny had some real talent for artwork.

Today was different, though, and no one seemed to notice the total chaos but Carol. She sat at the dining room table regretting the long trip she had made to visit the family and wondered to herself, "What in the hell is going on here?"

Carol looked around the room to try to take it all in and make some sense of what was going on. It looks like someone's nightmare in a scene from one of those obscure European movies, she thought. Some of the characters were moving in fast motion, others in slow motion: Jabbering that doesn't make sense. Talking that, in and of itself, is understandable, but doesn't fit the conversation. Conversation! Good God—this isn't conversation! I don't know what it is, but it isn't conversation!" She tried to listen to what everyone was saying; no one was really talking to Carol.

Her mother, Mrs. Williams, was nagging her sister Barb.

"Why don't you comb your hair? Put on some makeup. Land, you look a sight! Aren't you going to eat something? I worked all morning on this so you could all have a nice meal. Here, Barb, take mine. I've hardly touched the meat. I made the chicken for you. I thought you didn't like ham or I wouldn't have taken the last piece. You want it? Take it. You really ought to eat something. When was the last time you ate something? What was it—what did you have? Nothing good, I bet. Stuff from the drive-in. That isn't real meat they use, you know. Has filler in it. I read somewhere they use kangaroo. Can you imagine! Those places have dirty kitchens, too—roaches and rats running the place at night, leaving droppings. Then they come in the mornings and cook on those grills and use the utensils—Lord! Listen, Barb, you shouldn't let the kids eat there. See how spoiled they are on that awful stuff. Now they won't eat this good food I've fixed for you all either."

Mrs. Williams continued on about the food; it seemed she couldn't get her mind off it and talk about something else or really attend to what was going on.

Danny came in the door, sweating and all red in the face from riding his bicycle so hard in the heat. He sat next to his Aunt Carol and studied her face, looking for an answer. He said nothing, but Carol could sense that he wanted to ask her what was going on—what was wrong with his mother, why was everybody so frantic and crazy? She looked at her nephew and he smiled a bit. That isn't a real smile. It's more of a nervous twitch—the boy looks terrified, she thought.

Carol took another glimpse around the room at the family activity. Her little niece, Annie, was off in the corner alone, rocking and singing nursery rhymes. Jason, the 4-year-old, was draped across his mother's lap, kicking, screaming, and beating her across the breasts. He wanted something from her but amid the baby talk, screaming, and choking tears it was impossible to understand what he was trying to say.

Carol's sister Barb was sitting straight up in the chair with a blank expression, unaware that Jason was all over her, not hearing her mother's nagging about the food, unconcerned about and not noticing anything going on around her. She was having her own conversation. Carol tried to follow what Barb was saying.

With a faraway look and in an excited voice, Barb said, "It's really beautiful how it works between us, you know what I mean? People don't understand—Larry and I communicate without talking—Right now, he's talking to me—I mean I never knew what love was before—He just looks at me—People are so mean, especially women—I hate women—They talk about you behind your back, laugh at you and everything—You know what I mean—All this time I never had any feelings, and now I feel everything—He can read my mind, and I can read his—He just looks at me and I know what I'm supposed to do—I want to be with him all the time and he wants to be with me—He makes me so mad! I'm going to stop seeing him—I tried to stop seeing him once but he told me with his mind that I should come to see him—I can't stop myself—He really treats me like dirt but when I'm with him I know I'm beautiful—You just don't know how hard it is to find someone who really loves you—Rick always treated me like nothing—That's why I had to divorce him—I couldn't feel anything—I was dead. Did you know I died once? You don't believe me, but I was dead. Rick never talked to me—could read my mind like Larry."

Carol interrupted, "Who is Larry?"

Barb did not answer; she continued with her own monologue.

Carol turned to her mother. "Who is Larry?"

Danny spoke before his grandmother could answer. "He's Mom's counselor."

"How long has this been going on?" Carol tried to get answers from her mother again. "What does Danny mean, counselor? Is he a doctor? A psychiatrist? A psychologist? Or what?"

Mrs. Williams looked bewildered. She spoke hesitantly, "I don't know. Danny, take this trash out for Grandma, will you, hon."

Danny didn't budge. He wanted to be in on this conversation, thinking that maybe now things were going someplace. Aunt Carol would get some answers and straighten everything out.

"Danny, I asked you to take out the trash. Be a good boy now and help Grandma."

"Shit! Why do I have to do everything around here!" Danny slammed out of the house without the trash. Carol could see him take off up the street on his bike again.

Mrs. Williams turned to her daughter. "I don't know exactly what he is. He works at this center and they call him a counselor. Barb has been going out there since the divorce and has only gotten worse. Talks crazy like this all the time. I tell you I don't know what's going on. She goes out all hours of the night and doesn't pay any attention to the kids. When she stays home, she's up all night—talking like this and running the television." Mrs. Williams went on talking to Carol about her other daughter as if Barb weren't right there. It didn't seem to matter, though; Barb went on with her conversation as if the others were not there either.

Barb laughed to herself with a knowing smile on her face. She tapped on the table four times with a spoon. She laughed again and tapped four times again.

"You see," she said, "Larry is talking to me now. Four. That's important to us—4. He and his wife and two kids, that's 4. Me and my three kids, that's 4. I've been seeing him 4 months. You and Mom and Dad and me, that's four. Dad's been dead 4 years. We all have 4 limbs. There's a 4 in our phone number and a 4 on my license plate. In 4 more years, I'll be 34. Every 4 years we elect a president. Four can be divided by 2. Always let the phone ring 4 times. Look at my baby here. Jason is 4. You see how important it is?

Jason was still screaming and crying, trying to get his mother to pay attention to him. Carol attempted to wrench the child loose from Barb to comfort and settle him down. He resisted for a while and then gave in to his aunt. She held him in her lap and he fell asleep from the exhaustion of trying to break down the wall that was between him and his mother.

"What about the other kids, Mom? I can see how Jason is dealing with this, but what about Danny and Annie? Don't you think Barb needs something more than this counselor?"

Mrs. Williams looked at Carol and spoke with anger in her voice. "I think she needs to get back to God! I've been doing my best around here, but it isn't easy. I don't think everybody in the world needs to know what's going on here. It's nobody's damn business! Annie is just like other kids—she likes to play outside and she likes to rock and sing. Anything wrong with that? Danny had some trouble in school this last semester—bad grades. But what can you expect—he's rarely at home. He has his paper route and rides that bike all the time. Most of the time I don't know where he is! Barb needs to get a job and get her mind off all this Larry stuff. She hasn't done a thing in I don't know how long! Keeping herself busy could help. Work is good for a person. You can't just sit around doing nothing all the time. That's bound to make a person sick. And God knows, we need the income! With Barb and all the kids living here, I can hardly make ends meet. Just like now—I ask Danny to do a simple thing like take out the trash and away he goes. Nobody helps. You don't live here. You don't know what it has been like for me."

"Nobody's blaming you, Mom. It just seems like Barb and the kids need more help. Danny has never had bad grades. I don't think rocking and singing for hours on end seems very healthy. Jason screaming and crying all the time isn't normal. No reason to get mad at me. I'm just trying to figure this out. Danny seems so depressed. He used to get a lot of joy out of his artwork. Now he just sits and draws like someone is forcing him to do it. He's old enough to know something is very wrong. I think he wants help."

Carol continued to plead the case with her mother as Danny came back in, slamming the door behind him as hard as he could. He sat next to Carol and listened to the running commentary going on between his aunt and grandmother; he looked at his mother, who had not stopped talking about Larry and the number 4.

Carol continued, "It just might be good for all concerned if everybody could talk to someone about this."

"Do you think," said Mrs. Williams, "that I am going to allow us to be the laughingstock of the neighborhood! Everybody is just going to have to shape up here. That includes you, too, Danny! Grandmother has been letting you get away with far too much. I need your help around here. And I don't want any more trouble in school. We're all going to start getting busy around here. Keeping busy keeps people out of trouble. Can't have your mind on yourself all the time. Have to get your mind on other things."

Danny threw back his head as if in extreme pain, his face nearly purple with rage. People weren't making sense. Why wouldn't they fix things? Talk—just talk, talk, talk! He screamed in agony, "I hate you all, fuckers! I wish you were all dead! I'm getting out of here! I don't want to see any of you again! Ever! I wish you would just go to hell! Just go to hell!"

....

LOSS OF A PARENT THROUGH MENTAL ILLNESS

Unless an individual is entirely without relatives, mental illness affects not just one person but a whole family. Danny's story is intended to illustrate this, as well as to provide a picture of how children can be affected. The confusion about what to do and who to turn to, as seen in Danny's family, is unfortunately, more the rule than the exception.

This story is based on my experience with a number of children and their families. I believe this problem is more common than most people realize. In most cases, school professionals are unaware of children in this situation as long as one intact family member is representing the child at school. We find out about the situation only if a child begins showing extremely negative or alarming behavior. This does not always happen. Many of these children begin to show signs that something is wrong, but most of these signs are so subtle they go unnoticed: a slight drop in grades, less interest in school and school activities, some behavior problems—usually nothing so extraordinary that we can identify the problem immediately. Many of these children have been "taught" to keep it quiet. They are coerced into keeping the family secret. So, they go unnoticed, suffering alone.

Growing up with a mentally ill parent has not been well researched in the context of a loss. It is, however, a loss of great magnitude to a child. It is perhaps a more devastating experience than even parental death, so I am giving it special attention in this book.

Rapoport and Ismond (1984) present in their DSM III Training Guide a case study of a loss through mental illness. The 8-month-old child in this case was born to a mother diagnosed as paranoid schizophrenic. The mother was in an institution and the father was unknown. Since her birth, the child had received minimal care. The little girl was described as extremely underweight, apathetic, disinterested in people or toys, and unable to vocalize, and she appeared to have a sad expression.

The description of this child is very similar to that of institutionalized children who never had a parent. Reevaluation of the child after 6 months in a foster home revealed that the girl was very fearful and cried periodically without apparent reason. Although she had improved in some ways from the earlier description, the child's prognosis for normal development was not very bright.

The loss of a parent through mental illness is perhaps more tragic and traumatizing than loss through death. In death there is a greater possibility of resolving the loss. The parent is completely gone rather than physically visible but with no hope of ever returning to his or her former self. In mental illness, the parent is more often than not physically available but emotionally and cognitively unavailable to the child. Physically, it is the same parent, but in all other ways the parent is a stranger. This type of loss is not so easily resolved.

Considerable attention has been given to the children of parents who are psychiatrically disturbed, but the attention has been primarily for the purpose of identifying risk factors and behavioral manifestations indicating the development of psychopathology in children. In the literature on affective disorders there is evidence that children of depressed parents are at high risk for developing emotional problems in childhood and in adulthood (Anthony & Koupernik, 1974; Beardslee, Bemporad, Keller, & Klerman, 1983; Cohler, Grunebaum, Weiss, Gamer, & Gallant, 1977; Cytryn, McKnew, & Bunney, 1980; Livingood & Daen, 1983; Orvaschel, Weissman, & Kidd, 1980; Orvaschel, Weissman, Padian, & Lowe, 1981; Weissman, Paykel, & Klerman, 1972).

In one study researchers found that 43% of high-risk children (those who have a parent with a severe mental illness) also had psychiatric disorders. It was noted, however, that the type of disorder in the child was not significantly related to the type of disorder in the parent, that children's disorders express themselves in a variety of diagnostic syndromes, and that boys' disorders tended to be more severe and result in greater impairment socially and academically than did girls' (Orvaschel et al., 1981).

These researchers were primarily looking for a genetic link in psychiatric disorders. For the most part, the psychiatric literature approaches this subject by investigating the parents of a disturbed child or examining the child of a disturbed parent when they are fairly certain the child also is disturbed, usually with the intent of linking the types of disturbance in each. Generally, psychiatric research has lost interest in pursuing the theory that child disturbances are based solely on living in a chaotic, morbid environment that forces a child to adapt and survive. Psychiatrists are medical people and are currently interested in genetic and biochemical research. Most psychiatric researchers are, however, more inclined to discuss the possibility of a child being predisposed by heredity, with environment and learning as the final ingredients needed to precipitate the manifestation of a type of mental illness. The evidence for this hypothesis is particularly impressive in the case of such disturbances as manic-depressive disorder and schizophrenia (Andofer, 1984; Bauer & Bauer, 1982; Cytryn, McKnew, Zahn-Waxler, Radke-Yarrow, Gaensbauer, Harmon, & Lamour, 1984; Gaensbauer, Harmon, Cytryn, & McKnew, 1984).

A major study that attempted to sort these variables of heredity versus environment was reported by Segal and Yahraes (1978). They concluded that heredity seems more potent than environment as a cause of mental illness. They further stated that the quality of the parent–child relationship seemed to make little difference. This study was based on Danish government records of children and their parents. It did not include subjects from the United States who were not at genetic risk for mental illness and found that the quality of the parent–child relationship has an appreciable effect on mental health and mental illness.

It is understandable that medical researchers wish to investigate genetic factors rather than environmental situations. Genetic engineering, genetic counseling, and drugs would be a quick and easy solution. Obviously, the issue has not been resolved and is not likely to be for some time.

A Family Affair: The Big Secret

Certainly all three children in the story of Danny appear to be disturbed, but the intent of the story is not to imply that they have inherited their mother's mental illness; rather, it is to show what life and the environment are like under such circumstances. What caring family member would not be disturbed living day to day with Barb? The children, in particular, who need a mother to be there emotionally and cognitively, are bound to respond in ways that appear aberrant to others.

In this story, the family members are trying to cope, in their own ways, without professional help. The story highlights a situation that is all too often a common situation rather than the exception. Barb is receiving some type of professional treatment, although in her case it seems to be ineffective, while the others are getting no help. There is another element to the story that is based on many real-life situations: the family is eager to avoid others knowing about Barb's abnormal state or seeing her in that state. Perhaps the grandmother in this family sees that her daughter has not been cured by her counselor and therefore has no incentive to seek professional help for the whole family.

The other possibility is that mental illness is still so mysterious and stigmatizing to the general public that this family would be embarrassed if others found out about their situation. For most lay people, mental illness carries the same shame and humiliation as alcoholism, drug addiction, or venereal disease; a mentally ill person is "bad." For the most part, society's understanding of mental illness has not advanced much since the 19th century and earlier.

Without a doubt, there is a breakdown in the mental health service delivery system. Most frequently it is the patient, and sometimes it is the patient's spouse, who receives attention, but it is an uncommon occurrence when the whole family is brought in for treatment. Rarely does a person who is seriously ill mentally recognize or realize that others in the family might need help also; so, obviously, they do not make referrals. Even if the therapist inquires about others in the family, the patient usually cannot respond or provide reliable information. Often patients do not want family members involved. The therapist is theirs alone, and that person and time belong to them.

Other family members, then, must recognize that they are in need of help and take the initiative in seeking attention. Most often, though, they do not. Instead, they operate with benign neglect in an attempt to protect each other from whatever taboos they have attached to mental illness and psychiatrists. Some have the notion that the more they talk about such things, the worse the situation can become. In many cases it is common for no one but the immediate group to know about the family member who is mentally ill. The illness is hidden, as much as is possible, from other relatives, close friends, and, of course, the neighbors. In these instances, people cannot help solve the problems. Mental illness, to most people in our society, is both poorly understood and frightening.

Another problem is, of course, money. Good treatment is very expensive. People who are seriously mentally ill need the services of a well-trained professional (usually a psychiatrist); medications are involved, and frequent hospitalizations are often necessary until the individual is stabilized. Therefore, the family may be faced with fees of $80 or $90 an hour and up for the services of a physician who is trained in psychiatry, plus the cost of drugs and hospital fees. Insurance companies are notorious for their lack of generosity when it comes to paying for the treatment of mental illness—mild or serious. Without financial help, most people are forced to resort to county-supported agencies, where the training of the professionals frequently is limited to treating less complex problems.

Even so-called milder psychological problems (e.g., neuroses) often are beyond the scope of the agency professional's training. It is an interesting enigma that in this society, even today, people who recognize that they need help in improving their mental health status are punished when they seek professional care. They become stigmatized with a label ("you must be crazy to see a psychiatrist") and then receive minimal assistance in paying for their improvement. They find themselves in the odd position of keeping such professional help hidden from friends and coworkers for fear of losing their jobs. In actuality, they are doing society, friends, family, and employers a service by recognizing that, with improved mental health, they could be more fully functioning and more productive individuals.

What is readily understood, then, is that high premiums are not awarded for maintaining mental health; however, high penalties are levied on those who become mentally ill. This may explain in part why family situations like those seen in Danny's story exist.

Following are actual case examples of the effects on children when a parent is lost through mental illness. One case involves a father and one case a mother.

The Smith Family: A Case Study

The Smiths were a typical family, probably very much like your neighbors next door. They had two adolescent children who were in every way normal teenagers. At age 40, Mr. Smith had a mental breakdown. The family could not recall observing any unusual behavior exhibited by Mr. Smith prior to the manifestation of his severe psychiatric disorder.

Mr. Smith held a responsible position in the community and

Continued

provided well for his family. He appeared to his family and friends to be a normal, average person. Mrs. Smith began to notice changes in her husband's behavior but was not really alarmed until she woke up one morning to find Mr. Smith sitting up in bed stiff, immobile, and maintaining a fixed stare. She alerted her children and phoned the family doctor; the living nightmare began.

For approximately a year the Smith family was caught in the turmoil of visiting one doctor after another, having Mr. Smith hospitalized intermittently, living with but not understanding his bizarre behavior, and going through the agonizing experience of watching a loved one continue to deteriorate. Mr. Smith committed suicide.

The children

Terryl during the episode

Terryl was 15 when he became consciously aware of the manifestations of his father's mental illness—when the trips to the doctors and the hospitals started. He knew something was wrong with his father but did not know exactly what it was. He assumed it was some type of illness that was treatable like most illnesses, and he felt sure that eventually his father would be put on a medication that would cure the problem. As his father became worse, Terryl felt more angry. He stayed away from home and avoided his father as much as possible. His need to avoid his father stemmed from a fear that he might say or do something inadvertently that would precipitate another manic or depressive episode.

Terryl looked forward to his father's visits at home from the hospital. He was always hopeful that his father had improved and would be able to stay home and return to the normal routine. However, when he saw that his father was basically in the same condition, Terryl found himself in great conflict: he felt let down, wanting his father back but at the same time desperately wanting him to go back to the hospital and stay.

Throughout this episode (and even now, 6 years later), he felt he had to be the strong one in the family; that he could not let his guard down for a minute and could not let himself feel anything for fear that the rest of his family would fall apart if

Continued

he did not remain strong.

In many ways, Terryl assumed the father role for his family. He worried and feared (and still does) for their financial well-being. In response, he took as much part-time work as he could get. As he tells it, this was to help financially and also to allow him to escape being around his father when he was home. "I stayed away as much as possible." He involved himself in extracurricular activities at school and socialized with friends at every opportunity.

Help for Terryl through this family crisis was, for the most part, incidental. He felt that school was basically a sanctuary, although he had great difficulty keeping his mind on school matters and off the problems at home. His grades slipped a bit but not significantly. Terryl had one friend he talked to on only one occasion. This friend also had a relative suffering from some sort of mental illness. "We talked about it once and then dropped it—never mentioned it again." Overall, he felt great loneliness with his problem, and throughout this period his dominant feelings were anger, frustration, sorrow, and fear. One year later, at age 16, he was shocked at his father's death but felt a tremendous sense of relief that the ordeal was "finally over."

Terryl after the episode

Six years later, at age 22, Terryl talks of feeling depressed occasionally when he thinks of his father. He misses him and at times wishes he were still around.

He says his life is now dominated with feelings of anxiety, "like I must be prepared for anything. Anything at any moment could go wrong—like something may happen to the others." His inference is that he is mainly concerned about his mother's well-being. Clearly, this young man is still confused about just what went wrong and still has many unresolved feelings about the event.

Terryl's descriptions about the way he goes about his daily living indicate that he has the constant feeling of living on a precipice. He verified this when the interviewer suggested that it must be like trying to walk on eggshells. He responded, "Exactly!"

Continued

Although he made statements about not wanting to "open a can of worms" by talking about it, he volunteered to be interviewed. However, he is not fully prepared to rely on anyone, nor is he trusting that anyone could really help. He commented that he never wanted to "bring this up again." However, when the interview was obviously over he made an overture to continue the discussion by bringing up incidents and questions. He is still concerned that others will find out about his father, which would be painful for him. Most of his inquiries indicated that Terryl wants help, but he is afraid of it and is very concerned about his future.

Throughout the interview he was very nervous; his voice trembled when discussing the past and at times he was near tears. He is highly defensive and will not let go or let down. He gives the impression that he fears that if he lets his feelings show, even a little, his world will come down around him. Undoubtedly, his greatest fear is that he will become exactly like his father.

Terryl's condition and responses are all quite natural and understandable considering the trauma he experienced: watching the apparently unexpected and sudden mental deterioration of his father, followed by his suicide. Living with this tremendous crisis without professional intervention has left him with a number of unresolved issues. However, this young man has many strengths. His feelings have not been totally repressed or gone unrecognized. He allows himself to verbalize to someone else how he felt about his father. He did take the first step for the first time to talk to a stranger about what had happened. Somewhere within himself he has acknowledged that he needs some help in understanding what happened, in putting other things in perspective, such as clarifying what his actual role in his family now should be, and in the more general process of resolving the loss of a parent. With the proper intervention, in time, Terryl should become less anxious, less depressed, and able to live more comfortably.

Vicky during the episode

Vicky was 13 when her father showed definite observable signs of severe mental illness. She remembers thinking during this

Continued

period that he was different in some way but since his moods were primarily euphoric she told herself it was all right, although deep down she suspected that there was actually something wrong.

Her account of the story indicates to the interviewer that she was a terrified little girl, completely in the dark about what was actually going on and not really understanding any of what was happening. She expressed the need also, during this time, to be out of the house and away from her father as much as possible. Her age, however, did not allow her the same opportunities for freedom that her brother Terryl was able to find for himself. She could not have a job and was not old enough to drive a car, which restricted her to the house much more. She had given thought to and fantasized several times about running away to live with out-of-state relatives.

As her father became more debilitated (weak and disoriented) from phrenotropic drugs, she became afraid that it would embarrass him if she offered to help him do something he appeared to be having difficulty accomplishing. More than likely she actually was feeling like her brother Terryl, who was afraid that any innocent act or word would push his father into one or the other of his extreme moods. Vicky was simply terrified of her father, who was now a stranger.

Vicky verbalized feeling extremely angry with her father and wishing he would either get well or go away—preferably to stay in a hospital. At such times, though, she would become worried and frightened about who would take care of them without a dad in the house.

School apparently was some relief because it allowed her to get out of the house and away from the turmoil. Unlike Terryl, however, Vicky seemed to bring to school with her a different set of anxieties: someone at school would find out what was happening and then everyone would think they were all mad. These fears were exacerbated in her health class when the topic of mental illness was presented. Apparently the health teacher was not very knowledgeable about the subject because the class became silly and made fun of the material presented. Vicky became most upset with this turn of events and felt anger, hurt, and fear that her classmates would find out and think she was "crazy." Nothing more unfortunate could have

Continued

happened. Here was a prime opportunity to instruct the students about mental illness and help them become more aware of and sensitive to these issues.

Vicky had one friend with whom she spent a lot of time, and she often stayed overnight at her friend's house. Her friend had visited her house on occasion and had observed Vicky's father in his various emotional states; the two girls never discussed her father. Vicky, at that time, wished she had someone to talk to about the whole situation.

The day of her father's suicide, Vicky was the only one home. Her hair dryer was on, and she heard a muffled sound from another room but was unalarmed since the television was on and the sound was indistinguishable from television noise. Her mother returned and found her father. Like her brother, Vicky felt relieved when he died—the nightmare was over. Vicky expressed great anger with her father for not leaving a note, for "putting us through hell and then leaving no clue to explain why it all happened."

Vicky after the episode

Of the two children, Vicky seemed more willing and less anxious to be interviewed and to discuss the family crisis. Although young at the time, she was definitely old enough to retain more than she was able to retrieve in the interview: many of her feelings and memories are firmly repressed.

As with her brother, for Vicky this tragedy has not reached a stage of resolution. She reported that on some nights before falling asleep the thought comes to her mind, "My God, my father killed himself! Why did this happen to us?" She does recognize that she worries and fears that she might become like her father or that mental illness could happen to her mother or another close relative. However, Vicky blocks some of her feelings and seems to have a real fear of any intense feelings. She tells herself "that things were once really bad, so I should not get upset over things now. I have realized that mental health is not something to take for granted."

This attitude toward mental health is a strength and could become the impetus for Vicky to seek an appropriate intervention program that would help her to reach a resolution con-

Continued

cerning her father's illness and death. In addition, such a program would assist her in identifying her feelings, in losing her fear of having strong feelings, and in realizing that having strong, intense feelings is normal and something that people can handle. It does not indicate madness.

The loss of a significant person for any reason possibly can impede emotional development even when the psychological damage is not immediately clear. The violent death of a loved one can have an even greater overwhelming effect. Clearly, intervention is needed no matter what strengths youths possess. Knowing those strengths can help set the course of intervention, but knowing that there are strengths should not substitute for intervention.

Terryl and Vicky did not suffer the trauma of observing the actual suicide, but the impact was not lessened. There are more cases than we would like to believe of children who have witnessed the actual suicide or homicide of a parent or sibling. The magnitude of the psychological damage caused by such horrifying experiences is beyond the abilities of school personnel to handle alone. These types of tragedies require cooperative intervention programs of a highly intense nature with child psychiatrists or clinical psychologists.

The Adams Family: A Case Study

The Adams family is a case of the loss of a mother through mental illness. This is an ongoing case and Mrs. Adams is still alive. From all observable behavior, Mrs. Adams was a typical mother and homemaker. Prior to her divorce she did not work outside the home; she took care of her family and her house conscientiously.

When Mrs. Adams was 39, she and Mr. Adams were divorced and she had in her care five children: one adolescent, two pre-teens, one young school-age child, and a toddler. She was receiving minimal child support from Mr. Adams and relying on welfare to meet the rest of the financial obligations.

Her illness began with periods of extreme depression in which she could not get out of bed in the mornings to send her

Continued

children off to school, attend to the toddler, prepare meals, or clean house. The older children took over the responsibility of seeing that they all at least ate dinner during the periods when their mother was in a helpless condition.

Mrs. Adams sought help at a community mental health center, but her condition deteriorated into episodes of intense activity, sleepless nights, and eventually delusional behavior with hallucinations. From that point on, Mrs. Adams has been in and out of the hospital, each time receiving piecemeal treatments for short periods. Until another family member took charge, Mrs. Adams' children were basically on their own: sometimes eating, sometimes not; usually going to school in dirty clothing; unbathed and generally unattended to after school. The oldest children had tried to keep their mother's condition a secret, and when she was sent to the hospital for the first time (by a relative), the children became hysterical and angry; they swore at and fought off the ambulance attendants, threatening destruction to anyone who would harm their mother.

The children during this ongoing episode

The children in this family have been living with their mother's illness for the past 3 years. The onset of their mother's condition occurred when Andrew was age 10, Jackie was 9, Sophie was 8, Ben was 5, and Elizabeth was a few weeks old. Prior to their mother's mental breakdown in its most extreme form, the children were functioning normally as youngsters.

The oldest, Andrew, was usually an "A" student, with a variety of other talents and interests. This boy had, at one time, been identified as a gifted child. He was exceptionally talented in music and had the ability to master foreign languages quickly and proficiently. As his mother's condition worsened, his grades slipped to average performance. He lost interest in music, was dropped from the gifted program, and abandoned his study of foreign languages. He became more and more isolated from his friends (by choice) and discontinued most after-school activities. He stayed home, keeping in the house to himself, spending hours in front of the television.

Andrew, now age 13, is visibly depressed. He walks with his

Continued

shoulders slumped and rarely makes eye contact. He often seems not to hear when asked a question or fails to respond to people when they try to make ordinary conversation. His face is usually expressionless, and he does not see the humor in most jokes. He seldom spends time with friends or enjoys the common activities that most youths his age engage in.

At age 12, Jackie, in contrast to Andrew, is seldom at home. As soon as school is out she disappears with friends, does not return for dinner, and usually comes back home late in the evening, just before bedtime. Whereas at age 9 she was a solid average student, Jackie is now in trouble at school on almost a daily basis. Her grades are mostly Ds and Fs; she has been caught experimenting with drugs and alcohol; she spends most of her time with older teenagers who have been in trouble with the law for a variety of offenses.

Sophie, now age 11, is more like Andrew in that she primarily isolates herself from friends, staying in the house most of her free time. Her primary interests are the family pets, and she occupies her time talking to and taking care of the animals. She continually brings home strays to add to the collection of pets to care for. Her grades and behavior at school have, for the most part, shown no significant change. She is, in fact, more than conscientious about her schoolwork, spending hours on homework, doing more than required, and reworking assignments to attain her idea of perfection. All of this extra attention to academic matters has not, however, improved her grades.

Ben, age 8, spends most of his time after school playing outside with friends. His games usually end in fistfights and then his playmates abandon and ignore him for days following. He frequently is kept after school for misbehaving; he does not do his homework, attend to his studies, or listen to the teacher. He talks out in class, leaves his desk, throws books, and starts fights. He has been referred for a special education placement. There is no one in the family who seems to have any effect on or control over Ben. He starts fights with his siblings, throws food and makes a shambles of the house, refuses to go to bed when he should, and basically runs wildly around the house until his own exhaustion forces him to fall asleep.

Elizabeth was only a few weeks old when her mother became

Continued

ill. Now, at age 3, she barely talks and has only a few, single-syllable words in her vocabulary. She does not sleep through the night, is afraid of most people, including relatives, and will not allow people to pick her up and hold her. She refuses most foods, still clings to a baby bottle, and spends most of her waking hours alone in a corner rocking and staring at the floor.

Prognosis for the children

These illustrations of the children's behavior during this ongoing crisis do not foretell a very bright future. None of these children are receiving professional help, with the exception of Ben, who has been referred for special education. However, special education alone may not be enough for Ben, especially in the context of the obvious need for total family intervention.

With the possible exception of Elizabeth, each child has characteristics that indicate their futures need not be hopeless. Appropriate interventions, in a variety of forms, could turn things around for these children.

Andrew is intelligent and talented; receiving help with his emotional crisis could free him to put these gifts to use on his own behalf.

Jackie is a survivor and has found a means to escape the madness in her house, however misguided her tactics. This child does recognize the importance of and her need to be out of that environment. With proper help, Jackie could learn to channel those survival instincts into more constructive patterns.

Sophie has the strengths of compassion and knowing the importance of school. Her emotional condition has taken the form of compulsive and obsessive behavior, which explains why all the extra efforts she puts into her schoolwork are not getting her ahead. Obviously, she finds refuge in school and with help could become a strong student, which would brighten her future.

Ben is still very young; at age 8 he is already experiencing great difficulties in school. This should not be surprising because he was only 5 years old when his mother's illness became noticeable. At age 5 he was just starting school and did not have a good beginning. His aggressiveness, however, indi-

Continued

cates also a strong sense of survival. All of his fighting and obstinate behavior could be interpreted as signs of his frustration and disturbance over his mother's condition, but it is also evidence that he is attempting to fight the whole situation. Again, proper channeling of his strong sense of survival would work to his benefit.

Elizabeth's condition is the most alarming, as her behaviors are indicative of several severe childhood disturbances. She has never had a mother, so to speak. From Elizabeth's birth to now, her mother has not been emotionally or cognitively available to her during the most critical stages of development. She needs to be in the care of adults who can attend to her. I would hesitate to predict her future. It is impossible to know for sure the extent of damage this child has suffered.

Symptoms of the Children During a Parent's Mental Illness

All studies indicate that children of parents who are psychiatrically disturbed are at high risk of developing emotional problems of their own. Incidence figures are as high as 45%. The list of symptoms is long and varied (Beardslee et al., 1983; Cohler et al., 1977; Lidz & Bloth, 1983; Livingood & Daen, 1983; Orvaschel et al., 1981). For informational purposes, they are listed as follows: (a) attention deficit disorders; (b) major depression; (c) separation anxiety; (d) conduct disorders; (e) excessive rivalry with peers and siblings; (f) isolation; (g) withdrawal; (h) enuresis; (i) defiance; (j) rebellion; (k) cyclothymis (mood fluctuations from periodic excitement to periodic depression, often accompanied by a wide variety of physical complaints); and (l) impaired intellectual ability.

It appears from these studies that children with a depressed parent are more severely affected than even children of schizophrenic parents. It is important to bear in mind, however, that studies have failed to provide conclusive evidence of a genetic or hereditary factor in the etiology of psychotic disorders (Lidz & Bloth, 1983; Orvaschel et al., 1981).

A Word About the Future

There are at least three areas on which we should be concentrating our efforts regarding the loss of a parent through mental illness. I have already indicted, in a manner of speaking, the society in the United States for its shortcomings in reason, compassion, understanding, sensitivity, and concern for all who need help. Does not the right to mental health and treatment of mental illness, without harsh judgment, fall within the purview of human rights? We really do have a lot of hard work to do if, as mental health professionals, we are going to make changes that will respond to the needs of all human beings. Advancement or stagnation of the mental health system largely depends on the political administration in power. Once ground has been lost, it is most difficult to gain it back, let alone move forward. The mood of the bureaucrats who are in charge of the use of our money has, at times, been mean-spirited toward some citizens.

All professional organizations with vested interests in mental health will need to exert whatever power and influence necessary to reverse this trend. What good is a stable economy if massive numbers of people in this country cannot enjoy personal stability? People like to say that our children are the future of this country, but their behavior shows they either do not really believe it or do not actually care. This statement (about our future being our children) now sounds like a platitude rather than the axiom it really is.

The second area that needs attention falls on the shoulders of the mental health researchers. It would be most helpful if these researchers looked a little more closely at the long-term effects of living with a mentally ill person, giving as much attention to environmental effects as is given to the genetic connection.

Finally, as mental health practitioners, we need to find ways to get help to all involved in this family affair. Certainly, in the here and now it is easier to deal with one person than with two or seven, but attending now to all involved may prevent dealing with the other seven a few years down the road. The barriers and ethical considerations are clear and understandable, but we are clever people. Undoubtedly, we can find a way if we put our minds to it.

Sibling Death

A sibling plays an important and significant part in the family dynamics, and therefore the death of a sibling can initiate a psychological crisis for a child. A sibling's death can result in modification of a child's life situation if the grief of the parents renders them unable to maintain a healthy parent relationship with the living child(ren). The realization that death happened to an older sibling and can happen to oneself may lead a younger child to take on babyish behavior as a way of keeping himself or herself from growing to an age when death could occur. An older child may react with extreme fear and anxiety if ignored by the parents during the grieving period. Typically, older youths in this situation become preoccupied with a horrifying question about their own future: "Will it happen to me tomorrow, or next week, or next year?" In fact, it has been shown that having a sibling with a serious illness ranks among the most stressful of life events. In addition, it has been shown that the well child is in greater need of support than are other family members (Grollman, 1974; McKeever, 1983).

Some children feel that, to please the parents, they must act like the dead sibling did, even when such behavior is not appropriate for their age. The child sees the parents grieving and wants to make everything all right again. Other children become burdened by the feeling that they must take the place of the seriously ill or dead child. A sense of guilt can operate very strongly in this situation because of what a child believes was done to or not done for the brother or sister when he or she was alive. Many children go through the experience of feeling happiness because now the parents are theirs alone; however, this feeling generates unbearable guilt feelings in the child. If not recognized and dealt with during childhood, these guilt feelings, accompanied by depression, carry on into adulthood and in some cases become the precursors to suicide (McKeever, 1983).

Another extreme type of problem in cases of sibling death can occur when the living child becomes the scapegoat as result of a parent's own pathological variation of the mourning process. The sense of guilt and self-hatred the parent feels is displaced to the living child. Even if all of this is being acted out unconsciously, children feel the parent's recrimination and hostility and sense that they are being punished (Tooley, 1975). This was painfully portrayed and illustrated in the motion picture *Ordinary People*.

As with the death of a parent, it is possible for positive effects to be seen with the death of a sibling—effects that could indicate that a negative situation existed before the death. There is the possibility of the remaining siblings making some positive identifications with the dead siblings and taking on their characteristics. As an example, a child whose grades had been poor before the sibling's death now becomes the one who makes good grades in school.

There is limited material available on sibling death and its effects on the child. Because of the role parents play in psychological as well as physical and emotional development, the death of a parent is thought to be much more traumatic. However, the importance of the death of a sibling should not be underestimated. The reactions of the parents to the loss are keenly observed by the remaining children and will affect their reactions to the death itself, as well as their feelings about death and about themselves.

Surviving the Major Losses

In terms of working through this type of crisis, one factor discussed in the literature is the child's ability to mourn the loss (McKeever, 1983; Shoor & Speed, 1963). Mourning can be described as a working through of pain and grief, a letting go of ties to the lost object, and the ability to shift attention toward new objects. There appear to be three phases in the natural grieving or mourning process. The first is the phase of protest, when the child cannot quite believe that the person is dead and attempts, sometimes angrily, to regain the dead parent or other loved one. Next is the phase of pain, despair, and disorganization, when the child begins to accept the fact that the loved one is really gone. In the final phase there is hope, when the child begins to organize life without the lost person. It is believed that if children are able to turn loose from their lost loved objects and make healthy new ties, they probably will continue to develop healthy personalities (Grollman, 1974).

The work of mourning may take a year and is frequently characterized by pleasant associations as well as intense regret or guilt over real or fancied hurts. Dreams may take up the work of mourning, although the final resolution takes place by working through repetitive memories. Successful resolution implies that the deceased will remain a living memory but without the pain that originally accompanied the grief reaction. The survivor is then able to seek out others for affectional needs (Shoor & Speed, 1963).

How and if this process can take place is a subject of debate in the literature dealing with death in a child's family or sphere of influence. Many psychiatrists define mourning in a way that stresses the complicated mental structures and the need for an established structuralization of the mind. There are those who believe that children cannot mourn because of their lack of experience and their immature ego development (Birtchnell, 1969; Nagera, 1970). It is argued by these psychoanalytic practitioners that children cannot mourn for fear of the developmental vacuum that acceptance of the loss would entail.

It is a personal observation, and also well documented in the literature already cited, that children go through the same stages of grief reaction as adults. Depending on their age, children may not go through the stages with the same intensity, or for the same duration, or even in the same order; however, the similarities to adult reactions are close enough to indicate a definite mourning process. Lampl-de Groot (1976) felt that the age at which a child is capable of a real mourning process varies individually and depends on the rate of maturation and development. Psychologists' and psychiatrists' pessimism about the inability of children to mourn parallels their pessimism about a satisfactory outcome for children who have lost a parent. The key word here is "real." For some, it seems that if children experience events and react differently than adults do their capacity to feel in a real way is always suspect.

It is interesting to note how society's views of children have changed. It has gone from one extreme to the other. It was not really until the 20th century that we determined that children were not just miniature adults. Prior to this century, children were thought to be no more than little adults, savages actually, who needed to be trained and molded to behave like respectable adults. Our real understanding of children changed with the works of Anna Freud, Erikson, Piaget, and others who demonstrated that children perceive and think differently than adults. Even so, perhaps this knowledge has taken some researchers far off course, to the point where they question children's capacity to feel in a real way simply because they are not adults (Rochlin, 1967).

This attitude seems nearly as harsh as the old concept of children as miniature adults. Who can really dare to say what constitutes real feelings? Although some researchers have definite ideas on the subject, it is obvious that more thought and more study need to be given to understanding children. Certainly, cognition affects perception and perception affects emotions. The point may seem labored; however, the work of understanding children is not complete and perhaps never will be. But until more has been done, I cannot accept the viewpoint that only adults go through emotional experiences in some real fashion. Granted, these experiences are undoubtedly different for the child, but they are different and real.

Other researchers indicate that children can go through a mourning process and continue to grow and maintain healthy personalities. Furman (1974) noted that children's chances of coping apparently are better if they are older, emotionally healthier, and have the ability to understand death realistically. Bowlby (1960) believed that mourning, in an adult sense, is possible and can be observed in children as young as 6 months. Greenberg (1975) also concluded that preadolescent children experience bereavement and mourn.

To be fair, part of the disparity in the research is due to the differences in defining mourning: some define it in the classical Freudian sense and others do not. The one area of agreement in which there seems to be some certainty is that what happens after the death of a significant person is extremely important.

The next section focuses on another type of loss—that of a friend or classmate. While the effects may not be as devastating or long-lasting, this type of loss can be at least temporarily traumatic and does constitute a crisis for the child.

THE DEATH OF A FRIEND OR CLASSMATE

It is discouraging to find that little research has been done with children on the various kinds of loss they can experience in their lifetimes. As a society, are we insensitive to children? It is a fair question to ask since many important issues that can have a profound effect on children have not been adequately addressed in a formal fashion.

We refer to ourselves as a child-centered society, and perhaps we are in comparison to other societies and countries. In many respects great strides have been made, especially in comparison to some other societies and in contrast to the past, but clearly we have a long way to go. A search of the literature was done on this topic, with disappointing results. The death of a friend or close associate has a most profound effect on adults. For whatever reasons, the death of a child's friend or classmate has been given small consideration, both in terms of how it affects children and in comparison to the research on other losses. Perhaps people believe that children will outgrow whatever effect this type of loss may have had, but the point is that children go through crises, and those crises are accompanied by extremely painful emotions. This book is intended to have more of a here-and-now perspective of crisis situations, with less focus on the future.

Even if children do recover relatively quickly from this type of loss, they go through painful emotional experiences. Whether or not the feelings they experience are only fleeting is not what is important. What is important is that the children are trying to cope with a loss that evokes strong emotions. Generally, they are on their own in learning how to manage these feelings, and children should not have to struggle with these emotions alone. School mental health professionals, because of their training and experience, are in a prime position to help youths learn ways to cope with difficult and painful life experiences.

When the friend of an adult dies, it is a very sad and emotionally upsetting experience for that adult. He or she does not get over it easily or quickly and seeks the company of someone who can help to cope with these feelings. The death of even an acquaintance is a shocking and upsetting event. Most people have experienced that kind of loss, and if they search their memories they will recall that the death of someone they knew, even casually, also was not quickly forgotten. People react by seeking each other out to talk about what happened and about "how sad it is." For example, not too long ago a colleague of mine was killed. The man was not someone that I knew very well, and it was common knowledge that he was not someone that most people liked very well. Nevertheless, the day after his death the college community was preoccupied with what had happened. People talked at length about his death, relating the same details to first one person, then another. Both talker and listener touched each other frequently, even if they had never done so before and have not done so since. In other words, even when a person dies whom others know but do not like very well, the feelings of the survivors need quite a bit of attention to alleviate their strong emotional reactions.

The research that comes closest to dealing with how children react to the death of friends or acquaintances can be found in a few studies on the outcomes of disasters (Bertoia & Allan, 1988; Bloch, Silber, & Perry, 1956; Gleser, Green, & Winget, 1981; Perry, 1979; Perry, Silber, & Bloch, 1956). It appears from these studies that a child's behavior with respect to a disaster experience is heavily influenced by the parents' attitudes. The main defense mechanisms used involve denying or attempting to suppress a recollection of the experience. For the most part, parents feel that it is best to forget the experience as quickly as possible, and the general attitude is that it is best not to talk to the children about it because it would only upset them more.

In interviews following disasters, most parents admitted to avoiding any talk about what had happened and keeping the children busy so that they would not hear anything about it on the radio or television. In the study by Perry and colleagues (1956), one of the mothers interviewed admitted that her child "talked about it constantly until he got his mind settled." The mother, however, said all the talk about the disaster made her nervous; she tried to change the conversation and keep the child from people who would talk about it by sending him out to play or on an errand.

Many people have difficulty answering the questions children ask about disasters, especially when the questions deal with the death of other children or of people who were close to the children. This difficulty seems to be a general one, as evidenced in articles about children who asked questions about friends or siblings who had been killed in disasters. The articles conclude that few people can bring themselves to tell children what has happened. The authors also recognize that some individuals lie to the children in attempting to make the experience seem less frightening. The parents feel that it is best to get the children back as quickly as possible into the kinds of activities that they had been doing, without acknowledging that anything has really happened. Adults acted in this way at a high school in a town when children were killed or were trapped in a theater during a tornado. It was reported that the students in the high school resented the fact that no mention was made of their classmate who was killed (Bloch et al., 1956; Perry et al., 1956).

These studies reported several symptoms consistently seen in children who had lived through a disaster and who also have seen someone die or be seriously hurt during the tragedy. Many children experienced severe separation anxiety and expressed fear that if the parents left the house they might not return. The other most common reactions were depression, bedwetting, nightmares, stomachaches, fear of hospitals, fear of dying, fear of seeing others hurt, a variety of somatic complaints, and difficulty concentrating in school (Bloch et al., 1956; Dollinger, 1982; Franson, 1988; O'Brien, Goodenow, & Espin, 1991).

It was obvious that many adults had difficulty in accepting the reality of the experience themselves. Undoubtedly they became so anxious in recalling it that the only way they felt they could deal with this anxiety was by a process of suppression or by denying that the experience had really been as bad as it had been. For this reason they could not tolerate hearing their own children discuss their experiences. What the parents actually communicated to their children was that these things could not be discussed openly, which made the disaster even more frightening for their children (Perry et al., 1956).

Let us look back again on the event I recounted about the death of a colleague and recall the behavior that the adults exhibited. These adults needed to discuss the tragedy not once with one person but many times with many people. Why do we assume that children do not have the same needs? In fact, the youths at the high school were angry because no one even mentioned their classmate. In the cases described, not only were the disasters not discussed in front of the children, but the children were deliberately thwarted when they tried to talk about their friends or siblings who had been killed. This is not to say that parents and all adults are "bad" because of this behavior. Clearly they think they are doing what is best for the children at the time. However, it also is evident that they are sometimes mistaken about the best course of action.

In actuality, adults seem to be unaware that what they are doing really is not so much for the protection of the children as for the protection of their own feelings. Although it is difficult for adults to face a tragedy, the children seem to need to have things out in the open for discussion. They often tell us what is best to do, but adults do not always listen. We need to listen.

Children are often quite able to tell us what they need and what is best for them. In many ways they are stronger than we think they are; they are instinctively more perceptive about positive approaches to mental health remedies.

To give an example, I have kept some material written by children years ago. What follows is from a real incident. When I saved this material I had no idea that I would be using it now to illustrate something so important. I saved the material for three reasons: (1) the sensitivity of the children impressed me so; (2) the children's insight into what they needed to do for their own mental health stuck in my mind; and (3) I learned that ignorance can make us insensitive even when we think we are trying to help.

First the story of what happened, followed by what transpired: A youth in special education classes was killed while riding his bike in the evening near his home. The men driving the car were drunk and speeding through the neighborhood without the headlights turned on. The boy, whom I will call Ken, was killed instantly. Ken was 13 and had been diagnosed as having emotional and learning problems. He had been placed in a class with other children diagnosed as having the same problems. Some of the children heard the news of Ken's death for the first time over the school intercom—an extraordinarily impersonal and insensitive way to handle such a tragedy. The children who had known Ken best attended his funeral. What ensued in Ken's class after his death is not peculiar to children in special education—those with emotional and learning problems. I believe these children responded naturally and in the same manner as any typical child in a regular class.

Ken's classmates would not settle into the routine of the class and commence with their work as the teacher wanted. They persisted with questions about what had happened to Ken, when it had happened, what the funeral was like, and who the men were who had been driving the car. They also talked about things they remembered about Ken. The message from the children came through to the teacher that they needed to deal with the death, and the teacher responded with a request that the boys write eulogies about their classmate and friend. However, something happened to this teacher as the boys carried out their assignment, and what started out as an excellent idea and a sensitive way to handle the boys' fears, anxieties, and sadness failed miserably. I assume that what happened was the result of a need on the part of the teacher to defend his own feelings of sadness and shock. This teacher responded in much the same manner as the parents in the tornado disaster did with their own children.

This material is presented only as a means of elevating awareness, so that when similar situations occur the results can be different. If the teacher had known how to better handle the situation, I am sure that person would have done so. The eulogies written by Ken's classmates follow, along with their teacher's responses. Remember that these children have emotional and learning problems. The eulogies are unaltered and presented exactly as written.

The Boys in Ken Jones's Class

From Ian, age 12: Ken Jones he was a frend of mine and I met him in band and I am every sad he dyed and he was a cool guy fran as mcch as I no him and I glad that he had a good life for as longd as it was.

From the teacher to Ian: Thank you Ian. You misspelled friend, died, from, know. I will pick 6 words from your box so that you will have 4 new words and 6 review words on Friday.

From Karl, age 13: When I Think of Ken I see Laghfter, Friends, having Fun even in Math even when he hated it, and eating all the Time and Now one is add To The Death Toll in Highway DePartment. and a good

Friend is dead at list it was quieck For Him. But it may Not Be quieck For Me. Thend

From the teacher to Karl: This is one of the most beautiful things I have ever read. Thank you for sharing it, but you misspelled laughter, friends, least, quick. I will choose 6 words from your box on Friday for the test. So you'll have 6 review and 4 new.

From Butch, age 13: Ken was some one I did not very well but he semed like a pretty cool gie. Ken played the T-bone and really well. He just started last fall but learnd fast. Just last week some thing really bad happend to Ken a car hit him well he was riding his bike and he was killed. Last Monday I went to his funrel and man was it sad. I gussd that thet kind of thing happens to the best some times though.

From the teacher to Butch: Thanks, Butch. I'll choose 4 words from your box as a review. You misspelled pretty, guy, learned, while, funeral, guessed.

From Adam, age 12: He was a good friend. The people on are block has changed a lot because of it. It is going to be hardest for his dad because of he always helped him at his work, and at home. I also feel sorry for his family and for his girl friend he went to see her that night because she thinks it is her falt. A lot of people have learned alot because now alot of people will not ride bikes at night and also will not drink and drive. I know his sisters are takeing it real well.

From the teacher to Adam: Thanks, Adam. Misspelled fault, taking. I will choose 8 words from your box on Friday. Please study.

From Sergie, age 11. I stienk shat Ken was a neet gi. and he was fuey and He was responolbel he plade that houn good. and you can Depend on hem. and I shenck them gis cheud get sint in peresin. I shenk shat the cops chood looke ot fr mo speder and I woad shout them gis.

From the teacher to Sergie: Thanks, Sergie. Among others, you misspelled neat, played, horn, him, should, sent, think.

From Saul, age 12: Yesterday I heard that Ken jons was killed. His fenural was yesterday I heard it over the wall speaker. I hate to think what I would do if someone in our family would Be Killed. I know that Ken jons will be happy with my father in heaven.

From the teacher to Saul: Nice—I will pick 9 words from your spelling box on Friday. The word is spelled "funeral."

From Ricky, age 13: When I think of ken jones I think it is sad. I think it is sad because he might have said to his parents that he was going on a bike ride ad that was the last time they would see him alive.

Also I think it is sad because if the two guys in the car were not drunk and not speeding the incidint would not have happened. I think even if they were drunk and speeding if they had their head lights on Ken might hve seen them and had a chance of getting out of the way.

From the teacher to Ricky: Thanks for sharing your thoughts, Ricky. I will pick 10 spelling words from your box on Friday. So take them home and study!

What Happened?

In the studies on the effects of disasters on children, it was shown that for the most part parents tended to try to get the children to forget the incident and not talk about it with them or with others. Many of the children in those studies responded to their friends and others in the way their parents were responding: by trying in some form to suppress affect or communication. For example, when asked how they helped others to feel better about things and how they helped themselves, they gave answers such as, "I tell them not to think about it" and "I think of other things."

Other children, however, indicated they tried some form of communication and social support with friends who had also experienced a disaster. These children said that they "try to talk to them," "sympathize with him," and "go do things with him." Nevertheless, because of parental influence, for the majority of the children the conception of emotional support was primarily the idea that one should not dwell on such things, and if they did not talk or think about the event their feelings would be less painful.

Looking back, it seems that Ken Jones's teacher probably felt the same way about dealing with the tragedy of the death of a child in the class. Perhaps this is what the teacher had been taught as a child. The boys felt a need to talk about Ken and his death. The teacher took their lead in asking them to write eulogies and then seemed to buckle under to the notion that it is best not to dwell too long on such events—better to get back to normal as soon as possible. As it turned out, the boys in Ken Jones's class had more problems the rest of the year. They were more unruly than they had been before the child's death, were less inclined to do their classwork, complained more frequently of headaches and stomachaches, and requested permission to go to the nurse's office more frequently throughout the remainder of the school year.

We will never know for sure if the boys in Ken Jones's class have learned permanently that the way to handle tragedies is to try to forget them and return to normal as soon as possible. Perhaps they have, and perhaps someone, since the time of the Ken Jones tragedy, has shown them a different way—a way they would have preferred in the first place. Since then, we have learned quite a bit about people's needs when it comes to coping with death and dying. Unfortunately, this knowledge is not being implemented in the schools consistently and pervasively, if at all.

Considering the turmoil and controversy going on over what is being taught in the schools, I am fully aware that suggesting the school curriculum should, at least in part, concentrate on the affective needs and the affective development of children would be accepted less than enthusiastically. Even when the movement for humanistic education was at its height in the United States, the ideas were not embraced by the majority. It may be next to impossible to convince entire school districts that we need to focus on some of the other real needs children have, especially when people are proposing a "get-back-to-the-basics" curriculum. Unfortunately, only a few of us think that mental health is a basic need. For the time being, this means that individuals will have to take the initiative to find ways and places in the curriculum and the school structure to work within the affective domain.

In terms of what has been learned about affective development and the strategies for meeting these needs, the "back-to-the-basics" movement could become a reversion to a less advanced stage rather than a cure for the ills in education. We know for a fact that there are numerous children who need help and could benefit from up-to-date knowledge and skills that are now available to professionals in the schools.

Twenty years ago, most of us were not all that clear about how to deliver mental health services to children in the school setting. Now we have better ideas and new ways, but the majority of those governing the schools are not very receptive. This is more than discouraging at times, since it almost guarantees some of the same mistakes of the past will continue—the kind of mistakes that were made in Ken Jones's class.

THE TERMINALLY ILL CHILD IN THE CLASSROOM

Despite all of the advances in medical science, more schools than ever before are confronted with the problem of students who are dying. Medical technology has developed to the stage where life can be prolonged for many children with terminal illnesses. A child's life-threatening illness can range from one that is imminently fatal, such as acute cancer, to a disease that has long-range implications of fatality, such as cystic fibrosis, kidney disease, heart disease, and cancers that are in remission. The fact that the children suffering from these diseases are attending school creates a multitude of questions, such as the effects on the other children; the school professional's responsibilities; and the best way to help the child, the child's classmates and parents, and the adults in the school to cope with the situation.

In dealing with a dying child in the classroom, the school professional should realize that each case is unique. There is no proven procedure for school personnel to follow. Judgment must be made and compassion must be experienced. Each person involved must be knowledgeable about the situation before taking action. The variety of ways that people might respond depends on the diagnosis. There are common reactions, however, that professionals in the schools should know about.

Some of these children express feelings of fear and anxiety to people at school when they feel they cannot show them to their families. Often these children feel the emotional involvement of their families and try to protect them and keep from hurting them. One thing that has been found to be helpful to these children is the development and instigation of a plan of action with their families (Koocher, 1974b). It has been noted that it makes an ill child uneasy to be set apart from peers. These children want to be treated just like other children, and in most cases it is best to minimize the illness.

As some researchers have found out, some parents feel tremendous guilt when they have a dying child (Kastenbaum, 1974). While the guilt is irrational, the feelings are real. Parents blame themselves because they did not contact a doctor at a certain time or because at one time they wished (as all parents do at some time or another) that they had not had the child in the first place. These same feelings have been seen in school professionals at varying times. Some feel guilty because they had blamed the child for being slow before they knew about the illness. Out of guilt, counselors and teachers fall into the same trap of overcompensating by becoming too protective of the ill child (Formanek, 1974). Showing favoritism to ill children sets them apart from their peers and makes school very distressing. They want to be treated in the same way as other students, and it is very important to ensure that this happens.

Having a terminally ill child in the class also can be distressing to classmates. As they begin to notice real differences in the dying child, they too become fearful and anxious. When the other children see that their classmate is absent a great deal, cannot go out to the playground, has lost hair, falls asleep in class, or has a different appearance, they frequently become concerned that what has happened to that child also will happen to them. Children who are sick sometimes have strange physical characteristics. For instance, those with cystic fibrosis have barrel chests, kidney and liver diseases can give a green appearance to the skin, and chemotherapy can cause baldness and extreme weight loss. It has been demonstrated that children in classes in which no explanation has been given for these physical differences often become cruel to the ill child. On the other hand, there is evidence that when the classmates are given an explanation, they become understanding, sensitive, and accepting. In all studies, open communication about the illness has been best for all involved (Childers & Wimmer, 1971; Formanek, 1974; Koocher, 1974a; Tallmer, 1974).

It seems that there is a period of mourning or bereavement when a classmate dies—maybe not for all the children, but certainly for some. The extent of mourning depends on how well other children had known the ill child. In general, it has been found that, to a child, the death of another child whom he or she has known quite well can be a severe crisis (Kastenbaum, 1974).

Michael: An Illustration

In my second year of teaching, Michael was admitted to my fifth-grade class. Michael had spent most of the previous year in the hospital undergoing chemotherapy for cancer. When he was admitted to the class he was a frail-looking child; some of his hair had started to grow back, but it was patchy. Most of the children remembered Michael from the third grade, where they had been classmates before his illness. From all past information, Michael had been a popular child, well liked and respected by his classmates. He had been a good student with many friends, played Little League baseball, and was never an isolate on the playground. He had his best friends, like most children, and in every respect was an all-around typical child.

When Michael returned to school, not only had he changed in some respects but the attitude of his classmates had changed as well. Their initial reaction was to avoid Michael; they stared at him frequently but did not speak to him or invite him to join them in their activities on the playground. My initial reaction, unfortunately, was also to avoid Michael. I did not know exactly how to treat this child, who had been seriously ill and was likely to die before the school year ended. I had been informed that death was imminent and only a matter of time. In retrospect, I remember that this frightened me, and I had thought many times that if this was to happen I certainly hoped it would happen over the summer and not during the school year. It was not that I did not speak to the child; when I did interact with Michael, however, I was not really with him. Avoidance also meant that I did not make an effort to help the other children in the class understand why Michael looked different than when they had last seen him, and I did not explain or try to discuss with the class anything concerning Michael's illness.

As the months went by, children in the class became cruel. They began teasing him about his baldness. Michael's absences became more frequent, and when he did return it was painfully noticeable and the children seemed almost angry to see him. They began to ask me if I would let them change seats so they did not have to sit next to the boy, and they made these requests vocally so Michael could hear them and was well aware of how the others were feeling about him.

Fate was not on Michael's side, nor on mine. What I had been dreading happened: Michael died during the school year.

It is important to know that the school was a parochial school. It was therefore commonplace for the children to attend religious church services on a regular basis—before school, during school hours, and sometimes after school, depending upon the occasion. Funerals for people in the parish were a common occasion. Although I had completely mishandled the circumstances for Michael, the fact that this took place in a religious environment was of some help to the other children in the class. The whole school—principal, teachers, and all students—attended the funeral, along with members of Michael's family and friends of the family. The funeral was at 8 a.m. and when it was over we returned to the classroom to go on with the regular school schedule.

I was saddened and deeply shaken (and undoubtedly also feeling guilty) over the loss of Michael, and I had cried profusely at the funeral. Since we were to continue with the school schedule, I assigned the children some quiet work and just wished for that day to end. The children were quiet but not content to just go about their quiet work. They would not just simply forget the matter and go on as usual. At varying intervals, one by one, a child would come to my desk to whisper a question concerning Michael: "Why did he die?" "Why was he in a box?" "What are they going to do with his body?" "Did he go to heaven?" I tried to manage this situation on a one-to-one basis, but that became impossible. The question that kept the day from being a totally tragic and terrifying one for all of the children came from one of the boys who had been Michael's friend. He came to my desk and said for all to hear: "I saw you cry in church. Why were you crying?" The question made me realize that my behavior all year had made it appear to the others that I did not like Michael. Undoubtedly, behind that question must have been some uncertainty about my ability to like and accept them should they become ill. Behind it also must have been questions about what was appropriate behavior under such circumstances. Obviously, to them, returning to the usual routine did not seem appropriate.

The children and I talked the rest of the morning. I admitted to them that I had not mentioned Michael's illness when he was alive because I did not know what to say; I thought it would be too upsetting for everybody, but I should have talked about it sooner. I told them I cried because it was a sad thing to lose someone you knew and liked. When I said it was all right to cry some of the children then cried in class. Some of their questions were answered in a religious context because this was a religious school, and the children's beliefs were comforting to them and had to be respected.

For the rest of the afternoon the children worked quietly at whatever work they chose to do: some drew pictures of heaven and God, some wrote stories about what Michael was now doing in heaven, some wrote stories about things not related to the death, and others did the regular schoolwork that they most enjoyed. It was a relaxed afternoon—not because it was quiet but because the children seemed relieved and more secure.

What I did not realize at the time is that children often have an emotional and psychological maturity beyond that expected for their years, which enables them to face death, even their own, with acceptance and serenity. This is true provided that adults can face the situation with emotional and psychological maturity and are willing to work with the children on understanding and eliminating fears.

OTHERS NOT TO BE FORGOTTEN

Because I consult with and instruct special education teachers and counselors, the topics discussed in this book have been receiving greater emphasis in the courses I teach. Fortunately, there is reciprocity in the work I do as I also learn from the working professionals who from time to time return to my classes. They recently have brought to my attention that the death of a teacher is another type of loss—a significant loss that I should have thought of, having been myself at one time a teacher of children. The incident reported to me in my university class concerned an elementary school teacher who died of cancer over the spring break. The children returned to a substitute teacher taking over the class, and the death of their own "real" teacher was never discussed. None of the children were released to attend her funeral. Although some of the parents had inquired about the funeral, the administration felt it would be "inappropriate" and "too upsetting" for the children to attend; they decided that the children needed to adjust to the new teacher. Consequently, during the remainder of the year numerous behavior problems appeared and there was a steady flow of children from this class to the nurse's office reporting a variety of physical complaints not connected to any real illnesses.

The point of this story is not to villainize people for what they do or fail to do but rather to offer this illustration as a reminder of the sensitivities of children, and of the fact that they will need attention and intervention whenever they lose a person with whom they have established a relationship. This might just as easily have been a story of the death of a counselor or a principal or another teacher down the hall whom the children knew or of a cafeteria worker who was regarded fondly by the children.

Environmentalists have referred to us as a throwaway society. Great care must be taken to ensure that we do not give the impression, especially to the young, that we throw away human beings as well.

THE IMPORTANCE OF RESOLVING A LOSS

One recurring theme in the literature dealing with children during the loss of a significant person is its emphasis on how the work of mourning or the resolution of bereavement can be aided by giving a child some understanding of these emotions before the occurrence of the event itself. The dissolution of some of our social taboos would facilitate the process of preparing children and helping them cope with loss situations in a healthy way. Pattison (1976) was especially critical in his attack on sociocultural taboos, which he believed led to many observed pathogenic effects of the loss of a parent on a child and which prevented the child and family from coping with the loss. Pattison believed that the family system incorporates the cultural denial of death rather than the integration of death and loss with natural life experiences, and that the family deals with the event through the avoidance mechanisms of family myth and family mystification.

A positive step in helping children before the occurrence of a significant loss is to not avoid the subject or a discussion of the emotions that the topic and the actual event engender. Changing ideas emphasize the exposure to death as a natural part of the life cycle. The suggestion to use literature as a basis for discussions on death and examples of relevant material is a good one (Bertman, 1974; Delisle & McNamee, 1981; Somerville, 1971).

It is believed that this type of approach can provide creative experiences through which people can grow. The illogicality of refusing to discuss death is obvious in such questions as, "Who teaches death education to youngsters? Does putting the death question out of sight have anything to do with putting the question out of mind? What do kids do with their secret thoughts of death if there is no place that these thoughts are acknowledged or allowed to seep through?" (Bertman, 1974, p. 339).

Since we know that children like to deal in fantasy and magical thoughts, it is likely that what they fantasize with regard to death is much worse than the real thing. Anthony (1972) commented that when adults attempt to keep from the child facts about death or indicate beliefs that the child's own experiences have shown them to be false, the child may suspect deception and develop anxieties more morbid and persistent than those that reality would have aroused.

Misleading statements, such as "only the old die," can lead to anxieties when a child's firsthand or secondhand experience of the death of a young person shows otherwise. Such stories would never be acceptable, obviously, to the children in Michael's or Ken Jones's class. Not only would the children be confused about why the people are lying but they would be even more frightened about what terrifying secret the adults are trying to hide.

Stories and fairy tales about death may be imaginative fancy that gets in the way of the child's ability to distinguish real from pretend, especially if adults persist with these stories after the child reaches a higher cognitive level of development. If explanations about death are given that even the adult does not believe, then the child often is sensitive enough to know this and react negatively to the deception.

Another deception practiced by adults is the use of "soft" words to play down the reality of death—terms such as "gone away," "passed on," and "eternal sleep." These can be misconstrued by children, leading to greater anxiety.

The answer to the question of when to tell the child about death would obviously seem to be when a question arises or when a death occurs. Even if the child barely knows the deceased person, the parents' suffering can be seen and the child often wants to participate. This can be an emotional experience that may help children when, in the future, they must come face to face with a traumatic and tragic situation (Nelson & Peterson, 1975).

In families in which a member has a terminal illness there is the opportunity to develop a plan to help the child understand and integrate what is happening, which can ease the adjustment following the death. When this situation exists, reality should not be kept from the child, although its fullness can be presented over a period of time.

The need for the family to inform the school is obvious, as is the need for the school's cooperation in following such a plan. It is absolutely imperative that the family know how the child is being dealt with at school; how important it is for the child to understand what is going on at home; what kind of information is being given; and that all concerned, at home and at school, will take great care to reassure the child that physical and emotional security will not be lost when the significant person does die.

Most children have experiences with loss that, at least in some ways, help to prepare them for significant losses. Mahon and Simpson (1977) studied the reaction of a group of children in a classroom to the death of a pet. This provided an occasion to discuss death. The pet is considered a secondary object; parents and siblings are primary objects. Even with the death of a pet, a period of mourning was observed. It is generally held that this type of experience with a secondary object can assist children in the process of mourning, which can lead to greater coping skills in resolving the eventual loss of a primary or significant person.

As has been stated, the process of mourning is considered important to the child's mental health, and it needs to be facilitated by the remaining parent or by other important adult figures.

Furman (1974) offered specific suggestions for helping a child to maintain a functioning personality and be able to mourn the lost parent (see below). School personnel should be knowledgeable about these suggestions so they can advise and work with the parents when necessary.

1. The child must be able to remain with a close, loving person rather than left with strangers.
2. Changes in ordinary daily living routines should be minimal.
3. The child needs and must receive physical closeness and empathy.
4. Younger children, especially, need help in understanding the reality of death and in learning to differentiate themselves from the dead.
5. Pictures and objects of the dead person should be part of the environment. They will help in different ways, sometimes reminding children of their love for the parent and at other times helping them in their identification process.
6. Children need and must have support during one of the loneliest and most difficult periods: the end of the mourning period. This is an area in which school professionals can be particularly helpful.

Participation in funeral rituals provides an opportunity for children to solidify their place as an integral part of the family system. They are able to witness the grief of others so that they do not think of the dead one as expendable and then wonder about their own expendability.

Other ways to aid mourning include placing special emphasis on remembering, which can include both loving and unpleasant memories. It is believed that this helps release resentments, which are a natural part of every child's store of feelings about parents. There is agreement that a child should not be discouraged from crying nor pushed to display unfelt sorrow (Greenberg, 1975; Kliman, 1968; Mahon & Simpson, 1977).

It also has been noted that sometimes a child's behavior of quickly turning to play activities is confusing to adults. The general understanding is that the child often is more active than the adult and therefore needs the motor-discharge pathways to help in the mourning process (Mahon & Simpson, 1977).

The school setting can be most helpful in aiding the child who has suffered the loss of a loved one. The special education classroom (the resource room, in particular) and the counselor's office are prime places for providing the necessary opportunity for children to vent their emotions and discuss them with an understanding adult. The words used when talking with a child are not as important as the attitude behind the words. The content of communication is of course important, but the channels and patterns (the feeling tone) are more significant. Probably the most important trait is that of being perceptive and empathic to what the child needs and is feeling.

Interferences In The Normal Mourning Process

After the loss of a significant person in a child's life, there are markers to let us know if the child is progressing or has passed through a normal mourning period and will emerge free of major emotional disorders. Most reactions that take place following the event might be considered pathological only if they show unusual intensity or persistence. Also, there is the possibility that the child appears to have made a healthy adjustment but pathological problems surface years later. With this sense of caution in mind, Kliman (1968) proposed that the presence of any one of the following criteria numbered 1 through 6 or any two of the criteria numbered 8 through 24 indicates that preventive intervention following childhood bereavement may be necessary and is almost certainly desirable.

1. Suicide as a cause of a parent's death.
2. Very poor relationship between child and dead parent.
3. Very poor relationship between child and surviving parent.
4. Dead parent was mentally ill and living with the family during the year prior to death.
5. Remaining parent is mentally ill.
6. Maternal bereavement of a girl less than eight years old.
7. Any two of the following:
8. Age less than four years at bereavement.
9. Child at one time had a neurotic or psychotic illness.
10. Paternal death during boy's adolescence.
11. Death forces a geographic move or causes severe economic hardship.

12. No readily available substitute object of same sex and appropriate age.

13. Remaining parent has pathologic mourning.

14. Remaining parent has increasing physical intimacy with child.

15. Child over age eight years old sheds no tears in first weeks after death.

16. Child over age four years does not discuss dead parent or fact of death.

17. Child over age five years refuses to participate in family funeral or religious observances.

18. Child has unusually cheerful mood beginning first week after parent's death.

19. Death was abrupt and unexpected.

20. Terminal illness was more than six months.

21. The terminal illness was unusually disfiguring or involved mental deterioration or physical mutilation.

22. Death from childbirth, uterine, ovarian, or breast carcinoma (if child is girl).

23. Family did not explain illness or deliberately concealed illness.

24. Family delayed informing child when others knew for more than one day. (pp. 89–90)

Obviously, parents should be aware that the death of a significant person can be a traumatic event in a child's life; however, some parents are unable to notice another's pain when they themselves are suffering. If the experience of grieving and bereavement is not shared within the family, it is often reenacted with someone else who becomes a parent surrogate. Apparently, children's mourning differs from that of the adult in degree but not in quality. The work of mourning goes on in three areas: accepting the loss, reminiscing and giving up the psychic energy that had been concentrated on the lost object (decathecting), and establishing substitute object relationships. A child's activity in all three areas is an indication of a healthy and normal resolution of bereavement (Kliman, 1968).

Counselors, teachers, and social workers should not underestimate the role they can play in the child's life at this time. In addition to giving emotional support to the child directly, school professionals may be called on to play the intermediary between the child and classmates and provide opportunities for discussion of questions and feelings the event is bound to raise in the classroom. Special care should be taken to not avoid the subject if the child is present and a question arises. The child may be relieved to know that others have questions about death, and the discussion gives opportunities to provide help to the child by remembering the deceased and knowing that others remember (Nelson & Peterson, 1975). Modern funeral homes have prepared booklets that address the questions most young children have about death. If you are uncertain about how to answer questions, these booklets can be very helpful.

Whether death education should become a part of the educational curriculum will undoubtedly be argued both by those who feel you should not discuss the subject because it belongs in the home and not at school, and by those who believe there is a need to do away with sociocultural taboos dealing with death. Whatever the outcome of this debate, professionals in the schools will continue to face issues dealing with death. From the research, we know that if children have adults around them who are knowledgeable about and sensitive to their needs, the children can proceed through their periods of bereavement and emerge with healthy, intact personalities.

Child Abuse
and Neglect

Stacy

"Well, what do you think? Isn't your mother gorgeous? Could have been a movie star, you know! People tell me all the time how I look like a movie star. 'Course you came along and I had to give up all my plans and get married and have a baby. Anyway, I do still have a terrific figure!"

Rita Clark stood in front of the bathroom mirror putting the final touches on her makeup and hair while talking to her daughter.

Stacy was only half listening as she stooped in the bathtub, clutching her feet with her hands. She was not sitting all the way down in the tub yet—the water was too hot. She looked up at her mother, thinking about what she had just said. Yes, her mother was very pretty. Stacy even thought she was the most beautiful lady in the whole world, especially when she was fixin' up to go out someplace. She stared at her mother who was all dressed up and ready to go out and see people and have a good time.

A funny feeling came over Stacy as she compared in her mind how extremely different they were. She thought of herself and how ridiculous she looked and felt. There was her mother all dressed with makeup and hair in place, looking very beautiful. And Stacy naked in the bathtub, hunched over with her bare bottom in the air, scrawny, hair half wet and hanging in her face. She wished her mother would leave the bathroom and leave her alone. She hated looking like that even in front of her mother.

Stacy's funny feeling became stronger. It had started as a feeling of not really being in her body. She felt more like she was someone else watching everything that was going on between herself and her mother. The feeling intensified to a point where she felt like she was getting smaller and smaller and, if it continued, she would disappear and be gone forever. It was a frightening sensation that she had had many times before, and she could not understand where the feeling came from or why she felt that way sometimes. The hot bath water brought Stacy back into herself and reality.

"Put some more cold in the water, Mamma. It's too hot! I can't sit down—the water burns!"

"How many times have I told you not to call me Mamma! Or Mommy. Or Mom! None of that stuff! Are you completely dense? Call me by my name like everybody else. My name, as you know is Rita! My mother named me after her favorite movie star, Rita Hayworth—just the most gorgeous woman in Hollywood in her day, the most popular pinup of the soldiers during World War II. Don't kiss and hug and hang all over me, either. You're too big for that! Take your bath like I told you. You're holding up the show. I don't intend to be late and you won't be either. I've got plans, have someplace to go tonight. And you, you're going to your dad's for the weekend."

A flood of rage came over Stacy as she bit down hard on her lower lip to keep from shouting her thoughts at her mother. I hate you. All you care about is just you and looking in that mirror. I wish I was dead! I hate you more than anything!

She felt a trickle of tears run down the side of her nose. Nothing she felt made a difference to her mother. She wouldn't dare tell her what she was just thinking. Her mother didn't seem to care that the water was so hot that her feet and hands had turned as red as a lobster. In fact, Rita had not stopped staring at herself in the mirror long enough to notice Stacy's misery.

Stacy's feelings of rage dissolved into great sadness. Her chest ached and throbbed and felt like the heaviest part of her body. She considered what she had just wanted to shout at her mother and gave it more thought. She really did not hate her mother; she loved her. Her mother really did not do bad things to hurt her hardly even gave her spankings, and when she did, they didn't even hurt much at all. She just didn't pay attention to how Stacy felt or what she wanted. She wanted her mother to love her. That's what she wanted most of all. She wished her mother would take her out of the tub and wrap her in a towel and hug her and rock her. She wanted to feel that good way again like long ago when she lived with her grandmother. There were never hot baths then. Gram made happy times and would hug her tight while rocking her in the chair and singing songs.

Rita's voice broke into Stacy's memories almost as if she was reading her mind.

"I could have been a famous singer with my voice and looks. Want me to sing to you? What should I sing? Everyone loves to hear me sing. You know I have a real talent for singing. You like to hear me sing, too, don't you, Stacy?"

Stacy perked up a bit at the offer of something pleasant. Her mother knew that she liked to hear her singing. It was nice, and when she sang, Stacy felt lots of love for her mother. The pretty songs made her feel loved. Such a pretty voice singing nice words to Stacy felt like love. When she sang to Stacy how could she not love Stacy? There was one song in particular that made Stacy feel wonderful. It was a song with a delicate little melody that told of flying on the back of a butterfly, being in the sunshine and breeze, going anyplace you please. Stacy loved that song. It made her feel light and happy. Her chest stopped feeling so heavy as she looked up at her mother with expectation.

"Sing the one about the butterfly. I like that one. It's my favorite!"

"What in the hell are you doing? Why haven't you sat down in that bathwater yet?"

"See, my feet are so red. The water burns. Please put more cold in. I don't want to sit down, it's too hot! The water is too hot!"

"Hot baths are good for a person. Gets all the dirt out of your pores. The stink, too, I might add. You did that nasty thing at school again today. I'm telling you, Stacy, I don't want that school calling me again to come and get you because you wet yourself. You're a big girl now; 8 years old is far too big to still be having those accidents. God, sometimes I wonder just whose child you are! You certainly are nothing like me. My dear own mother used to say what a beautiful, perfect child I was. I certainly never did such nasty things."

Tears came to Stacy's eyes again and blurred her vision. She could not see the expression on her mother's face but she did not have to look at her. She knew there would be no butterfly song, no nice words or pretty sounds. Her good feeling disappeared as the memory of the whole horrible day was brought back to her by what her mother had just said. Her chest became very heavy again and now she wished she would disappear.

"It wasn't my fault, Rita. I got mixed up again. I thought it was the lunch bell, not recess. I didn't mean to leave school before I was supposed to—thought it was lunchtime, not recess."

"Of course you don't know what's going on! Your teacher said you sleep in class all the time. I'm getting pretty tired of you embarrassing me in front of people! The school calling me up there all the time about one damn thing after another. It's endless and I'm getting sick of it, Stacy! I wish to hell you were living with your father permanently! Can't take much more of this!"

Rita Clark worked, so Stacy could not go home for lunch and her mother never had the time to make a sack lunch for her to take to school. Stacy only remembered feeling good when she heard the bell and ran out of the building to go to lunch. Her mother gave her money and permission to leave the grounds to eat in a little diner close to school. She liked that a lot because she always got to eat what she liked; the same friendly waitress was always there and talked to her about school and such; and, best of all, when she had money left over she put it in the music machine and listened to some favorite song. When she didn't have leftover money the waitress in the diner would play the machine. She would always ask Stacy, "What should we listen to?" Then she would play just the song Stacy wanted to hear. The nice lady in the diner would say, "That's exactly what I wanted to hear, too." It was the most pleasant part of her day, something she looked forward to—a lunch she liked, the lady in the diner to talk to, and some pretty music.

Stacy listened to her mother rave on and on about her numerous failings. She was still crouched down in the tub clutching her red feet because the water was too hot. She thought about what happened that day at school and she felt embarrassed. She couldn't think clearly about the whole confusing incident. It left her mind feeling numb because she didn't understand how it happened. School was mostly something to be endured. Things always seemed to go wrong at school and she didn't understand how they happened. Like this thing today. Stacy was shocked and completely surprised when she returned from the diner to find that the others were just leaving for lunch. Her teacher grabbed her by the arm and asked her where she had been but did not believe it when Stacy said she thought it was lunchtime. So the teacher put her in the "bad corner" for the rest of the day to be ignored. Those were the rules. Once in the "bad corner," you had to be ignored.

She just sat in the corner that afternoon feeling far away, like she was shrinking to a very tiny size, like she would disappear, until the urge came. She tried to get her teacher's attention to let her go to the bathroom, but she was ignored. The ignoring went on and on as Stacy tried more and more desperately to get her teacher's attention. It went on too long. Her stomach started to hurt, and she couldn't hold it any longer. Stacy pressed her body down harder on the chair and squeezed her legs tight, trying with all her strength to stop it, but it was too painful. She gave in to the inevitable humiliation. First a small trickle and then the chair was flooded and ran over the edges to the floor. That's when the others noticed. They heard the noise and all turned to look. The giggles and calling to the teacher started. "Stacy did it again in her pants, Teacher." "Stacy's a baby, Teacher." "She stinks." "Send her home!"

Stacy looked up at her mother who was still preening before the mirror, getting ready for a fun night out. "I really did think it was lunchtime. I couldn't help it today, Mamma. I can't sleep. I'm afraid of those bad dreams. I get so sleepy. Mamma, do you love me?"

"What kind of a stupid question is that? I'm your mother aren't I? Stop trying to change the subject! Wetting yourself. How shameful, Stacy! What an embarrassment you are to me! And sleeping in school! I've been putting you to bed earlier; you get enough sleep! I suppose I'll have to start sending you to bed right after school, if that's what it takes! Get down in that tub and finish your bath! You'll be late when Beatrice comes to pick you up. I don't intend to hang around here with you. You're not going to mess that up for me. I don't want you here when Gary comes. You embarrass me at your school, but you're not going to embarrass me in front of my friends."

She wished her mother did not feel embarrassed. She felt very sad and her chest ached with such heaviness that it was hard to breathe. Her throat tightened like her own blood vessels would strangle and crush her neck. She would suffocate! Stacy fought back her tears and words. Rita did not like it when she cried. She let her daughter know plainly that her reasons never made any sense. Stacy felt stupid and ugly. She must be stupid and ugly or else her own mother would not hate her so much. There seemed to be no hope that her mother would ever love her as long as she was so bad, always doing stupid and nasty, ugly things.

Stacy wanted her mother to make her feel better and to understand how bad she felt. She had learned, though, that it was useless to try to explain things to Rita. So she said no more about what happened that day. Stacy was tiring of the bathtub and of talking about it all again. She just wanted to put on some clothes and be alone in her room for a while before her stepmother came to get her.

"Can I get out now? I've been in the tub long enough."

"I will not—do you hear me—will not allow you to go visit your father smelling like a dirty old bathroom. Although he probably wouldn't even notice. He has no class whatsoever. What a disgusting man! You're a lot like your father, do you realize that, Stacy? Never would have married him, but there you were. So, that's what I get I guess. Anyway, he wouldn't notice your dirty old bathroom smell but that damn wife of his would and then she would say ugly things about me to other people. There I'd be, embarrassed again!"

"Do I have to go to Dad's? Can I have a babysitter instead? I wish Gram was here! There isn't anything to do at Dad's house. Could I stay home this weekend with you?"

"No, you cannot have a babysitter! I can't afford it! These days, kiddo, my poor, dear, dead mother wouldn't want anything to do with you. Thank God she can't see how you've turned out. She would be real disgusted with you, Stacy, just as I am. I need the weekend to myself—can't have you around all the time or I might start acting as crazy as you do!"

"What time will Beatrice be here to get me? Who's going to bring me back? How long am I supposed to stay with them?"

"Not long enough, that's for sure. That damn new wife of his won't allow you to stay with him. I tried—told him he should take some of the responsibility for his mistake. That's you, you know, his mistake and mine. But, oh no! Beatrice wouldn't have any of that. She has too frail a temperament, couldn't have a kid around all the time, both have to work too hard, long hours. Damn them both! I work hard, too, and don't have near the money they have! I ought to just leave you on their doorstep sometime, let them figure it out!"

Stacy's thoughts turned to her father. She was not really looking forward to their visit. He didn't talk to her much when she was at his house. They were like strangers to each other. It was a mystery—the two of them, father and daughter, and yet they did not know each other at all. He asked the usual things anybody would. "How're you doing in school? Like the teacher and other kids?" If Beatrice was nowhere around, he would occasionally ask about Rita and how she was doing.

Stacy considered his questions for a few minutes but gave him the usual answers back. Everything was fine. She sensed he would not really be interested in hearing how hard things could be at school sometimes and that she did not have any friends. From what Rita had said about her father, she had long ago put away her thoughts of what it would be like for her if Rita and her dad were still married. Once she had thought that Rita would be happier and love her more if she had him back. In turn, she thought her father would get to know her and then he would love her. But Rita hated him, so she gave up that dream. Her dad always seemed restless and eager for the weekend to pass and then finally relieved when her mother took her back home. Most of the time they left Stacy with her stepmother's sister while the two of them went out to dinner and a movie.

It wasn't only that her father seemed like a stranger that kept

Stacy from wanting to go to his house. It was mainly Beatrice. Beatrice always found something wrong with Stacy. In many ways, she was a lot like Rita, just not always as blunt. She could make Stacy feel like crying, too, just by the way she said things. Her dad heard Beatrice's insults but never said a word to defend Stacy. Sometimes he looked sadly at Stacy but still never said anything.

Stacy had some good feeling for her father, though. He always gave her a hug when he saw her. He never yelled at her or said ugly things. Once he actually told her he thought she was getting prettier all the time. Her father bought her nice presents and even seemed to get excited about the toys he gave her. Sometimes it was like he was about to offer to play and enjoy the new things with Stacy, but then Beatrice would take over and always seemed to find a way to separate them. Stacy knew Beatrice wanted to keep her away from her dad. She didn't want them to get to know each other.

Stacy felt sad and confused thinking about it all. She could not make any sense out of a big, grown man not being able to do or say what he wanted. She felt very mad at him for doing nothing about the situation, always doing what Beatrice wanted. She hated Beatrice for keeping her father away.

"Rita, does Daddy love me?"

"How should I know what your father thinks or feels! Besides, isn't it obvious? What did I just say? Don't you think you would be living with him if he loved you? You better get with reality, kiddo. Stop being such a dreamer. Okay, so you're clean enough now. Get out of the tub and get dressed. That woman will be here any minute to pick you up."

Stacy put on her clothes. Her mother had laid out her prettiest dress and good shoes. Even Rita said she looked nice in that dress. Her mother came in and brushed her long hair. It was dry now and fell down in waves. Rita was satisfied that Stacy looked presentable enough to go to her father's "without being an embarrassment."

"There's the horn. That fat-ass Beatrice! The queen is waiting out there in her big fancy car. Get going. I'll be picking you up Sunday, so when you hear me honk, hurry out! I don't want to have to see those two for even a minute! Have a good time. Don't do anything to embarrass me! Go on, Stacy. Love ya."

Stacy turned to give her mother a hug good-bye but Rita had already returned to the bathroom and was looking in the mirror again, brushing her hair. She yelled bye-bye, but Rita did not respond. She was singing for herself the butterfly song.

Stacy skipped her way up to the car, forcing a smile. She could feel the sweat break out on her face and her hands turn cold and clammy. Her heart was pounding and it was getting hard for Stacy to breathe. She opened the car door.

"Hi, Bea! How are you? What a beautiful new car! When did you get it? Blue is my favorite color, too. It's almost the same color as my dress. Will Dad be home from work when we get there? I hope so! Do you think we could all go to a movie? I don't mean right now, but maybe later tonight or tomorrow?"

"Make sure the door is closed tight and lock it. Don't want your mother suing us if you fall out and crack your head open or something. I see you could use a haircut. You'd look more presentable with shorter hair. People are going to start wondering if you are animal or human! Oh, well, don't worry, I've made an appointment for you tomorrow with my very own hairdresser. She can do wonders, even with the worst of messes. Can't change the color, though, you're too young to dye your hair. Someday....But I'm sure we can get you fixed up some better for now. Anything would be an improvement! You really shouldn't wear blue. It doesn't go well with your complexion, and it makes you look too tall and skinny. Hope you put on some weight. Right now, can't tell if you're a boy or a girl.

"Your father will be too tired to go out tonight. He and I will go out tomorrow night, and you will get to stay with my sister. I'm sure you'll enjoy that. You wouldn't enjoy the movies we like to see, anyway, Stacy."

Stacy looked out the back window of the car as it moved down the street away from her house. Rita was going down the walk with her friend Gary. She looked very happy with her arm wrapped around his. Stacy wiped the tears away from the corners of her eyes so Beatrice would not see her crying, then turned around in the seat for the rest of the ride to her father's house.

....

Someday, maybe, there will exist a well-informed, well-considered, and yet fervent public conviction that the most deadly of all possible sins is the mutilation of a child's spirit; for such mutilation undercuts the life principle of trust, without which every human act, may it feel ever so good, and seem ever so right, is prone to perversion by destructive forms of consciousness.

—*Erik Erikson*

Stacy's story is an illustration of only one type of child abuse: emotional. The story will be given more attention in the section on that subject, which is the first type of abuse discussed in this chapter.

Each year, in the United States alone, approximately 1 million children are abused by their parents or caregivers, and this is considered a conservative estimate. Children are subjected to cruel and unusual punishment: physical beatings, emotional abuse, sexual molestation, physical neglect, torture, and even murder; approximately 2,000 of these children die each year. In most cases, these acts are committed by adults who should be providing love, security, and trust. For many of the children who survive, the damage inflicted on them impacts their entire lives (National Center on Child Abuse and Neglect, 1991).

It is said that child abuse affects us as a nation and destroys our children, who are the nation's resources. Historically, accounts of abuse have been reported repeatedly by delinquents, adult criminals, adolescent drug offenders, and prostitutes. Agencies and governmental committees that talk of the financial cost to society of dealing with the results of child abuse say that it is astronomical. More importantly, the cost in human suffering and wasted potential cannot be calculated.

The latter cost is the reason why this chapter was written, and it should be the only real reason for our involvement. Financial liabilities to the nation are inconsequential in comparison to the human suffering, wasted lives, and wasted potential. That is why we should be so concerned.

Definitions of child abuse range from acts of commission [willfully inflicting physical injury to a child (Kempe & Kempe, 1976)] to omission [wasting a child's potential by failing to provide conditions necessary for optimal development (Gil, 1976)]. Child abuse includes intentional acts of commission or omission on the part of the caregiver that result in physical or emotional injury or damage to a child.

This chapter focuses on the traditionally recognized types of abuse: emotional, nonaccidental physical injury, physical neglect, and sexual molestation. In addition, the more recently identified ritual abuse also is discussed (Oates, 1989; Williamson, Borduin, & Howe, 1991). Since the definition of abuse includes the idea of obstructing a child's optimal development, abuse has strong implications for professionals dealing with children, particularly in educational settings. Child abuse can no longer be overlooked. In the past, physicians and social workers made nearly all the reports of abuse, but today all states have laws regarding child abuse, report-ing procedures, and the responsibilities of certain adults who know about any type of abuse being perpetrated against a child (Sorenson, 1991). Even were there no legal repercussions, we would not want to ignore these rulings, no matter how temporarily unpleasant, uncomfortable, or difficult they might make our own lives.

In the ethical sense and by the guidelines of their own profes-sion, counselors are required to get involved. The American School Counselor Association (ASCA) adopted a position on child abuse and neglect in 1981 and published the recommendations in 1983. The statement included the requirement that school counselors not only be able to identify abuse and neglect but also must know their role in dealing with such cases. The ASCA guidelines state that report-ing suspected cases is the responsibility of school counselors. Counselors are warned that failure to report even suspicions of child abuse may result in legal penalties (ASCA, 1983).

In fact, there could be legal penalties for most professionals working with children should they fail to report any type of child abuse. All 50 states have some law against abusing children, although the legal definition of what constitutes child abuse may dif-fer from state to state. For instance, all states have clear laws about physical and sexual abuse, but when it comes to emotional neglect and abuse the issue is less clear and the laws are less definite (Smith, 1988). Where school personnel are concerned, there are 7 states that do not require the reporting of emotional neglect, 3 states that do not require the reporting of abandonment, 1 state that does not require the reporting of children at risk for abuse, and 1 state that does not require the reporting of general maltreatment. In addi-tion, only 3 states do require that the exploitation of children be reported (Sorenson, 1991). Although not all school personnel are required to report all types of abuse in all 50 states, each state does have at least one statewide agency that is required by law to receive and investigate reports of any type of child abuse.

The problem of child abuse is not only one of physical batter-ing. Neglect and emotional and sexual abuse have equally devastat-ing effects on a child's development. Except for the children who are permanently brain damaged or killed, the most tragic aspect is the permanent adverse effects on the developmental process and the child's emotional well-being (Cantrell & Prinz, 1985). Stacy's story, which opened this chapter, dealt with the type of abuse that people know and understand the least about: emotional abuse.

Emotional Abuse

My attempt to illustrate emotional abuse in Stacy's story was the most difficult of the vignettes to write. The children who suffer this type of abuse are subjected to mental and emotional torment that is somewhat difficult to depict. Although people have attempted to define emotional abuse, it is still very difficult to describe what is happening to a child in a way that would show it as abuse. In contrast to physical or sexual abuse or even physical neglect, this type of abuse is more nebulous. The outward signs are hazy, indistinct, and confused. Unless adults in the schools are really knowledgeable about this subject (and few professionals of any sort truly are) and really know the child and the family, these children for the most part go unnoticed.

Definitions that are used for legal and social services purposes will be given later, but first an example is given of why it is very difficult to try to describe abuse. Emotional abuse is analogous to prejudice—not the obvious kind in which a cross is burned on someone's front yard or people are beaten or hung. Instead it is an insidious type that is stealthily treacherous but inconspicuous to outsiders while having a grave, injurious effect on the self-esteem and emotional life of the person. Even adults who experience this type of prejudice find it difficult to describe to others what is actually happening to them. They cannot tell someone that so-and-so beat them up, spit in their face, or pulled their hair. Some types of discrimination or prejudice are so subtle that people who have tried to describe an example will tell you that when they relate what transpired it sounds almost silly and trivial.

Now let us turn to the emotionally abused child. What could Stacy tell people about what was happening to her? How could she describe her mother? Her stepmother? What could she say to someone that would make her abuse obvious. Chances are that Stacy could say nothing that would make her abuse obvious? Chances are that Stacy could say nothing that would make any adult become alarmed at seeing an emotionally abused child. Stacy would not say, "My mother thinks I'm ugly," or "She thinks I'm stupid." Instead, she says, "I am ugly," or "I am stupid." Stacy, or any young child for that matter, cannot interpret parental behavior in a logical fashion, testing it for reality. Young children do not think, "My mother thinks such and such." To do so implies that they recognize the parent thinks something and that it may or may not be true. To a young child, what a mother or father thinks is the actuality.

I once heard a woman who runs a preschool for disadvantaged black children describe how she thought children responded to what adults say to them. This perceptive woman said, "Watch any young child when a parent or an important adult says to them, 'Aren't you beautiful?' The child replies, 'Uh-huh.' 'Aren't you smart?' The child replies, 'Uh-huh.' And the reverse operates just as strongly. If a child is asked, 'Aren't you ugly?' The child will reply, 'uh-huh.' The child will also agree that he or she is stupid, worthless, unlovable, or bothersome to have around. But, if these questions are not put to the child directly but the adult behavior says the same thing as loudly and as clearly, then the child concludes that the adult's inner voice is saying, 'Yes, you are ugly, stupid, worthless, bothersome, unlovable,' and the child agrees, 'Uh-huh, uh-huh, uh-huh.'"

Stacy's abuse is more subtle than the abuse in most cases recounted in the literature. She is not physically neglected or physically injured. People cannot see anything actually happening to her. We don't know from the story how this mother appears to others at the school, only how she treats her child in the privacy of their home. Chances are, this mother seems to others pretty much like any other mother. Stacy has decent clothes, and she even has the money to take herself out to lunch—enough money, in fact, to spend on a luxury such as playing the jukebox. Although she exhibits signs that would alert a knowledgeable professional (lack of concentration, disorientation, enuresis), more than likely her teacher sees her as "one of that bothersome kind of child" that you get now and then.

No one should be blamed for not recognizing this problem. It is a tough one to identify. Even lawyers have a difficult time preparing a case alleging emotional abuse. And if it presents problems to lawyers it will present even greater problems to those who are not versed in dealing with such cases. I cannot even guess how many children whom I taught in my years as a regular education teacher might have been emotionally abused. In most cases, when I taught children who had been diagnosed previously as disturbed, there was no question, but in my regular classes, I cannot even begin to suspect. When searching my memory, I recall children who acted like Stacy: those who had occasional accidents; would fall asleep, never seemed to be quite with it, and would do some things that they surely knew were wrong. Emotional abuse? I had never even heard the term. It was not in any of my textbooks; my professors never mentioned it; and there were no television movies about it, nothing in weekly news magazines, no talk shows to inform me, and no pamphlets that described it. Now more information is available—not a lot, but some and that is one of the purposes of this book: to make professionals better informed, more aware, and more capable of providing some help to these children.

The National Committee for Prevention of Child Abuse (1983) defined emotional abuse to include the following:

> ... excessive, aggressive, or unreasonable parental demands that place expectations on a child beyond his or her capabilities. Emotional abuse can show itself in constant and persistent teasing, belittling, or verbal attacks. Emotional abuses also include failures to provide the psychological nurturance necessary for a child's psychological growth and development—no love, no care, no support, no guidance. (p. 5)

The foregoing quotation describes some of the main features of Stacy's abuse. She is constantly belittled by both her mother and her stepmother. In Stacy's own words, her mother "hardly even gave me spankings, and when she did, they didn't hurt much at all." The only events that Stacy doesn't seem to give much thought to are the hot baths she is given for her accidents. Chances are that Stacy's mother does not give much thought to them either, in terms of whether or not she is mistreating her child. The vignette about Stacy does not suggest that the baths scald and burn the child, as is often seen in cases of physical abuse.

There is, however, an element of physical abuse involved in Stacy's emotional abuse. Although the child is not injured, the bath is meant to be an unpleasant experience; the intent is to punish the child and make her suffer. Many parents guilty of emotional abuse are not even aware of their motives for inflicting unpleasant physical experiences on their children. The belittling and berating that goes on in emotional abuse is sometimes done under the guise of teasing but the intent is malicious. These characteristics are seen in Stacy's stepmother.

Some of the things parents do that constitute emotional abuse have been described by Garbarino and Garbarino (1984). The authors described parents who knowingly refuse to allow attachment and bonding to take place between them and their infants. Frequently, the parents punish their child for showing signs of positive, normal behavior such as walking, talking, smiling, and exploring their environment; for exhibiting signs of positive self-esteem; and for trying to form social relationships and friendships outside the family.

This description certainly seems to define the problem well; that is exactly what emotional abuse is all about. However, what is missing in their explanation is a concrete behavior that people can see for themselves and that could lead to court action. Dean (1979) tried to clarify the legalities better by describing several court cases that have been adjudicated. Legal interpretations of abuse may vary from court to court, but most courts are reluctant to get involved unless the effects of emotional abuse are very clear and unusually extreme. Of the three court cases successfully presented, all involved one or more of the following characteristics: "an act that in itself is sufficient to establish abuse; differential treatment of one child in the family; [or] a reduction in the child's functioning that can be linked to abusive treatment" (p. 19).

Dean said that when preparing for court it is necessary to document which of the characteristics of abuse are present and to show that the emotional abuse has had a detrimental effect on the child. She gave several examples of cases of emotional abuse that reached the courts. One case involved a child who had to wear a sign on herself wherever she went that told of the wrongdoing she had committed. Another case concerned an adolescent who was forced to stand in his front yard in diapers as punishment. The third case described a child who was the family scapegoat and whose mistreatment was obvious and observable. These cases involved extreme public humiliation, and the courts ruled that a child has a right "to reasonable and just discipline in the privacy of the home. Subjecting a child to public scorn was not considered reasonable or positive discipline" (p. 19).

It is good, of course, that these cases reached the courts, where intervention could take place to help those children. What is distressing about these rulings, however, is the courts' usage of the language "in the privacy of the home," so that, when it comes to emotional abuse, the courts in effect have said that parents can treat their children as they please as long as they do it in private. Would the hundreds, thousands, or millions of children who are treated like Stacy find that particular ruling very comforting or satisfactory? I doubt it.

Signs of Emotional Abuse

Before the National Committee for Prevention of Child Abuse distributed material defining all the types of abuse, some local child-protective agencies developed definitions of their own that were based upon the research of the most noted authorities on the subject. Rarely was emotional abuse mentioned. One local child-protective agency put together a paper for its newly hired social workers. This paper talked about physical abuse, physical neglect, and what is termed "emotional neglect." Surprisingly enough, sexual abuse is not mentioned at all.

Concerning emotional neglect, the agency listed certain signs to look for in children, such as moodiness, withdrawal, aggressiveness, difficulties in school adjustment, temper tantrums, and stuttering. The symptoms sound like ones that can be observed in a child experiencing any number of problems or crises. The agency's paper went on to say that if these symptoms are observed, the child undoubtedly is emotionally neglected and is probably being subjected to family friction, marital discord, or rejection. Also, it warned that a child will be emotionally neglected if one or both of the parents are disturbed by neurosis or psychosis.

Another paper from a local agency also listed signs of emotional neglect with the intent of alerting social workers. Among others, this paper posed questions such as the following: Is the child loved or hated? Is the child constantly scolded, scapegoated, and discouraged? Is there excessive alcohol consumption in the family? Does the excessive use of alcohol cause behaviors that create severe family conflicts? Does the child appear lost in the family setting? Is there a stepparent who is jealous of or who resents the child? Is the child rejected?

These are, indeed, all behaviors that are related to emotional abuse as we understand it today. Social workers who have access to the home are in a better position to determine the existence of these behaviors. It is more difficult for counselors and teachers to make such determinations, unless the behavior of the child at school is obvious and serious enough to warrant a home visit. Even then, teachers and counselors typically do not, and often are not allowed to, visit unannounced or as frequently as social workers, and therefore they commonly find the parents on their best behavior when they do make a visit. The social services agencies should, however, be given credit for recognizing years ago that children can be abused emotionally and mentally, even if the definitions offered by these agencies were not precise enough to be helpful to those outside the profession. Today, it is still difficult to be precise, since the definitions have not been consolidated, nor has the entire issue even been clarified (Criville, 1990; Dean, 1979; Foreman & Seligman, 1983; Junewicz, 1983; Kavanagh, 1982; Lourie & Stefano, 1978; Whiting,

1976).

The list that follows describes a number or signs of characteristics of children who have been emotionally abused and is drawn from the literature that exists on this topic.

1. self-destructive behavior
2. apathy, depression, and withdrawals
3. academic failure
4. developmental delays
5. hyperactivity, tantrums, and conduct disorders
6. pseudomaturity
7. lack of trust
8. rigid, compulsive, and disorganized behavior
9. feelings of inadequacy and poor self-esteem
10. role reversal (the child takes care of the parent)
11. excessive fantasy
12. fearfulness and hyperalertness
13. lack of creativity
14. poor peer relations or peer dependence
15. lack of familial attachment
16. gender confusion
17. lack of empathy
18. excessive anxiety and night terrors
19. obliviousness to hazards and risks

The literature from which the above list is drawn includes the following: Linn-Benton Education Service Digest, 1991; Emery, 1989; Garbarino & Garbarino, 1984; Lourie & Stefano, 1978; Money, 1982; Moss & Moss, 1984; Rohner, 1975; Straker & Johnson, 1981; Whiting, 1976.

Obviously, the symptoms noted are not exclusively symptoms of emotional abuse; they appear over and over again in material related to any childhood crisis. They appear as symptoms in children suffering from family strife and divorce as well as in children suffering the loss of a significant person because of death or mental illness. They appear too as symptoms in children physically and sexually abused. There are only so many ways a child can respond to tragedies and crisis-ridden lives. The point is to keep emphasizing the symptoms so that professionals are alerted to children whose mental health is threatened. First the child has to be identified; then the differential diagnosis follows.

The Parents and How They Behave

The first question usually asked about parents who mistreat their children is "How can people possibly abuse children?" Phrased that way, the question is unanswerable. The attention has to be focused on the particular situations and the characteristics of adults who typically are involved in the abuse of children. As is true of all types of abuse, these parents come from all racial, religious, economic, and ethnic groups; many were abused as children themselves. The only certain characteristic of abusive parents is that they are people struggling with a combination of stresses that they experience as overwhelming and for which they do not have coping skills.

Situational factors. Frequently these parents find themselves in isolation from family, friends, or other adults who could provide them with emotional support. They generally are people with low self-esteem who do not like themselves or know how to fulfill their own emotional needs. In many cases, although not all, higher rates of abuse are associated with undesirable economic conditions (Linn-Benton Education Service Digest, 1991; Otto, 1984; Steinberg, Catalano, & Dooley, 1982).

It is not uncommon to find that these parents suffer from forms of mental retardation, drug and alcohol abuse, and such types of psychopathology as severe personality disorders and sadistic psychosis. Some of these parents have unrealistic ideas about the needs of children and just do not understand how to care for them. Apparently the most common situation leading to emotional abuse is when parents feel unable to resolve their own stress and control their own lives; the child becomes the target for mistreatment when the parents are unable to cope (Emery, 1989; Garbarino & Garbarino, 1984; Garbarino & Gilliam, 1980; Justice & Justice, 1976).

In an article (Junewicz, 1983) from the field of social work, this type of mistreatment of children is divided into two parts: (1) emotional neglect, defined as parental omission in the child's care by providing no stimulation, and (2) emotional abuse, defined as parental acts toward children that overstimulate the children, such as verbal rejection and fear-inducing language or behavior. This article reported the results of a study conducted over a 3-year period that delineated five family environments producing emotional neglect or emotional abuse: (1) mental illness, (2) abuse of drugs or alcohol, (3) serious stress in relationships, (4) inadequate adjustment to life, and (5) serious personal conflicts. One hundred children from such family environments were studied, and the majority of the children were found to be either emotionally neglected or emotionally abused. The family environments that seemed to produce the most abuse were the third item listed above (serious stress in relationships) and the fifth (serious personal conflicts). The other family environments were split almost evenly between abuse and neglect, with the exception of the second (abusing drugs or alcohol), in which the majority of the children were judged to be predominantly emotionally neglected.

Parental behavior. It is consistently extreme behavior that is cause for concern. Isolated traumas apparently are not as damaging as a constant and pervasive pattern of emotional neglect and emotional abuse (Oates, 1989). This style of interaction was depicted in Stacy's story as it became clear that emotional attacks were part of the day-to-day routine in her life with her mother. The emotional abuse was continued by her stepmother, and school too was unpleasant, which left Stacy with no place to go where she could feel loved, lovable, and worthwhile.

With the exception of Dean (1979) and Bowlby (1984), who described situations in which the child was punished for normal activities, the literature on emotionally abusive behavior tends to focus primarily on what parents fail to do rather than what they actually do to their children.

Typically, emotionally abusive parents do not provide consistent love, acceptance, and praise that tells their children of their own self-worth. There is a notable lack of affection, continuity of care, guidance concerning behavior, and opportunities and approval for learning and growth. In addition, emotionally abused children are not allowed to become independent beings or to engage in relationships that do not involve the family. Generally, the parents fail to provide an adequate standard of reality or feelings of security. The parent–child relationship is, for the most part, characterized as cold and rejecting (Bowlby, 1984; Burgess & Conger, 1978; Garbarino & Garbarino, 1984; Rohner, 1975; Steele & Pollock, 1974; Whiting, 1976).

Rejection is a major theme that runs through the literature on emotional abuse. Can a child be rejected by one or both parents and still not be emotionally abused? I don't know the answer to that question, and I present it to show how muddy the waters remain. It is probably safe to say that the two are related. Rejection must be there if a child is emotionally abused, but abuse may not always be the outcome of rejection. It is important then, to divide this type of mistreatment into the two phases of abuse and neglect. With some degree of certainty we can say that, at the very least, rejection of a child will lead to the child's emotional neglect.

In his interesting book, *The Rejected*, John Evoy (1983) said that rejection is a reported subjective experience. Evoy's book is a report of clients he has treated over the years who felt rejected as children. Their experience of rejection is described as "emotionally toned knowledge that they were not loved and wanted for themselves by one or both parents" (p. 14).

Another question: What if one parent rejects the child but the other parent is accepting and loving? Can we say for certain that the child will be emotionally neglected? I don't know the answer to that question either. Evoy stated that his different patients sensed varying degrees of rejection that ranged from knowing they were hated and viewed as worthless to feeling that their parents thought they loved their children or wished they did but were simply unable to give them love. Evoy noted that others have tried to put rejection on a scale ranging from *benign* to *malignant*, but he did not believe there was "any substantial difference of hurtful experiential and/or behavioral characteristics in the rejected that appeared to be directly associated with their perceptions of different degrees of rejection by their parents" (p. 15). The major problems Evoy's patients, who had been rejected as children, experienced as adults fell into the broad categories of damaged self-esteem, fear, guilt, depression, anger, hostility, and aggression.

We all realize how important parental acceptance is, but we do not have a good understanding of just how much rejection, and in what varying degrees, a child can take, or how much difference it makes whether the rejection comes from one or both parents and which parent is doing the rejecting. We assume that the effects are drastic, and they probably are. But could any parent be taken to court for not loving his or her child? What could be accomplished by legal action if the child is not obviously and overtly abused? Would the courts be able to stop the parents from rejecting their child? More importantly, could the courts make parents love their children?

Obviously, legal action is not possible or even desirable unless it leads to counseling and education in parenting, with the goal of increased mental health for the whole family. Seen from the vantage point of a parent who has a child that he or she does not love and would rather not have, life cannot be very joyful for that parent, either. Some of these parents might welcome help or a change, but they may not seek it out because they have not recognized at a conscious level how they feel about their child or why.

For now, perhaps Dean's (1979) position of proving there has been a detrimental effect is the only realistic way to handle emotional abuse. Clearly, as with so many other societal problems and mental health issues, the key lies in prevention.

Chuy

"Come on, Chuy, tell the doctor what happened. You've been hurt pretty bad. This doesn't seem just right. Your mother said you fell down the ravine behind your house. Is that what happened, Chuy? We don't think so. The doctor just wants to help but you have to tell him the truth. Este hombre es bueno. Es mi mejor amigo. Hablar verdad, por favor, niño!"

Chuy peered up at the nurse leaning over his bed and whispering in his ear. He could see just enough to notice that she looked much like his mother. Through half-closed eyes, he noticed the doctor too. A white! An anglo just like his stepfather. He would tell him nothing. No matter how nice the nurse is, he would not trust either one of them, even if she did speak to him in Spanish. Spanish would not make him trust her. He did not trust his own mother. She lied—didn't protect him—let Sergeant Pate get away with anything. Chuy closed his eyes all the way shut and pretended to sleep.

The nurse and doctor gave up for the time being and left his room muttering to each other about his condition and how they were sure it had nothing to do with a fall down a ravine. When the door closed softly behind them, Chuy tried to open his eyes again and roll over on his side. A piercing pain shot through his stomach and he turned over on his back again. He couldn't see too well, but he had a cast on one arm—that was for sure—and tape around his stomach and chest, squeezing him so tight he could hardly breathe. He was alone in the hospital but not scared the way some kids would be; he had been in the hospital before, many times. It was really all right to be here, he thought. It was a safe and quiet place.

If only he did not hurt all over so bad. But it was good to be here, and if they would let him, he would never go home. Never see Sergeant Pate again. But then he wouldn't see his mother either. He gave some thought to that and felt sad and scared. They warned him that if he talked about what had happened he would have to go away forever. His mother cried when Sergeant Pate made those threats. If it were up to him, Chuy would be sent away. Sergeant Pate declared he would leave Chuy behind when he got his next transfer orders. Then Rosa would cry and plead with Pate not to leave the boy and not to be so cruel. She even threatened to leave Pate herself from time to time. That was something else that would get it started. Pate would get red in the face and start swearing and hitting Rose across the face until her nose bled and eyes swelled shut, just as Chuy's were half shut now.

Chuy thought about last night and how it started this time. He was late getting home from school; the teacher had kept him after for fighting again and not having his homework. Sergeant Pate was home when he came in—he was off duty early. Chuy ran in the front door expecting to see his mother and get a hug, but there was Pate sitting in the living room with his beer.

"You're late, you little spic bastard!"

"It wasn't my fault. I . . . ."

"No excuses! You're just supposed to say, 'Yes, Sergeant'! Goddamn you, you little shit! How many times have I told you! You were going to lie, weren't you! I already know why you're late. Called your school. Kept after again—fighting again! Making me look like a fool, like I can't run my own house!" Pate threw the beer bottle and hit Chuy straight in the mouth. "Think you're some tough Mexican kid, don't you! A real, regular, goddamn, son-of-a-bitchin' matador! And your lousy old man wanted you named Jesus! Ha! A little bastard with a name like that! That's really something! What an ignorant son of a bitch your old man was! You're as goddamn worthless as he was! I'm not having you in my house, shaming me. I'll kill you first!"

Rosa came in the kitchen back door just as Pate threw his fist in Chuy's face—and then again in the face. Chuy fell to the floor and looked up at Pate begging him to stop. Rosa tried to stop Pate but he turned and slammed her against the wall. Her head hit with a thud and she slumped to the floor in almost a sitting position. She didn't move anymore to help Chuy. She just covered her face and cried as she heard what was happening.

"I'm sorry, Sergeant! I won't fight anymore! Please stop!" Chuy found himself staring at the black boots Pate was wearing. They still had a spit shine. He tried to look up at Pate towering above him, but he could not see him well now—his eyes had started to swell shut. He put his hand up to protect his face, and Pate grabbed his arm and twisted until Chuy heard his bone crack.

"Here—you want to be a little Jesus! Take it like the real Jesus! You think you're goddamn better than anybody else! Maybe this will straighten out your thinking!" Pate drew his leg back and threw his boot into Chuy's side. The child rolled over on his back holding his ribs and begging his stepfather to stop. Pate wouldn't stop. He lifted his spit-shined boot and stomped it down as hard as he could into Chuy's stomach. Chuy vomited and then slipped into unconsciousness.

Rosa put her boy in the car and drove him to the hospital. "You mustn't tell anybody what happened, Chuy. Do you understand Mamma? You can't tell. They'll put Tom in the Army jail. There will be nobody to take care of us. Welfare will take you away from Mamma. Promise you won't tell, niño—no matter what they say. You fell down the ravine. Kids are always doing that, hurting themselves when they play by the ravine. Don't tell. Be strong like your real father was. He named you, you know. How proud he was when you were born. Jesus—that was his name too. Do you remember?"

Chuy could hear his mother talking but she sounded very far away. Long ago he thought his name, Jesus, was beautiful when it was pronounced the way it was supposed to sound in Spanish—not the way Sergeant Pate said it. The English way. Pate mocked it and made it sound ugly. Yes, he remembered his father. How he wished he were still alive and living with them, taking care of them. He wished he could talk to his father again like he used to. All the stories about the past. Like his nickname, Chuy. His father was called Chuy and so was his grandfather. All the men in his family as far back as anyone could remember—all the way back to the Conquistadors—were named Jesus and called Chuy. The nickname was so you would never get a big head and think you were better than anybody else because you had the honored name Jesus.

"You should be proud," his father had said, "but don't think your name makes you better than another person. Only your behavior makes you stand above others. Be strong, not afraid. Always remember what I have told you, Chuy. Then I will be proud. Take care of your mother. She needs someone to take care of her. She can't go it alone. You have to help her in any way you can. Then you will be a man that can be proud." Those were the last words Chuy's father said to him before he died. It was the last thing Chuy remembered thinking about in the car before waking up in the hospital.

"Chuy, are you awake?" The nurse was speaking softly, once again trying to encourage him to tell what had happened. "Chuy, tell the truth, niño. How did all this happen? How did you get so hurt? You have nothing to be afraid of. We will protect you. Tell me the truth, now. Be a brave boy. What really happened?"

Chuy looked at the kind nurse. "I am brave. I fell down the ravine—didn't even cry. I wasn't supposed to play there but I did. That's the truth. Just like my mother said. I fell."

....

Physical Abuse And Neglect

Chuy is an illustration of a typical case of physical abuse. From his story we can be certain that the boy is neglected as well; it would be unrealistic to believe that the stepfather, who obviously despises the child, is providing for all the child's basic needs. The emotional abuse that goes along with this type of situation is self-evident.

It is not uncommon in homes in which one parent physically abuses a child to find that parent also batters his or her spouse. In these situations, if the other parent does not find a way to stop the abuse of the child, that parent is just as guilty, by omission, as the parent who actually perpetrates the attacks. Chuy is like many other children who are victims of physical abuse; in his efforts to protect his mother he goes along with her lie about the way his injuries were incurred. Since the severity of his abuse is life-threatening, we are left to wonder if he can survive another brutal attack. Clearly, the stepfather is capable of murdering the child and, if he is not removed from this home, the child's death may be the result of the next attack. While the abuser in this story is a stepparent, the reader should be reminded that just as many, if not more, child abusers are the biological parents.

The abuse of children by their caregivers is recognized as a major national health problem. Depending on the source, the figures on the number of children who die as a direct result of physical abuse range from 2,000 to 5,000 each year (Cantrell & Prinz, 1985; Kurtz, Kurtz, & Jarvis, 1991). Most authorities believe that only one in five cases is actually reported, so the actual extent of abuse is unknown. Children are beaten, burned, strangled, kicked, and brutalized in every way conceivable, and in ways that are inconceivable to most people. Physical abuse is defined as: any physical injury to a child that has been caused by other than accidental means, including any injury that appears to be at variance with the explanation of the injury (Linn-Benton Education Service Digest, 1991, p. 9).

Before 1960 only a few scattered reports concerned with child abuse could be found in the literature. Dr. C. H. Kempe and his coworkers first called attention to the problem in a study of over 300 cases of abuse in the United States. It was reported in this study that 11% of these victims died and 28% had permanent injuries caused by the abuse (Kempe, Silverman, Steele, Droegemueller, & Silver, 1962).

It was not until 1967 that Elmer concluded in his study that 90% of the abused children showed evidence of residual damage and only 10% remained free of intellectual, physical, and emotional problems (Elmer, 1967). Kempe and his associates (1962) had found that approximately 55% of the children who had been physically abused had IQs of less than 80. Other researchers did not find incidence rates of mental retardation quite as high, although the figures were still disproportionately high. Martin (1976) reported that 33% of his subjects had IQs below 80 and 43% were neurologically damaged. The children with normal intellect in his study did, however, show delay in learning to speak.

Morse, Sahler, and Friedman (1970) found that 29% of the children they studied were considered mentally retarded and 28% were significantly emotionally disturbed. The question of cause and effect was raised by Sandgrund, Gaines, and Green (1974) when they concluded that there were almost 10 times as many children with IQs below 70 in the abused group as in the nonabused group. Morgan (1976) noted that there is a higher incidence of all types of disabilities among children who are abused, and that the abused constitute a disproportionate percentage of the clientele of special education classrooms. The question is, are many of these disabling conditions the result of abuse and neglect, or are children with disabilities more vulnerable to being abused and neglected?

Children victimized by severe violence are two to three times more likely to have failing grades and become school discipline problems, have difficulty in peer relationships, show physically aggressive behavior, be involved in vandalism or theft, use alcohol or drugs, and four times more likely to be arrested than nonabused children (Emery, 1989; Oates, 1989; Smith, 1988). Studies by Howing, Wodarski, Kurtz, and Gaudin (1990) showed that abused children exhibit severe social skills deficits. They tend to be shy and inhibited in social contacts and do not initiate peer interactions. They lack problem-solving skills and have deficits in receptive and expressive language skills. Weston, Ludolph, Misle, Ruffins, and Block (1990) found that severe abuse takes a toll on cognitive functioning. They found that a high percentage of the abused children they studied had IQs below 80 and were language delayed.

Malnutrition and Neglect

During early infancy permanent, irreparable damage to the nervous system can occur as a result of malnutrition and neglect, which can depress the adaptive and intellectual capacity of children. The impact of neglect on neural development is most critical during the early years of life (conception to 6 years of age). During this period the brain achieves 90% of its growth. Neglect and malnutrition during these years cannot be corrected after the child reaches school age. Neglected children inadequately integrate intersensory information. There is additional evidence that mild malnutrition in an older child may reduce the child's ability to focus, orient, or sustain interest in learning tasks.

Neglect is usually part of the physical abuse but not always. There are children who are neglected but not physically abused and physically abused children who are not neglected. Neglect constitutes undercare by the caretakers—underfed and/or malnourished, underclothed, undereducated, and undersupervised. Neglected children are left with the responsibility for their own care. They are on their own to feed themselves, take baths, shampoo their own hair, dress themselves, get to school, and so forth. Neglected children are obvious because of their reduced ability to focus, orient, or sustain interest in learning tasks. Perceptual deficiencies, fatigue, and irritability also have been documented in neglected children (Oates, 1989; Smith, 1988).

The environment can contain elements of deprivation, neglect or undernutrition, or forms of unstable family functioning that can all lead to specific types of disabling conditions. Neglect can have a detrimental effect on the child's development even without malnutrition, deprivation, parent disturbance, or low socioeconomic status (Martin, 1976; Martin & Rodeheffer, 1976; Powell, Brasel, & Blizzard, 1967a; Powell, Brasel, & Blizzard, 1967b).

Family disorganization, poverty, minimal cognitive stimulation, and lack of love are known to impede neurological and intellectual development in growing children. Environmental factors may not only result in impaired thinking but also may be the basis for tremors, uncoordination, impaired perception, impaired balance, and delayed language abilities. Often, children with learning disabilities are products of milieus that are insensitive, imposing, punishing, and abusing (Abram & Kaslow, 1976; Baron, Byar, & Sheaff, 1970; Martin, 1976).

Environmental Factors Leading to Abuse and Neglect

In general, abusing parents seem to be isolates in their own communities, mistrusting others and receiving little support from relatives or friends. They often appear beset with anxiety, hostility, and depression, making their responses to ordinary events inappropriate, impulsive, and excessive. Adequate social adjustment appears to be rare in these parents. More than half of the abusing parents lack self-confidence, and more than a third seem to be irresponsible and unreliable. Also noted is that the parent who does not inflict the injuries is passive and ineffective in protecting the children (Johnson & Morse, 1968).

Elmer (1967) found that abusing mothers were less able to control themselves and their households. They experienced more negative feelings toward their children and their home lives. Furthermore, it was noted that these families do not know on whom to rely and live under a constant stress of a kind and degree unknown to those who are nonabusive. An extensive study of black parents who abuse their children found that these parents suffer from poverty, social isolation, and stressful relationships with each other and with other family members (Daniel, Hampton, & Newberger, 1983).

According to some researchers, there are certain stresses within and outside of the home that can cause normally nonabusive parents to become abusive, including such factors as a pregnancy that results in a forced marriage, an illegitimate child, a disability that causes unacceptable behavior viewed by the parent as deliberate, some type of interruption in the mothering process, marital and interfamily conflict, cultures that accept violence as a means of socialization, and the belief in corporal punishment (Delsordo, 1974; James, 1975; Welsh, 1976a).

Characteristics of the Child

Infants born with certain kinds of problems or with differences in personality seem especially vulnerable to physical abuse. It has been suggested that some children are born with a predisposition to abuse. Some of the prominent ailments of abused infants that are most frequently reported are colic, asthma, eczema, sleep disorders, irritability, and excessive crying (Martin & Beezley, 1974; Ounsted, Oppenheimer, & Lindsay, 1974).

Other researchers found that a high percentage of abused infants showed aberrations in social interactions and general functioning in the year prior to the abuse incident. There appears to be a strong correlation between psychological and behavioral problems and abuse (Gil, 1976; Soeffing, 1975). Kline and Christiansen (1975) found that aggressiveness and withdrawal were the most commonly observed traits in abused children. Specific characteristics they found to be associated with physical abuse were fearfulness, poor social relationships, destructiveness, aggressiveness, and withdrawal. Most of the abused children in this study exhibited one or more of these traits.

In a similar study, Kent (1976) found many of the same characteristics, including poor peer relationships, tantrums, excessive disobedience, withdrawal, and aggression. Kent's subjects were described by observers as being more aggressive and more disobedient and as having more problems with peer relationships than children who were neglected or nonabused.

The question arises as to whether these constitutional characteristics bring on abuse or are the result of it. None of the studies distinguish between cause and effect. The studies described in the next paragraph come closer to an answer, and to common sense.

Elmer (1967) found that abused children show poor impulse control, poor self-concept, and frequent anger. In this study, anger was the most differentiating characteristic of physically abused children, and those who had remained in their environment had more severe emotional problems than abused children who had been removed from the home.

Overt and fantasy aggression in physically abused children who had been placed in foster homes also was studied by Rolston (1971). He found that these children showed significantly less overt and fantasy aggression. They scored lower on truancy, quarrelsomeness, and destructiveness. These children were characterized by their docility, somberness, compliancy, noncompetitiveness, and eagerness to please. They did, however, engage in more self-stimulatory activities, such as thumb sucking and masturbation. Fantasy aggression was seen in children who were abused before the age of 3 and who had a history of prolonged, severe abuse rather than a series of isolated incidents.

There is an overwhelming amount of research on emotional problems associated with physical abuse. Bakan (1971) found that abused children developed traits that made them difficult to like and invited further mistreatment. He cited such traits as fear of being alone, continual whining, shyness, depression, fear of new situations, hypersensitivity to pain, overreaction to hostility, hyperactivity, destructiveness, inability to help themselves, tendency to turn anger inward, and self-blame.

Morgan (1979) found behavioral and social differences between emotionally disturbed children who were physically abused and those who were not abused. Abused subjects in this study demonstrated more impulsiveness, anger, and aggression. The abused subjects' acting-out behaviors consisted primarily of yelling, making loud noises, sulking, and making angry faces and obscene gestures. These behaviors were followed almost immediately with overtures to make amends, in very disingenuous ways, with the teacher. In terms of their social behavior, the abused subjects' positive responses to their classroom teachers' authority did not transfer to other adults in the school. They were reluctant to try different things and displayed an exaggerated fear of failure by trembling and crying when confronted with a new lesson, activity, or situation. They often did not fight themselves but provoked and encouraged other children to fight with each other. Their own aggression took the form of teasing and tormenting others with rude remarks, but they quickly retracted their behavior by telling their peers, "I was only kidding." They were as disingenuous with their peers as they were with their teachers.

When all of the research studies pertaining to behavioral and emotional problems of physically abused children are examined, four basic styles of interaction are found consistently: passiveness, aggressiveness, regressiveness, and interpersonal relationships (Bakan, 1971; Elmer, 1967; Galdston, 1974; Greene, 1974; Justice & Justice, 1976; Kinard, 1979; Martin & Rodeheffer, 1976; Morgan, 1979; Morse et al., 1970; Ounsted et al., 1974).

The passive child. Galdston (1974) likened the passive child to the adult who suffers from shell shock, and Ounsted and associates (1974) used the term *frozen watchfulness.* Frozen watchfulness is seen as a child's attempt to cope with unpredictable parental behavior, when basic trust and a consistent environment have not been established.

Older children may not withdraw to the extent of frozen watchfulness, but they may become extremely passive and withdrawn. These children show little initiative and avoid attracting attention to themselves, making few if any demands, and trying to act as if they were not a part of the environment. Typically, these children do not take action until they are fairly certain of what the reaction of the adults might be. Rarely do they express their own thoughts or ideas, since they have learned that this can be very dangerous in an abusive environment (Court, 1974; Justice & Justice, 1976).

Another behavior associated with the passive child is termed *hypervigilance* which is intently watching the adults in the environment and becoming acutely sensitive to their mood changes. Hypervigilance is a sharply developed perceptual skill that these children use out of a necessity to avoid further attacks and injury (Emery, 1989).

Since abused children are appreciated only when they meet parental needs and expectations, they often take on, along with hypervigilance, pseudo-adult behaviors. This frequently results in role reversal between child and parent. The children become their parents' caregivers, both emotionally and physically, which gives them the appearance of being mature, charming, considerate, and sensitive to the moods and wishes of others (Einbender & Friedrich, 1989).

Studies tend to cite passivity as a major distinguishing feature of the abused child. Because the characteristics of passive children may go unrecognized by school professionals, these children may be more at risk psychologically than their more aggressive peers because they are not identified as having problems (Kurtz, Kurtz, & Jarvis, 1991).

The aggressive child. Severe physical punishment has been associated with a lowering of the aggressive threshold and appears to be a major factor in the development of deviant behaviors such as anger and violence, distractibility, social ineptness, impulsiveness, and the antiauthoritarian attitudes prevalent among delinquents. It has been noted that battered children's hostility often gets channeled into inappropriate and destructive patterns, such as acting out their anger on others. This acting out may take the form of stealing, in an effort to buy gifts that can be used to buy friendships (Kurtz, Kurtz, & Jarvis, 1991).

Aggression may not always be focused toward others. Often as children get older they develop self-hatred, blaming themselves for their parents' mistreatment and then turning their aggression inward. This self-hatred can be seen in passive aggressive behavior used by the child in an attempt to hold on to some sense of integrity in a family in which the child's rights as a person are constantly denied. Passive aggressiveness allows the child to defy authority without confronting a person directly and openly. An example of such behavior is the child who acquiesces verbally to some request but then does just the opposite and, when confronted, acts incompetent or as if the request was misunderstood.

Physically abused children have been found to go through an aggressive phase as they come out of their extreme passivity. It has been suggested that such aggressive behavior is a way of testing new relationships and also of reinforcing the child's own negative self-concept and internal guilt (Emery, 1989).

Many of these children seem to have poor impulse control, which is understandable when we realize that they come from abusive environments in which the parents have poor impulse control. This leaves the child with little else to imitate. This can certainly be viewed in two ways: either the battered child's aggression, hostility, and anger are so intense that they come out directed indiscriminately at peers; or the child has identified with the parental model (Kurtz, Kurtz, & Jarvis, 1991).

It has been stated repeatedly in the literature that battered children who are especially aggressive must in some way provoke their own abuse and neglect. They are identified early on as troublemakers and begin to encounter serious difficulties with peers and other adults, who may become abusive in return. More knowledgeable professionals quickly recognize this assaultive, aggressive behavior as the child's cry for help. The schools need to be aware of the cause of an abused child's bad behavior so that they do not exacerbate, with corporal punishment, the abuse the child already receives at home (Morgan, 1976).

Regressive behavior. Some children regress to inappropriate behaviors as a way of coping with an abusive environment. These children frequently become enuretic, cry easily and often, masturbate, suck their thumbs, act immature, and withdraw into fantasy worlds. Their behavior is often paradoxical in that they tend to be overly dependent while at the same time withdrawing from even a kind human touch. Their regressive behavior seems to be an attempt to gain sympathy by exaggerating their helplessness (Smith, 1988).

Interpersonal relationship deficits. The abused and battered child has been characterized as lonely, asocial, and joyless; as often isolated from friends; and as having shallow parental relationships and superficial, albeit friendly, attitudes toward adults (Morgan, 1979). Galdston (1974) believed that the quantity and quality of gratification that the physically abused child experiences with other human beings is so deficient that the ego skills needed to relate to others and to progress to more mature levels are prevented from developing. As a defense, many children in abusive homes are forced to restrict various autonomous ego functions, resulting in withdrawal and inhibition of personal drives and impulses. The inconsistency of an abusive environment also makes the development of trust nearly impossible. Since people in the home are constantly in flux, the child must keep changing behaviors to adapt. This lack of consistency precludes learning appropriate interpersonal relationship skills, since what is acceptable one day probably will not be acceptable another day.

Finally, these children have poor self-concepts and practically no sense of autonomy. This is a direct result of not being valued unless they meet the needs and expectations of the adults in their environments. Impaired interpersonal relationships serve only to reinforce the child's negative self-concept and to perpetuate the cycle (Williamson, Borduin, & Howe, 1991).

Abusive Parents

Abuse does not always begin at birth. Some parents have children so that they, the parents, can be needed. An infant is in constant need and so fulfills the parent's need to be needed. A critical stage in the parent–child relationship begins when the infant starts to show signs of independence, such as walking, playing with others, and then wandering greater distances from the parent. It is at this point in the child's life when love and trust are really learned and when a parent who needs to be needed can become abusive. The main caregiver, who is usually the mother, can react to this new independence in at least two adverse ways: by restricting the child's development and thereby promoting extreme dependence, or by rejecting the child and thereby causing a disruption in the development of a sense of trust and self-worth (Brunnquell, Crichton, & Egeland, 1981).

Why do such parents need to feel needed? Many parents, as children, experienced deprivation and abuse themselves. As adults, they hope to find a human being to fill the emptiness they have felt since their own childhood. They hope that a child of their own will fill that need. Abusive parents seem to have a pervasive feeling of never having been taken care of, and they consequently feel lonely, depressed, and anxious. Characteristically, they have low self-esteem and feel inferior, which makes them jealous and suspicious of even their own children. As an outgrowth of these needs, they feel that their children should be capable of adult behavior, and they expect them to obey immediately, to perform adult activities, and to recognize and respond to every need of the parent (Bowlby, 1984; Court, 1974; Davoren, 1974).

Whether or not these expectations are realistic, many abusing parents view their children as abnormal in some way or another. As was noted previously, some abused children do have disabling conditions that make them the target of parental attacks. In other cases, however, there are parents who just see their children as bad or as a competitor or burden that must be obliterated, or, at the very least, made to suffer (Brunnquell et al., 1981; Delsordo, 1974; Gil, 1976; Ounsted et al., 1974; Soeffing, 1975).

Spinetta and Rigler (1972) cited in some detail the personality characteristics of the abusing parent. These investigators classified abusing parents into four groups: (1) those with constant, pervasive hostility and uncontrolled aggression; (2) those who are self-indulgent, rigid and compulsive, lack warmth, and blame their children for their problems; (3) those who are extremely dependent, passive, immature, depressed, unresponsive, and moody, and who compete with the child for the love and attention of the spouse; and (4) fathers who are unable to support their families and stay home while their wives work. Apparently, the fathers in the last group are frustrated and threatened by this type of role reversal and turn aggressively on their children.

Mahler's work (1968) on separation–individuation is of interest in the sphere of the causal relationship between the abusing parent and aggression. According to Mahler, the child develops first in a phase of symbiosis with the mother. During this phase, the child behaves and functions as though the two are an indistinguishable system. The child learns to depend on the mother and experiences her as a love object. Martin and Rodeheffer (1976) state that abusive parents, having a distorted object relationship themselves, are not able to tolerate the separation–individuation process in their children. Mahler concluded that when this process is impeded, for whatever reason, there is a surplus of unneutralized aggression.

Masterson (1976) further developed this concept of separation and individuation in his theory about the borderline psychotic adult. He stated that the mother's own borderline syndrome is projected upon the child, making the youth a nonperson. Children react by ignoring their own potential to retain approval from their mothers. This type of relationship creates conflict and produces fear of abandonment. Abandonment conjures up a variety of feelings: fear, anger, guilt, depression, helplessness, and emptiness, all of which are manifested in varying degrees as the child goes through normal developmental traumas. The abandonment feeling is an internal experience on which the actual separation has only a precipitating influence. The depression involved may have the motivational power of suicidal despair.

Lystad (1975) noted that some research shows a relationship between infanticide and subsequent suicide attempts or actual suicides of parents. She stated that this may be the result of a fusion of identities between the mother and infant that took place during a postpartum depression. Masterson (1976) believed that in the adult borderline personality, the anger and rage felt toward their own mothers may be projected onto their own children in the immediate situation. Fear of separation can dominate the adult and conceal both depression and rage. When the threat of abandonment is used as a disciplinary technique, it enforces compliance from the child but also creates fear. When children reach the stage at which they feel a need to become individuals and this is met with disapproval and withdrawal from a most significant person, strong feelings of guilt and fear develop. When these children reach adulthood, to suppress this guilt and fear they resort to becoming clinging and dependent, which leaves them open to overwhelming feelings of helplessness.

These are very dynamic and complex theories, not easily understood at the abstract level. To put the theories into better perspective, Chuy's story serves as a good illustration of what these theorists propose. The stepfather is an example, perhaps, of a man with low self-esteem who feels jealous of another man's child. Clearly, he is one of those adults who expect adult behavior and prompt obedience from the child. Pate even extends this to expecting Chuy to behave in the same manner required of Pate in his role as a soldier.

Obviously, the child is different from Pate in a very identifiable way; he has a cultural and ethnic background that differs from Pate's and that Pate despises. To the stepfather, the child is bad, as well as a competitor for the attention and affection of his wife. Pate finds this an intolerable burden for which the child must suffer; indeed, if the situation is allowed to continue, he will do away with Chuy altogether.

In some way, it is possible that Mahler's theory about separation–individuation is relevant to Pate's behavior. Perhaps Pate, as a child, had never been allowed to become a separate, independent individual himself. Studies have been undertaken of people who are attracted to lifetime military service; results have suggested that some of the people attracted are incapable of living independently, making decisions for themselves, or structuring their own lives. They have been described as extremely dependent, requiring an authority who will tell them what to do and who will, in reward for their dependence and obedience, take care of them and see that their physical needs are met. If it is indeed the case with Pate that his own separation–individuation process was obstructed, then Mahler's notion of a surplus of unneutralized aggression would fit as part of the explanation for Pate's behavior toward a child who does not meet his needs and who seems so different. Also, Masterson's theory of the borderline psychotic adult fits Pate in the sense that he projects his own problems onto Chuy ("Making me look like a fool, like I can't run my own house!"). Pate may sense his own extreme dependence and actually mean that he cannot run his own life, not just his house. Clearly, little of what Pate feels actually has much to do with Chuy.

Chuy's mother also fits into this theoretical framework. She may, like her husband, serve as an example of concealed depression and rage; for her, however, it is manifested differently. Why does she stay with a man who beats her and brutally attacks her child? Perhaps, at some level, she finds a sense of pleasure or relief in Chuy's abuse. If she is filled with depression, anger, and rage but is unable to express it overtly, Pate's actions may provide the outlet for her own intense hostile feelings. Her own separation anxiety is so overwhelming that it prevents her from protecting herself or Chuy. She has become clinging, dependent, and helpless. Although telling the truth to an authority would prevent her own abuse and the possible murder of her child, her fears of separation and her sense of helplessness will not allow her to take the appropriate action. She would rather suffer and risk her child's death than lose someone on whom she is very dependent. Instead, she encourages her son to keep quiet and lie about his injuries: "You mustn't tell anybody what happened, Chuy. They'll put Tom in the Army jail. There will be nobody to take care of us." It apparently never occurs to her, or she doesn't want to consider at all, that they could somehow manage on their own. In some of my early professional experiences it was always a puzzle to me why some battered women, who also allowed their children to be battered, found it more frightening to be alone than to continue living with a person who was capable of taking their lives or the lives of their own children. I think I understand it better now. At least I have, if not empathy, sympathy for the emotional trap in which they find themselves.

Chuy's story gives a brief glimpse of how Chuy is affected now and a hint as to his future development. He responds in ways that have been described in the section on the abused child: he gets into frequent fights, trusts nobody, and is uninterested in school. He also fears abandonment and the loss of his mother's love more than he fears anything Pate will do to him. This is shown by his willingness to support his mother's life in order to stay with her. What is in Chuy's future—if he lives? Turning to delinquency or substance abuse would not be surprising. Many abused children turn to drugs and alcohol to deaden their emotional and psychological pain. As an adult Chuy would be likely to perpetuate the cycle of abuse, projecting onto his own children the surplus of anger and rage he carried all through his childhood.

Irma

"This is your stop, Irma. I said, this is your stop, Irma! Irma! Irma, get off the bus. You're home. This is your stop!"

The bus driver got no response from Irma. She was still in her seat, staring out the window. "Are you asleep, girl? This is your house. Come on now, get off the bus. You don't want me to drive you back to school, do you? You'd have to stay there all night. Bet you'd love that, huh?" The other kids on the bus laughed uproariously at the notion that anyone would like staying overnight at school. They chimed in with the bus driver, urging Irma to get off the bus so they could go home too.

Irma wrapped one hand around the railing on the back of the seat in front of her and slowly pulled herself to her feet. Staying at school all night did not sound horrible to her the way it did to the other kids. She thought of her teacher that she loved so much and wondered if she were still at school. The idea raced through Irma's mind that maybe if she let the driver take her back, she could stay with Mrs. Zigler—that her teacher would take her home with her. Irma had even asked her once if she could go to her house to live, but Mrs. Zigler just smiled and patted her head. "I don't think that would make your parents very happy, do you? They would miss you very much. It would be fun for a while and then you would miss your own mom and dad. Besides, Irma, I have my own children at home. What do you think they would do if I started bringing home all my second graders?" Mrs. Zigler laughed a little. Irma realized her teacher thought she was just talking, that she didn't really mean it. But she really did mean it.

Irma knew the bus was stopped in front of her house. She had seen her house a block back when she had pressed her face against the window to try to see if her mother's car was in the drive. It was not there. That meant her mother would work late tonight and she wouldn't see her until the morning. It meant just her dad would be there tonight.

The doors on the bus slammed shut and the driver and other kids left, still laughing at the joke about staying at school all night. Irma stood on the sidewalk for a while, staring at her house. She hated to go in there when her mother wasn't home. It seemed dark and lonely. Her stomach tightened and she felt funny. The "funny" feeling was a lot of things that Irma could not put into words. She felt kind of afraid. She felt like she was a bad girl.

Irma took the key from under the mat and opened the door. She was resigned to the fact now that her mother wouldn't be home tonight and that she could not stay with her teacher. She put her things down and went into the kitchen to look for something to drink. Her throat felt very dry. She took another drink of her juice and looked at the clock. Daddy would be home when the little hand was on 5 and the big hand was on 6. Her throat tightened; she pulled the bottle away from her lips and began gasping and spitting the juice on to the kitchen floor. Irma gave more thought to her father and poured the rest of the juice down the sink. She loved Daddy but did not want to be home with him when her mother wasn't there. He made her feel funny—like a bad girl. She turned on the TV and sat on the floor to watch the after-school cartoons.

The cartoons were over and the news was on. Irma did not understand the things they were talking about on the news and it bored her, but she did not leave her place on the floor in front of the TV. The news meant it was time for her dad to come home. He always came home when the news was on, when the little hand was on 5 and the big hand on 6. Irma heard his car in the drive and then the key opening the front door.

"Well, there's my little Kitten! Give Daddy a kiss and tell me all about school today." He bent down and gave Irma a kiss on the cheek. "I see your mother isn't home. That means she took another shift at the hospital, so it's just you and me, Kitten. Another night to fend for ourselves. But we do okay, don't we?"

Irma did not look up at her father. She sat glued to the floor with her back stiffened, pretending to be engrossed in the TV. She would not let her eyes or a muscle move until she heard him walking down the hall to his bedroom.

He shouted to Irma from the back of the house. "As soon as I get out of this tie and am more comfortable we'll figure out what we are going to do tonight. You know I always take good care of you, Kitten, when your mother isn't here. We'll do some fun things—like we do—you know. Then, maybe we'll go get some pizza and Coke. You like that a lot, don't you, Kitten? Come back here, Kitten, with Daddy. I have something to show you. Thought you were going to tell me about school. You don't like to watch the news. That's boring stuff."

Irma did not move. She put her hands, clenched into fists, down into the carpet to brace her position on the floor. She stared straight ahead at the TV, trying desperately to listen only to what the anchorman was saying and not to what her father was saying. She heard what he said, though, and began to feel funny as she heard him coming down the hall to the living room.

"Hey, Kitten, what's up? You're not mad at your old dad, are you? Something happen at school today? How's your teacher you like so much? You haven't been telling our secret, have you? Remember, even if you do like your teacher, you can't tell her our secret. It would get us into trouble. You don't want Daddy to get into trouble, do you? 'Course you don't. I'd probably have to go away forever, maybe even to jail where all kinds of terrible things would happen to me, and you and Mom would never see me again. You can't ever tell our secret to Mom, either. You remember? I've told you that lots of times. Mom would get real mad at you for telling such stories and she would send you away. Then none of us would ever be together."

Irma let her eyes move ever so carefully to the side. She could see her father standing next to her. His feet and legs were bare. She did not look up at him. Her heart started racing and the funny feeling grew stronger. She loved Daddy, but he frightened her when he talked about going away forever, and maybe she would have to go away too and never get to see him or Mommy again.

He went to the chair behind Irma and sat down. "Oh, come on, Kitten. You know Daddy loves you more than anybody in the whole world. Don't I buy you everything you want? What do you want now? Just tell Daddy and I'll get it for you! We'll play our little game and then go for some pizza and Coke and then off to the shopping center to get you what you want. Do everything I've shown you and then we'll go. If you don't, I'll have to tell your mother you were a bad girl tonight. You don't want to be a bad girl, do you? You do love Daddy, don't you? You're making me feel awful, Kitten.
I don't think you love me anymore. You're going to make Daddy cry."

Irma got up from the floor, pulled her dress over her head, slipped her panties down, and stepped out of them. "I do love you, Daddy. Don't cry. I don't want you to go away forever!" She ran naked to her father, who was waiting in the chair. "Can I have one of those new dolls, Daddy—the cabbage one?"

"Just as soon as we play our game, Kitten. Up here on my lap, now, and give Daddy a big kiss, lots of kisses, just like I've shown you. We're going to have a lot of fun tonight."

....

SEXUAL ABUSE

I opened this section of the chapter with Irma's story because incest is the most common type of sexual abuse. Incest rarely makes newspaper headlines or lead stories on the national news. The problem, however, has been given some attention by the media over the last few years. It has been the topic of television talk shows and a made-for-TV movie and was even discussed on ABC's "Nightline."

Irma's story is a typical story of incest; it is not unusual or unique. It is a true representation of the many cases that take place each year. Irma is a little girl who loves her father and can be cajoled into a relationship that somewhere within her consciousness she knows is wrong. There is no hint of any other type of abuse; she is not being beaten or treated in a sexually brutal way. It appears that her suffering is on the emotional level rather than physical. She doesn't want the kind of relationship she has with her father and tries the only tactics she knows to avoid another sexual encounter with him: she ignores his requests, pretending to be engrossed in the television in the hope that he will leave her alone, and she avoids eye contact, hoping that will discourage him. As in typical cases of incest, he uses his tactics to entrap her into another sexual encounter; he plays on her feelings of love for him, bribes her, scares her with the possibility of losing his love and her mother's love, and threatens to reveal her "badness" in a way that feeds into the guilt she already feels.

Irma shows some of the outward signs of a sexually abused child: she prefers to stay at school rather than go home and even asks her teacher if she can live with her. These signs can be easily misunderstood because Irma does not show any other signs of abuse. Her case is more subtle, as are many incest cases, in that she does not have the morbid physical symptoms sometimes associated with sexual assaults.

Parameters of Sexual Abuse

Not all of the types of sexual mistreatment recognized by mental health professionals are considered criminal offenses, and not all of them are listed in state statutes on child abuse and neglect. As child advocates, we cannot allow our concerns to be limited exclusively to what is legally recognized, legally defined, or legally prosecutable. Our interests are in any interference with the development of positive mental health. A child can be sexually abused by a variety of means other than actual physical contact, ways that can leave permanent psychological and emotional scars.

Most people are aware of sexual molestations that include touching and fondling a child's genitals; vaginal, anal, or oral intercourse or rape; attempted but uncompleted intercourse; incest; prostitution; and the use of children in pornography. But children can also be considered sexually abused, from a mental health standpoint, without actually being physically molested. Such abuse comprises the acts of exposing children to the sexually explicit behavior of adults with the intention of arousing or shocking them, obscene phone calls, voyeurism, and exhibitionism. It also is sexual abuse when an adult stares lewdly at a child to the point of causing discomfort, worry, uneasiness, fear, or intimidation. And although some people will disagree vehemently, another behavior that can be considered sexual abuse is any use of children in media or theatrical productions that involve them in sexually explicit or sexually subtle activities, regardless of parental consent or intent and regardless of whether or not the parents or paid professionals believe the child has the ability to understand and cope cognitively and emotionally (Briggs & Lehmann, 1989; Einbender & Friedrich, 1989; German, Habenicht, & Futcher1990; Greenwald, Leitenberg, Cado, & Tarran, 1990; Williamson, Borduin, & Howe, 1991).

Incidence

The problem of sexual abuse of children is of unknown national dimensions. Almost on a daily basis, the news and research literature point to the probability of an enormous national incidence of sexual abuse many times greater than even the reports of physical batterings. Senator Paula Hawkins of Florida (herself sexually abused as a child) stated on national television and at the Senate Children's Caucus hearing on child sexual abuse, "My fear is that the number of children who have this problem may be in the millions." We have no way of knowing the actual figures, but cases could well number in excess of 1 million. The Manhattan Beach incident, in which alleged sexual abuse was perpetrated by all of the preschool teachers, went on for more than 10 years. More than 400 children were interviewed before the trial, and the majority admitted to being sexually abused in some way. Prior to these pretrial disclosures, 99% of the children had never mentioned the abuse to anyone (Sheehy, 1984). So the estimate of more than 1 million child sexual abuse cases a year is not preposterous (De Jong, 1982; Khan, 1983; Koch, 1980; Shah, 1982; Williams, 1981).

Reliable data are not available, partly due to the secrecy and taboos that surround this issue and that prevent the reporting of such cases, particularly when incest is the offense. Sexual crimes against children may be reported to law enforcement agencies but never reach the state abuse agency to be included in their statistics. Also, not all the states categorize sexual abuse separately from physical abuse (Khan, 1983; Merrill, 1975; National Center on Child Abuse and Neglect, 1991; Williams, 1981).

In the United States, estimates range from 45,000 incidents a year to more than 1 million cases annually, depending on the source of information. Another factor that clouds the incidence issue is which cases get reported. Some sources report figures only for girls and do not include sexual attacks on boys, whereas others report on both girls and boys. Some have an age limitation, reporting only cases that involve children under age 14; others report cases involving youths up to the age of 16. National studies reveal that one in five cases of sexual abuse happens to children under the age of 7. However, children in the most danger of being abused are those between the ages of 8 and 12. Even infants and toddlers are subjected to sexual abuse, as has been determined by medical examinations. Finally, for the most part, child prostitutes, victims of pornography, and victims of nontouching offenses are excluded in many estimates (Sheehy, 1984; Williams, 1981; Williams, 1983).

Until recently, our society has closed its eyes to the needs of children who are sexually abused. At one time, some law enforcement officials operated on the premise that children could not be believed until they were at least 12 years of age (Sheehy, 1984). Even among psychiatrists and psychologists, sexual abuse has been clouded over by hasty conclusions and misinformation, partly because of the influence of Freudian theory, which proposes that many children (girls in particular) fantasize about such events. When the research is reviewed, it is strikingly evident that this is a real problem that both the professional and the lay community need to consider and give their full attention.

Symptoms of Sexual Abuse

There are a number of physical and behavioral symptoms indicative of sexual abuse, which include the following:

1. physical injuries to the genital area, such as vaginal tears
2. sexually transmitted diseases
3. difficulty in urinating
4. discharges from the penis or vagina
5. pregnancy
6. fear of aggressive behavior toward adults, especially the child's own parents
7. sexual self-consciousness
8. sexual promiscuity and acting out
9. inability to establish appropriate relationships with peers
10. running away, stealing, and using alcohol or drugs
11. withdrawal, regressive behavior, or behavior that makes the child look retarded

12. use of the school as a sanctuary, coming early and not wanting to go home

13. complaints of frequent nightmares

14. indirect hints indicating fear of going home or fear of someone in particular at home

15. information that children relate involving sexual encounters (which should be taken absolutely seriously, since almost always what they say about such encounters is true and not just a story)

The foregoing list of physical and behavioral symptoms of sexual abuse in children is taken from the following sources: Cohen, 1988; Fontana and Schneider, 1978; Giarretto, 1982; Greenwald et al., 1990; Jones, 1982; Morgan, 1984; Mrazek, 1980; National Center on Child Abuse and Neglect, 1991; Shamray, 1980; Swift, 1979; Williams, 1981.

The Perpetrators

The shock of learning that an adult has sexually molested a child prompts the most commonly asked question: "What kind of a person does such a thing to a child?" There are a number of other questions, however, that also concern researchers and mental health professionals, such as the following: (1) What are the characteristics of the different types of child molesters? (2) Do certain environments tend to produce this type of offender? (3) Are there patterns of behavior seen in childhood that may be predictive of such behavior in adulthood? (4) What does the adult sex offender think and feel about his or her own behavior? (5) Can treatment cure?

There are two categories of child molesters: (1) family members, who may be either heterosexual or homosexual , and (2) pedophiles or strangers, who also can be either heterosexual or homosexual. The reader should be aware too that there are accounts of children sexually attacking other children. These are not always cases of adolescents preying on smaller, weaker children. The cases include young children who happen to be stronger and more aggressive attacking other children their own age, younger, or even older than themselves. In one study, De Jong (1982) found that 10% of the 416 children admitted to an emergency room for sexual abuse had been attacked by assailants 10 years of age or younger.

The family member. Incest is defined as sexual intercourse between persons who are blood relatives. Incest has recently become a widely studied area of research, with many questions about the causes and effects of incest on the whole family. It cannot be viewed solely as concerning only the offender and the victim. Usually the entire family is involved in some way in continuing the situation, and the entire family is affected by it (Emery, 1989).

Most investigators report that brother–sister incest is the most frequent type, although it is rarely reported. Mother–son incest is believed to be very rare. Father–daughter and stepfather–step-daughter incest are the most prevalently reported forms of incest. Stepfather–stepdaughter is reported most frequently (Anderson & Shafer, 1979; Cohen & Mannarino, 1988; Giarretto, 1982; Walters, 1975; Williams, 1981; Woodling, 1981). It may well be that father–daughter incest is just as prevalent as stepfather incest, if not more so, but perhaps wives report stepfathers more readily.

The experience of incest appears to be more traumatic than other forms of childhood sexual abuse. One fact may be stated with certainty: healthy families do not find themselves in the midst of incestuous relations. Incest is seen as a clear manifestation of a disturbance within the family, and when it occurs between father and daughter it develops most often from a background of disharmony and disorganization. Most investigators note that incest occurs predominantly in families with lower social prestige but who, on the average, are comfortable financially. Incestuous relationships do not appear to be episodic but are more drawn out, lasting at least a year and usually more. Despite the fact that some of these relationships can go on for many years, rarely is it the mother who reports the offense. In most cases, the authorities find out through some outside source (Cohen, 1983).

It appears that there is a complicated interpersonal triangle, in which contributions are made by the nonactive members. On the basis of research findings, the following components create a climate for incest. The incest usually begins following sexual estrangement between husband and wife, most frequently as a reaction of the husband to some real or perceived loss of the wife. For instance, it can begin in reaction to death, divorce, separation, mental or physical illness, marital strife, or a new job that takes the mother out of the home for extended periods. Generally, the wife is extremely dependent and immature, and feels inadequate as a mother and a woman. This causes her to reverse roles with her daughter and to push the child into adult responsibilities. Collusion by the mother is made possible through very strong denial of the incestuous relationship. Some mothers have been known to directly encourage father–daughter intimacy. Frequently, the daughters see their mothers as cruel and rejecting, making the relationship with the father extremely important as a means of taking revenge on the mother and also as a source for the affection and attention denied by the mother. A climate for incest also develops when the mother is emotionally unavailable because of mental illness and the father is the only source of affection (Anderson & Shafer, 1979; Cohen, 1983; Gordy, 1983; Maisch, 1972).

Fathers. The fathers involved in incest have been found to range from mentally average fathers who take care of their families adequately to men who have problems with alcoholism and show little self-control. Incestuous fathers range from the psychologically normal to the psychologically abnormal, with no consistent personality patterns dominating. Overall, however, the fathers do have some characteristics that reappear in many studies. They try to control the lives of all the family members by whatever means possible. They try to justify and rationalize the incest by claiming to be protecting their daughters from outside influences and teaching them the "facts of life." Their needs for attention and affection cannot be met through nonphysical or nonsexual means. They are considered emotionally immature (Anderson & Shafer, 1979; Gordy, 1983).

Mothers. With the exception of mothers who are definitely mentally ill and do not, or cannot, stop the incest, most mothers have been described as normally intelligent and not psychologically unfit in any observable way. In general, they have been described as weak, submissive, depressed, and sometimes promiscuous. Some have come from deprived backgrounds in which they were deserted by their own parents. Generally, they give up their role as wife and mother and turn this role over to their daughters, including the sexual role, in an attempt to be nurtured as if they were the child. Many had incestuous pasts as well and are unable to avoid or terminate relationships in which they are mistreated. They may have such sexual problems as frigidity or latent lesbian tendencies, and in some cases they do seek out lesbian relationships (Anderson & Shafer, 1979; Cohen, 1983).

Daughters. The majority of girls involved in incestuous relationships have been found to be normal in personality and intelligence. Although a few have been observed to be underachievers in school, most are average or above average, dispelling the stereotype of girls involved in incest as being slightly mentally retarded or socially offensive in some way. Usually the girl is the eldest in the family, mature although not necessarily sexually mature. She does not feel like a part of the family, and since she fears rejection or breakup of the family she does not ask for help. Most girls involved in incest have been given the care of siblings and other household responsibilities. Nearly all the girls think the only way to cope is by keeping silent.

Whether the girls had relationships with their real fathers or a father substitute, there seem to be no apparent differences in how they are affected psychologically. It appears that the younger the child, the more likely it is that she will suffer the psychological consequences of personality disruption. The consequences for an adolescent are presumed to depend on her ego development before an incest incident. Delinquency, school problems, and suicide attempts have been reported. Most of the girls have strong feelings of guilt, depression, anxiety, and confusion over sexual identity. Some girls search for punishment, whereas others want forgiveness from their mothers; however, this forgiveness is related to the disruption that the incest incidents cause rather than the incest itself. At puberty, some girls develop mild to moderate disturbances and have difficulty relating to boys in any kind of relationship, but most particularly in dating relationships (Anderson & Shafer, 1979; Cohen, 1983; Gordy, 1983).

The pedophile. Pedophilic offenses fall into two categories: heterosexual and homosexual. Heterosexual pedophilia is of an immature nature, meaning that the behaviors are usually restricted to fondling, exhibiting, looking, and masturbating, with no attempt at coitus. Although the majority of sexual acts involving female children are of this type, there are pedophiles who do rape children. In cases involving male children, the sexual acts are usually more aberrant, aggressive, and brutal (Brant & Tisza, 1977; Ellerstein & Canavan, 1980). The number of sex offenders who are female has always been thought to be extremely small; however, this small number has been open to question and research since the disclosure of the California preschool case, which involved several women and one man.

The pedophile commonly has been stereotyped as a "dirty old man," but the age distribution actually falls into three groups: (1) adolescents characterized by a lag in psychosexual maturation; (2)

those in their middle to late 30s, who experience a breakdown in adjustment to the demands of the adult world and to family relationships in particular; and (3) lonely and impotent men in their late 50s to early 60s (Peters, 1976; Tilelli, 1980; Woodling, 1981).

In terms of a psychiatric profile, child molesters often are diagnosed as psychopaths or sociopaths who are passive aggressive and extremely immature, with strong feelings of inadequacy and insecurity. Pedophiles have been assessed with every conceivable psychological test and consistently show high levels of anxiety, dependency, and regressiveness. It also appears that they have considerably low self-esteem and are extremely lacking in sensitivity to the needs of others. A small percentage of the pedophiles have been diagnosed as schizophrenic or paranoid (Ellerstein & Canavan, 1980; Woodling, 1981).

Frequently, pedophiles are alcoholics who do not relate well to their adult peers and have poor relationships, if any, with women. Gigeroff (1968) found that 45% of the pedophiles he studied were alcoholics or very heavy drinkers and that economic stress made them more prone to pedophilia as well as a variety of other types of antisocial behavior.

Pedophiles seem to need some unusual or unique experience to stimulate their sexual drives. Whether they are heterosexual, homosexual, or bisexual, the majority of them are psychosexually infantile, with a predilection for young children. They are very adept at attracting the attention of children and gaining their confidence and friendship, thus luring them into situations where sexual abuse can occur. Pedophiles own personal sense of inadequacy creates a fear of impotence, and after repeated unsatisfactory sexual relationships with adults they turn to children (Woodling, 1981).

Background of the pedophile. As has been stated several times in this chapter, abused children may become abusing adults. Abuse begets abuse. This is true of the adult who becomes a pedophile. Pedophiles come from predominantly low socioeconomic areas and as children were often neglected and abused, although not necessarily sexually abused.

A common finding is that pedophiles never received adequate or accurate sexual information during their developmental years and instead experienced continuous traumatic reactions to normal sexual experiences. They treated normal childhood sexual experiments, such as masturbation, as great transgressions, and they typically feared and received retribution from their parents for such activities. A substantial proportion of the case histories of pedophiles revealed that they had experienced, in early childhood, incestuous and homosexual attacks. Those who had been involved in homosexual incest had pronounced fears of impotence, sterility, and physical disfigurement (Adams-Tucker, 1982; De Jong, 1982).

According to the available information, most of these individuals come from unstable homes where they felt rejected by their mothers and where their fathers were characterized as alcoholic, cruel, and domineering. Their homes were dominated by stress and strife, with the parents in constant conflict with each other (Gigeroff, 1968; Woodling, 1981).

Apparently, many of the pedophiles experience great guilt and contrition for what they have done. There is always the question of whether, even after treatment, recidivation will occur since pedophiles seem to have such a wide variety of emotional problems. Heterosexual pedophiles show more positive signs for recovery than do homosexual pedophiles. The difference is supposedly because the homosexual pedophile has more deeply ingrained problems (double deviation), whereas the heterosexual pedophile's actions are often related to strong situational factors (Jones, 1982; Walters, 1975).

Child molestation is a broad topic that includes incest, rape, indecent exposure, child prostitution, genital touching, and sodomy. Incest has already been covered, so in this section molestation will be broken into two major categories: rape and prostitution.

Rape

Rape is used here to include sodomy, which is anal intercourse. The word *rape* elicits a strong emotional reaction in people. Perhaps it evokes a greater response from the general public than any other sexual offense. This is especially true when children are involved, since the children are seen as being brutally forced to engage in sexual intercourse without a knowledge or an understanding of the consequences. Child rape victims are also considered to be more traumatically affected by the experience than any other age group (Adams-Tucker, 1982; Schultz & Jones, 1983; Shah, 1982; Tilelli, 1980; Woodling, 1981).

One of the most complete studies on this subject was done in 1976 by Peters at the Sex Offender and Rape Victim Center in Philadelphia. This investigator studied the social and psychological effects of rape and other sexual assaults on child victims from 2 to 12 years old. Peters's study also included general findings from adult patients suffering emotional problems who had experienced sexual assaults in childhood.

At the time of the offense, in this study, almost three fourths of the children were enrolled in school, and most were average or better-than-average students. Few child victims, unlike adolescents, had displayed such behavior patterns as problems in school, running away, truancy, or drug and alcohol abuse. Most of the children got along well with friends at school and in their home communities. In other words, at the time of the offense these were apparently well-adjusted, normal children.

One of the major findings in this study was that the rape of these children involved less physical force than with any other age group. Threats of physical harm or other verbal threats were reported in 31% of the cases. Physical force was not used at all in 54% of the incidents involving children. The lack of physical force was because 80% of the attackers were familiar power figures to the child: grandfather, father, uncle, babysitter, or friend of the family. At the time the offense occurred, nearly all the children had been left by the mother in the care of the attacker. This in itself may be a principal component in explaining why childhood rape is often the basis for psychiatric problems later in life. The victim may continue to be anxious and confused about trusting men, while also feeling unprotected in the society.

Assaults by unknown persons seem to lead to less complex psychological confusion. The entire family, the police, and the courts will consistently and sympathetically stand behind the child who has been raped by a stranger. Take, for example, the child in Buffalo, New York, who was raped by a pedophile in 1984. That story made the national news. Why? Children are raped in large numbers on a daily basis, and their cases do not make the national news. This case involved the response of the father, the neighbors, and the police. The father and some of his neighbors found the attacker before the police arrived. The child's father was beating and kicking the man while the neighbors, news media, and police watched. Eventually, the police intervened and arrested the father and the attacker. The police and the judge showed sympathy for the father and hesitated to prosecute a man who had a just right to such anger over the sexual abuse of his child. The neighbors collected money for the father's defense. These events were the only ones that were shown on the television news broadcast. There was no mention of what people might have been doing for the child, or about her feelings, or whether the neighbors were contributing money toward any treatment she might require as a result of the attack.

While this is not a book on sexual discrimination or feminism, it is appropriate to ask here the question of who was offended in this case. The point is not that the child should have been shown or interviewed on television—certainly not. I am asking why more consideration was not given the child in this story. Somewhere in this case lies the implication that children, especially females, are still the property of men. Therefore the emphasis is placed on the damaged father and not on the damaged child. Would such furor have been evoked if it had been the father who molested his own child and another irate family member had beaten him? More than likely, no one in the neighborhood would have gotten involved and the rest of the family would have tried to keep the situation quiet.

What happens when children try to protect themselves from their own abusive parents? Take, for example, another infamous case of physical and sexual abuse that made the national news: the two youths in Wyoming in 1982. The father in this case sexually abused his adolescent daughter and physically abused both his adolescent son and his wife. Since no one would help, even when the children told their story to a counselor in their school and asked for help, they decided the only way to stop the abuse was to kill the father, which they did. The mother, also abused, tried to keep all the events quiet and did not seek help for her children or herself. A trial resulted in the sentencing of the son, who had killed the father.

In this case it was society that was really on trial—and won—but it was the children who lost. Although the boy's sentence was commuted, he was not exonerated and is still guilty in the eyes of the law and has a police record. What would have happened if someone had listened to the children? Possibly the father would have received help for his problem. This was, after all, a family matter. But righteousness, at times, still takes the place of common sense, and children still take a backseat in society and the justice system. Since they had asked for help and had not received it, what was their alternative? What would have happened if a stranger had come over on a regular basis and beaten the boy and sexually molested the girl? People would have listened. If no one had done anything about the stranger and the children had killed him, would that have been a clear case of self-defense? Probably so, since those children were not the "property" of the stranger.

When the attacker is a family member, support is often split between the offender and the child. Whether or not the child has long-term emotional damage depends on the way significant people react and respond to the event. In many such cases, adult attitudes range from concern for the child's emotional well-being to anger toward the child and concern about how the whole incident will affect the family. In these situations, adult attitudes exacerbate the problem and create tremendous guilt within the child (Peters, 1976).

Many children do not tell anyone until much later about incestuous attacks because they fear parental reactions and revenge from the attacker. Although children who are attacked by strangers do not, in general, react as severely as those who are attacked by a father or father substitute, they do develop problems following such incidents. Typically, they have eating and sleeping problems, they develop negative feelings toward men they know as well as men they do not know, they become fearful of leaving their houses, and some of them drop out of school entirely (Adams-Tucker, 1982; Gordy, 1983; Peters, 1976; Tilelli, 1980). The parents of the children who were attacked in the Manhattan Beach preschool reported that their children had frequent nightmares and cried in their sleep. One child asked his parents if the scary thoughts would ever go away.

Peters (1976) surmised that victims of incestuous rape react with less observable emotional response, possibly because the incidents are less harsh, less violent, and less threatening. It is believed, however, that the children regress into emotional withdrawal when they are unable to express their feelings because the parents avoid talking about or dealing with the problem. These are the cases of incestuous rape in which everyone involved in the problem reacts with confusion, anxiety, and silence. The mother decides to protect either her child or her spouse, and if she decides to protect her husband, the child feels alone, unprotected, and guilty for the breakdown in the family (Cohen, 1983; Peters, 1976; Shamray, 1980; Summit & Kryso, 1978; Woodling, 1981).

Prostitution

The scope of our information about the prostitution of children has become greater over the years, and we now know that it includes much more than the individual sale of a girl or boy for sexual use. The knowledge that the general public and many professionals had about child prostitution formerly extended only to those children who had been abandoned or had run away from home and fallen into the hands of pimps. We now know that the problem is much more pervasive and that children are exploited in a wholesale manner for sexual use and pornography. The shocking case in Manhattan Beach, California, has jolted us into the realization that these things can happen to children of any age who are ordinarily well cared for, that these things do not just happen to children who are homeless, addicted to drugs, and on the streets at the mercy of any degenerate who picks them out for such exploitation (Hunt & Baird, 1990).

In fact, we have learned that there are parents who will sell their children for such use in order to maintain their own drug or alcohol dependency. There are parents who will allow, even push, their children into participating in films, theater productions, and magazines whose focus is the sale of sex or whose whole theme is illicit sex. These things are done, according to some parents, under the pretense of developing an artistic career and building a financial future for their child.

Prostitution of boys was studied extensively and found to have its basis in family and school problems (Lloyd, 1976). Most of the boy prostitutes came from backgrounds of neglect. In school, many of these boys faced constant failure and frustration and could not find acceptance, approval, or attention in either environment—home or school. These boys would run away and then find themselves in situations in which they could not survive without selling themselves for sexual purposes.

In an even earlier study, some similarities were discovered in cases of prostitution of boys. Reiss (1964) found that the boys involved came almost exclusively from lower-class homes. They regarded street hustling as an alternative to other delinquent ways of getting money. Generally, they saw their situations as temporary and did not view themselves as homosexuals. In contrast to the boys in Lloyd's study, the boys in Reiss's study were not controlled by pimps but belonged to peer groups, which to them were not the same as delinquent gangs. The peer group taught them the rules of behavior and how to carry on their business transactions. It also controlled the conditions and amount of activity in which the boys could be involved. As the boys got older, according to group norms it was no longer appropriate to continue in prostitution. Most older boys gave up hustling and became involved in vocations that conformed to conventional lower-class society, although some did turn to criminal behavior. Although boys in these situations do not usually become hustlers or homosexuals as adults, the overall experience is thought to be extremely emotionally damaging to them (Ellerstein & Canavan, 1980; Lloyd, 1976; Reiss, 1964).

In cases of prostitution of girls, beyond the factors already mentioned, some believe there is an evolutional process involved. It has been discovered that, in many cases, other family members are sexually promiscuous and that their promiscuity began at a young age. The girl may become involved sexually with her father, brothers, uncles, cousins, or neighbors and eventually move on to selling sex to earn money for herself or her family (Anderson & Shafer, 1979; Hunt & Baird, 1990; Walters, 1975).

Some researchers also view the prostitution of young girls as the outcome of a lack of positively reinforcing public education. Young girls, particularly girls from lower socioeconomic environments, may leave school to face life without a vocation, trade, or any means of earning a living (Giarretto, 1982; Walters, 1975; Williams, 1981). Anyone who has ever worked in ghetto schools knows what this means. It is not the school professionals who are at fault; this is a much broader social problem. Many teachers, counselors, and social workers employed in inner-city schools feel the utter hopelessness of trying to make positive changes in their students. They see, on a daily basis, girls and boys who come from homes where the family is surviving on welfare payments or by illegal means and teaching the children their own "trades." There is much more money to be made from prostitution than can be received from welfare or earned from unskilled jobs.

Many of these girls feel that life, their parents, and the schools have all given them a bad deal. Prostitution is a way to rebel and act out their feelings of hostility, hurt, anger, and aggression. It also allows them to break away, earn money, and possibly find the love that they do not receive from their own families (Hunt & Baird, 1990).

Emotional Consequences Of Sexual Abuse

Before delving too far into this section of the chapter, I intend to explain to the reader where I stand on the issue of children's so-called involvement in their own sexual abuse. To some it may sound like a harsh stance, unempathic and out of date, and there are many who will not agree with me. But this book is about children and not about what they are like when they are no longer children; it is about child advocacy. It is not intended to advocate for the position of disturbed adults; they have their own advocates, and quite a few books have been written about them. This book is for and about children. Since the adult perspective is important from a standpoint of prevention, a short look at the events of their childhood that made them what they are today is necessary and appropriate.

Some very famous and highly respected scholars (Bender & Blau, 1937; Bender & Grugett, 1952; Kinsey, Martin, Pomeroy, & Gebhard, 1953) have said, in so many words, that some children become disturbed over the reactions of the adults around them rather than the sexual attack itself, and that there are children who are not innocent victims but actually seduce adults into sexual liaisons.

The first question that comes to mind is, are these theorists asking us to believe that the adults in such cases are innocent because they perceive a child as sexy? Attractive, cute, charming, engaging, fun, interesting—yes. But sexy? The second question is, are these theorists suggesting that the blame should be shared because the adult thinks a child is seductive? We should not forget that adults are expected to have at least some control over their impulses, no matter how sexually attractive a child may seem to them. The following quotation from Bender and Blau (1937) may be revealing:

> It is true that the child often rationalized with excuses of fear of physical harm or the enticement of gifts, but these were obvious secondary reasons. Even in cases in which physical force may have been applied by the adult, this does not wholly account for the frequent repetition of the practice . . . the emotional placidity of most of the children would seem to indicate that they derived some fundamental satisfaction from the relationship. (p. 514)

Although the foregoing observations were made in 1937, Bender and Grugett repeated the study in 1952 with children age 5 to 12 who had "typical" sexual experiences with adults, and reached the same conclusions. These same attitudes hang on today in the minds of some law enforcement officials and even some professionals. Schultz and Jones (1983) cited work that showed that when psychiatrists are exposed clinically to cases of incest their assessments of damage decrease. Old notions from the past are still with us today because some people retain these same ideas about rape in general, and rape of females in particular (be they child or grown): somehow the victim asked for it (Sheehy, 1984).

The idea that a child is sexually seductive derives from followers of S. Freud—for example, Bender. Earlier in this chapter, it was pointed out that the notion that girls fantasized seduction by their fathers is based on Freudian views. Freud made great and significant contributions to psychological theory; however, to cling to his older notions is, in my opinion, out of date. Since there are people who allow righteousness to take the place of common sense, there are others who will allow a phantasmagoric theory to replace their own common sense. We are asked to be sympathetic to the adult; after all, it was he or she who was seduced by a very sexy child.

It is a well-known fact that children are normally curious about sex. They want to look at pictures, look at their bodies, look at others' bodies, feel their own bodies, play house, and play doctor. Adults are not allowed in these games. They are games that are a natural part of a child's development. But playing these games does not mean that children want a full sexual experience.

Freud has been misunderstood and misinterpreted by many of his own followers; of course he contradicted himself over the years in his attempt to develop his ideas about psychopathology and psychotherapy. At one time Freud recognized the strong connection between certain emotional problems and early childhood sexual abuse. In his early work, he was on the right track and saw the associated problems as they related to sexual abuse. It was not until several years later that, for whatever reasons, he reversed himself and proposed that women had only fantasized sexual attacks by their fathers; they had not actually occurred. Nevertheless, in 1897, before he advanced this new theory, he said:

> Girls who are involved in father–daughter incest are, without exception, severely damaged and plagued with serious psychiatric problems. Their disturbances are manifested by an aimless promiscuity, severe masochism with tendency to self–mutilation, overwhelming dependency needs and the occurrence of transient psychotic episodes. (1954, p. 217)

More recent studies exist that dispute the notion that sexual encounters with adults are not emotionally very consequential for a child. For instance, it has been shown that the combined effects of all the problems involved in incest cause in some children reactions close to psychotic states, such as prolonged confusional periods and rage reactions. A great variety of physical and emotional symptoms may occur following sexual assaults, including enuresis, fears, hyperactivity, altered sleep patterns, phobias, compulsive play, learning problems, compulsive masturbation, depression, and anxiety (Deblinger, McLeer, Atkins, Ralphe, & Edna, 1989; Greenwald, Leitenberg, Cado, & Tarran, 1990).

Although done a number of years ago, a study by De Francis (1969) is still one of the most respected investigations conducted on the emotional effects of child sexual abuse. De Francis studied child victims of incest, rape, sodomy, and other forms of child molestation. In this study, two thirds of the children evaluated were judged to be emotionally disturbed by the offense and its consequences. Nearly one fourth of the disturbed children had suffered severe, acute damage to their mental health. Some of the reactions shown by these children were anxiety, guilt, hostile aggressiveness, delinquency, antisocial adjustment problems, damage to self-esteem, and repetitive imitative behavior of the sexual attack. De Francis also reported that the victims of incest are especially vulnerable, and the guilt is often too enormous for the ego to accommodate, causing serious emotional damage, sometimes to the point of schizophrenia. It has been found that grown women who had been sexually abused as children abuse themselves with alcohol or drugs or develop anorexia nervosa. It is clear that if professionals do not support children effectively after a sexual attack, the chances of these children for positive mental health and development in the future will be diminished (Einbender & Friedrich, 1989; German, Habenicht, & Futcher, 1990).

Crisis intervention

Immediately after the incident of abuse, crisis intervention is needed. Experience with child victims indicates how important it is that the child be given the opportunity to ventilate. Children who express in their own words what happened, and particularly how they feel about it, seem to adjust with fewer traumatic changes (Gordy, 1983; Schultz & Jones, 1983). Parents often make the mistake of thinking their children will be better off if they do not talk about the incident, if they just forget the whole thing.

As professionals who work day to day with children, we know that they do not just forget the whole thing because it was not talked about. In spite of the data affirming that most children are afraid to talk about abuse incidents, experience has shown that, even though afraid, many children desperately need to talk to someone and wish that someone had talked to them (Orr, 1980).

Schmitt (1975) reported that in some cases a sexually abused child will confide in a favorite teacher or counselor—usually a man if the child is a boy and a woman if the child is a girl. If anything like sexual abuse is mentioned, the teacher or counselor should not show distress. The child should be taken to a private place where she or he can speak freely and should be gently encouraged to relate all of the details of the incident. Later, the child's account should be recorded precisely as told since some children do become frightened and try to deny their accounts of the incident.

Belcher (1983) proposed the use of literature to prevent child abuse and to help the abused child maintain a positive self-image. Using literature is suggested as one way to make children aware that abuse is unacceptable in society and that adults are aware that incidents of abuse do occur, so that children do not believe that they are alone or that no one will believe them if they tell their story. Belcher's work included a list of books, together with references to the type of abuse, the child's sex and race, the abuser's relation to the child, and the appropriate reading age. All this material can be used in group counseling sessions. Care should be taken that children are not left on their own with the reading material. They need the guidance of a skilled counselor or teacher who is familiar with the material.

We are just now beginning to see programs brought into the schools that are designed to teach young children about sexual abuse, how they can avoid molesters, and what to do if they are approached or attacked. It will take some time before we know the effects of this type of sex-education program.

For children too young, too afraid, or too shocked to talk, a number of therapists have developed techniques, using puppets and art therapy, to assist children in talking about their experiences and their feelings. These techniques are becoming better known and available for the use of other professionals.

Legal Intervention

Stoenner (1976) noted that a number of psychopathic parents cannot be helped by any means. Apparently, these are people who do not know right from wrong and who repeatedly abuse their children. The only recourse is to remove the parent or the child from the home, depending on the situation.

The trend today is to not remove the child or the parent in the belief that punitive action is not always needed and that such action may stand in the way of a successful therapy program. Keeping the family together at all costs is almost a rule, although some family therapists realize that the abuse continues even while counseling is ongoing. Clearly, some of these therapists do not understand that just because a group of people are living together they do not automatically constitute a family. The concept of a family is much, much more than merely people living together. In any case, the first order of business is to protect the child. Perhaps family members can return to the family situation later, but a great deal of work has to be done with some adults before the child or the parent should be allowed back into the house.

Why make such an issue out of the trend toward family therapy? Why do I seem so negative about this strong emphasis on keeping the family together? An example of an actual case may help explain my skepticism. Lee was 12 years old and in a special class for emotionally disturbed children. He was volatile and could be quite aggressive, especially when an adult came near him, and most especially if anyone so much as put a hand on his shoulder or head, even in the most gentle and harmless manner.

Lee was one of eight children, all of whom had been sexually abused. The Department of Social Services was aware of the situation, and the court ordered family therapy; however, the parents subsequently divorced and the mother remarried. End of problem? No, not by a long shot! As time went by for Lee in his special class, and after he eventually learned to trust the teacher, he told his story. When his real (biological) father was living with them, all of the children, both boys and girls, were being sexually abused by the father and the mother, and the older children were sexually attacking the younger children. Nearly everyone in the family was heterosexually and homosexually attacking other family members. The mother had sex with sons and daughters. The father had sex with sons and daughters. Older siblings had sex with brothers and sisters. When Lee's real father was gone and he had a stepfather, the routine had not changed. The same sexual activities were occurring; the only difference was that now the stepfather was involved instead of the real father.

Once again, family therapy was ordered. For what purpose? This so-called family was finally abolished and the children were placed in foster homes. Then and only then did Lee show any improvement in his special class. It took pressure from the teacher to force a reevaluation of how this case was being handled. Sometimes ordering family therapy as a solution is only a quick way to rid the courts and social services of very complicated problems.

Prosecution has to be handled very carefully. If the prosecution of extremely serious cases fails, the child is in even more danger. Schoepfer (1975) warned that it is very important for social workers to establish strong working relationships with probation officers, police, and the judges who hear cases of physical and sexual abuse. Judges, by virtue of their training, more often protect the constitutional rights of adults. Social workers need to be more in touch with school personnel as well. Many counselors and teachers have access to information, received from the children, that no one else has.

Physicians are generally loath to testify in court since they would be spending much of their time in court proceedings instead of in their offices. Arrangements should be made to allow physicians to testify quickly and then return to their offices.

While it seems a drastic measure to some, in many cases the interests of children would be served by their temporary or permanent removal from the home. Removal requires court orders. Cooperative planning that keeps the best interests of the child in mind will help decide whether a child should be placed elsewhere, so that it can be determined whether such a threat motivates the parent to reform, whether a period of protective supervision will rehabilitate the family, or whether parental rights should be terminated permanently.

Whatever the ultimate decision, it will be a judge who makes it, and that decision will be based in part on whatever additional psychosocial information has been provided. This is where the critical role of the school professional comes into play and why it is so important that school professionals be as knowledgeable as they can be. A child's life may be in their hands.

RITUAL ABUSE

The facts about ritual abuse are being uncovered at an accelerated rate, disclosing the reality of brutal and devastating experiences encountered by children and adults of all ages. The ritualistically abused child is trapped in his or her own hidden world of affliction and will remain bound to that world until he or she can be guided to freedom by someone with the right knowledge (Stratford, 1991).

According to the Ritual Abuse Task Force of the Los Angeles County Commission for Women (Ritual Abuse Task Force, 1989), ritual abuse is defined as "a brutal form of abuse of children, adolescents, and adults, consisting of physical, sexual, and psychological abuse, and involving the use of rituals. Rarely consisting of a single episode, it is an attack against innocence."

Most victims, both during and after the abuse has taken place, are in a state of terror, mind control, and dissociation in which disclosure is extremely difficult (Ritual Abuse Task Force, 1989). Since they are impressionable, virtually helpless, and easily de-programmed and reprogrammed, children are the principal targets of ritual abuse.

Purposes of Ritual Elements

The Ritual Abuse Task Force (Ritual Abuse Task Force, 1989) identified three characteristics of ritual abuse, which are usually carried out by members of a cult: (1) rituals in some groups are part of a shared belief or worship system into which the victim is being indoctrinated; (2) rituals are used to intimidate victims into silence; (3) ritual elements (e.g., devil worship, animal or human sacrifice) seem so unbelievable to those unfamiliar with these crimes that these elements detract from the credibility of the victims and make prosecution of the crimes very difficult.

Pazder (cited in Ritual Abuse Task Force, 1986) shared other purposes of the ritual elements. He stated that in ritual abuse "every assault has a purpose." Each action is premeditated, part of the process aimed at humiliating and producing guilt in the child. Another purpose is to inculcate the child into the primary satanic group. The thinking is that, if they are programmed at a young age, these children will be more recruitable when they are teenagers.

Types Of Ritual Abuse

Psychological abuse. Psychological abuse involving the use of rituals is devastating and involves the use of ritual indoctrination, including mind-control techniques as well as the use of mind-altering drugs (Ritual Abuse Task Force, 1989). Furthermore, it involves ritual intimidation, imparting in the victim a discerning fear of cult members as well as the evil spirits that they feel the cult members can command (Ritual Abuse Task Force, 1989). The extreme terror and mind-control techniques to which victims are subjected are so severe that most of them dissociate their memories of the experience and lose their sense of free will (Ritual Abuse Task Force, 1989; Stratford, 1991). Some reported examples of the psychological abuse endured by victims are threats of punishment, torture, mutilation, or death (Stratford, 1991). Children often are told that their families are secretly cult members who intend them harm and have chosen to have their children ritually abused. Children often are placed in coffins and told to "practice being dead," confined in cages or closets with dead human or animal parts, and photographed in sexually provocative poses (Steacy & Bethune, 1989). Moreover, children have had their own bodies smeared or covered with urine or feces, or have been forced to ingest urine, feces, or semen (Ritual Abuse Task Force, 1989; Steacy & Bethune, 1989).

Physical abuse. Physical abuse in satanic rituals is so severe that it often gets to the point of torture, and young victims frequently are abused without their parents' knowledge because they are sub-jected only to physical abuse that is not easily detected (Ritual Abuse Task Force, 1986; Ritual Abuse Task Force, 1989). Detectives and law enforcement personnel have expressed extreme frustration in dealing with ritual abuse cases because of the lack of evidence in most cases. It is nearly impossible to be able to come up with the physical evidence necessary to take criminals to court (Steacy & Bethune, 1989; Watters, 1991).

Some less detectable forms of physical abuse involved in ritu-als include having pins or "shots" inserted into genital areas or into sensitive areas of the body (i.e., between digits or under fingernails) (Ritual Abuse Task Force, 1989). Victims often have received electric shock in these body areas. Other types of abuse include being sub-merged in water with the notion of drowning, having food withheld for extended periods of time, or being hung from crosses in mock crucifixions with sexual abuse occurring in such positions (Ritual Abuse Task Force, 1989; Stratford, 1991). Some of the more detectable forms of abuse include physical beatings, the use of cuts, tattoos, branding, and burns, as well as removal of body parts (e.g., digits).

Watters (1991) shared the experiences of a victim who testified against her father in court. She spoke of having a nail driven into her arm and having pliers used to open up her "private parts" so men could have sex with her. She remembered being burned with smoldering sticks and cut with knives when they needed blood for the ceremonies. At one point she told of her mother using the pliers to put a piece of a dead baby's arm inside her. At another ceremo-ny, instead of a baby's arm, they used spiders.

Sexual abuse. Ritual victims are sexually abused in extremely bizarre, sadistic, brutal, and humiliating acts. As well as being an end itself, its purpose is to gain total dominance over the victim (Ritual Abuse Task Force, 1986; Ritual Abuse Task Force, 1989; Stratford, 1991). Some of the abuse involves assaults by men, women, and other children (often occurring in a group), or repeated fondling, oral copulation, rape, and sodomy. The use of instruments such as symbolic objects (e.g., crucifixes or wands) or weapons are used for penetration of body orifices. Victims may be forced to have sexual contact with dead or dying people, or forced to perform sex-ual acts with children and infants, and even animals (Ritual Abuse Task Force, 1986; Ritual Abuse Task Force, 1989; Stratford, 1991).

Types Of Rituals

Birthing rituals. According to the Los Angeles County Ritual Abuse Task Force (cited in Ritual Abuse Task Force, 1989), ritual victims often report of having been forced to participate in a "birthing ritual," in which the victim is placed in the carcass of a dead animal or human body, symbolic of being born into membership with the group.

Marriage rituals. Victims also have been forced to participate in a mock marriage taking place between a child and a member of the abusive group, between two children, or even between the child and Satan.

In both birthing and marriage rituals, the victims are made to feel acutely connected to the abusive group or to the "powers of evil" (Ritual Abuse Task Force, 1989; Stratford, 1991).

Magic surgery. Children who are ritually abused are often drugged or hypnotized and told when they wake up that they have had a "magic surgery." They are told that the blood smeared on their bodies is from the surgery, that a bomb has been placed inside of them, and that it will explode if they tell anyone of the abuse (Stratford, 1991). At times, children are told that they've had a monster, a demon, or even "the devil's heart" placed inside them, attacking if they disclose.

Human and animal sacrifices. Victims of ritual abuse often are forced to participate in the killing of animals, babies, children, and adults, with the understanding that they will acquire "magical powers" (Ritual Abuse," 1986; "Ritual abuse," 1989; Stratford, 1991). Drinking blood and practicing cannibalism are said to be ways for the abusers to acquire the spiritual powers of the victim.

Even more repulsive is the fact that many female victims are raised in satanic cults for the sole purpose of becoming "breeders" (Stratford, 1991). They become impregnated by cult members and are forced to sacrifice their babies to Satan (Ritual Abuse Task Force, 1986; Watters, 1991). Since there is never a public record of the birth of these babies, they are never missed when they are abused or killed (Steacy & Bethune, 1989; Stratford, 1991). One victim said that, at age 16, the cult aborted her unborn child with a sword, then cut up the fetus and laid it across her stomach (Watters, 1991). Another victim reported being impregnated at age 9, and again at age 11, and being forced to sacrifice both babies. When questioned about the validity of her statements regarding pregnancy at such a young age, she indicated that the cult members/perpetrators start "stimulating" the genitals and "stretching the vagina" of young babies just after birth, so that by the time the children are 8 or 9 years of age, their bodies are mature enough to give birth. Children marked for ritualized abuse are often subjected to excessive use of enemas to stretch and prepare the child for massive sex use of the rectum, as well as to get control over the child (Ritual Abuse Task Force, 1986).

Other bodies used in human sacrifices come from the ranks of the homeless people, as well as from an unknown percentage of missing children and adults (Ritual Abuse Task Force, 1989; Steacy & Bethune, 1989). The lack of evidence of the remains of these human sacrifices can be explained by cannibalism, cult access to mortuaries and crematories, frozen storage of body parts, and the retention by cult members of bones and other body parts for further "magical practices" (Ritual Abuse Task Force, 1989).

Mind Control

As indicated by the Ritual Abuse Task Force (Ritual Abuse Task Force, 1989), mind control is the cornerstone of ritual abuse. It is the principal element in controlling and silencing the victims and is achieved through a complex system of brainwashing, indoctrination, programming, hypnosis, and the use of mind-altering drugs (Ritual Abuse Task Force, 1989; Stratford, 1991). Most frequently and persistently, satanic cults tend to focus their efforts on achieving mind control with children under the age of 6 (Ritual Abuse Task Force, 1989). Some of the elements of cult indoctrination used to achieve mind control have been identified in *Cults, Quacks and NonProfessional Psychotherapists* by West and Singer (cited in Ritual Abuse Task Force, 1989):

1. isolation and manipulation of the environment
2. control over channels of communication and information
3. induction of uncertainty, fear, and confusion, with joy and certainty through surrender to the group as a goal
4. alternation of harshness and leniency in a context of discipline
5. insistence that the victim's survival (physical and spiritual) depends on identifying with the group
6. assignments of monotonous or repetitive tasks such as chant-

ing or copying written materials

7. acts of symbolic betrayal or renunciation of self, family, and previously held values, designed to increase the psychological distance between the victim and his/her previous way of life

Children are more susceptible to indoctrination and other techniques used for gaining control over their minds and their behavior (Ritual Abuse Task Force, 1989).

Trance states can be achieved through elements such as chanting, isolation, sensory deprivation, pain, hypnosis, and hypnotic drugs. Those who have survived ritual abuse often can be called back into the cult years by a cult member who knows the trigger words or signs to use to access their programming (Ritual Abuse Task Force, 1989; Stratford, 1991).

Both cognitive and religious beliefs are impaired by mind control and ritual abuse (Stratford, 1991). Victims begin to believe that there is no escape, that they are completely controlled, that they are incapable of protecting themselves, that the cult is their only true family, and that disclosures are dangerous. Furthermore, they begin to believe that Satan is stronger than God, that God does not love them, that God wants to punish them, and that their life is controlled by Satan (Ritual Abuse Task Force, 1989; Stratford, 1991).

Warning Signs

Some indicators that a child may possibly be involved in ritualistic abuse include abrupt emotional changes, a preoccupation with sex, sudden irrational fear of being left alone, changes in school habits, use of verbal or written words that are "strange" or written backwards, sudden change in normal toileting practices, and an unexplainable fear of being in small spaces (Criville, 1990; Stratford, 1991). Davidowitz (1989) also has noted that mood swings, a loss of interest in friends, withdrawal from family, and a sudden fascination with death may also be indicative of involvement in ritualistic abuse.

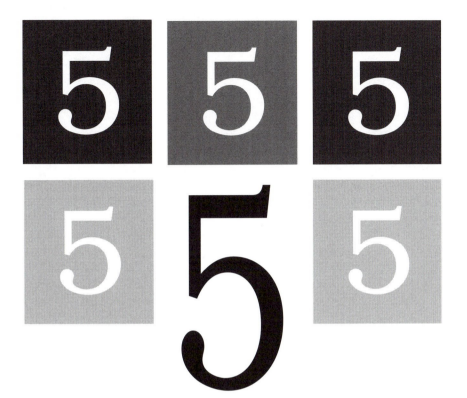

Depression and Suicide in Children and Adolescents

Remy

"How can they know? How do they know the answers? I don't understand! I can't think! How do they know those things? I can't do this! I can't do this work! Don't make me do this work! I don't know how! I wish I was dead! Dead!"

Remy ran around the room screaming, his face nearly purple and twisted in a horrified expression. Tears, saliva, and mucus from his nose were gushing down and drenching the front of his shirt. He grabbed at the wall like he wanted to dig a hole into it and bury himself inside. He clawed at it as if he could climb to the ceiling where nobody would be able to get to him. Remy kicked the wall and slumped into a heap on the floor, writhing and rolling, first on his stomach and then on his back, banging his head on the floor, smashing his fists against the leg of the table nearby. He coughed and gagged, and more saliva spewed from his mouth, making a slick puddle on the floor. In his twisting and flailing his head was in the saliva puddle, but he didn't seem to know or care. He was totally out of control—like a pathetic, trapped little animal, wild-eyed and terrified.

Mrs. Gregory moved toward the boy to try to comfort him but he drew back his legs and kicked up and out, keeping her at a distance. "I want to help you, Remy. But I can't if you don't settle down. This work is not so important. If it doesn't get done today, then tomorrow, or sometime when you are able to do it. Everybody can't know everything. I'll help you with your work. That's what I'm here for, to help."

"No! Ooooh, no, you don't understand! I don't know things! I'll never know. Not tomorrow—ever! You're going to hurt me! Let me go! Let me go home! I feel sick. I'm going to throw up! Go away! Get away! How can I do this? How can I do this work? I can't! Can't! Can't! I can't think! Let me die! I want to die! It'll never be all right! Things are all wrong, all mixed up in my head! Ooooh, my heart hurts! My head hurts! Can't breathe! Can't breathe! Can't sleep anymore! Dream scary things! I'm scared! I'm scared!"

"Remy, Remy, you can't breathe because you're so upset. Calm down and you will breathe okay. It's very scary when you feel so bad, when you feel like you can't breathe." Mrs. Gregory's voice was soft and gentle as she tried to calm Remy. "Nobody wants to die, Remy. You shouldn't say that kind of thing. Let me wipe your face with this cool towel—you'll feel better.

Mrs. Gregory's voice had calmed Remy, so he let her wipe his face. He looked up at her kind face and felt like crying some more. She did not understand how he felt. Nobody did. It was hopeless. His mom and dad didn't understand. Dr. Sandberg didn't understand. All they said was that someday things would be better—when he learned like the others, he would feel much better. If he played more with other kids, made friends, things would be much better. They weren't. Nothing was better. He didn't want to play with the others. He couldn't do anything right—always missed the ball, couldn't hit it, couldn't catch it. He wanted to, and his dad wanted him to. Remy could tell his dad was real disappointed he couldn't play better. His mother was disappointed he couldn't read and write yet. They all hated him, didn't love him. He hated himself. Nothing was right and wouldn't ever be. His heart ached and his chest felt like lead.

He wanted to close his eyes and go to sleep forever, like when his Uncle John died. Everybody said nice things about Uncle John and they felt sad he was gone, they all said how much they loved him and would miss him. Remy wanted to die like Uncle John. Then everybody would love him, and when he woke up after a real long time, everything would be all right. He would be all changed—would be able to do all the things everyone wanted him to do.

Nothing was good now, everything bad. He only liked to ride his bike, to be alone, to go down to the creek where nobody would bother him. He could be alone in the woods and sit by the creek and put his bare feet in the water, listen to the birds, and try to catch the dragonflies. It was peaceful there; he didn't have to know things or do things he couldn't do. He could go up on the cliffs and see a far distance. He could look down at the creek below. It was beautiful there—so quiet, so peaceful—a nice place to sleep.

"Remy, you seem very calm now. Do you think you could get up and get cleaned up? It's almost time to go home. Your parents can't pick you up today. I know you don't like to ride the bus but it's the only way home today. You do want to go home, don't you?

Mrs. Gregory helped him to his feet and wiped his face again and brushed his hair back out of his eyes. She gave his shirt a final tuck in the back where he couldn't reach. "Will your sister be there to watch you until your parents come home?"

"I suppose so." He spoke with the most serene voice now. No one would ever dream that he had just been through such an emotional upheaval. "Good-bye, Mrs. Gregory. Have a nice day."

Mrs. Gregory watched as the children went to catch their bus. Some of them were running with their shirttails hanging out and waving their jackets high above their heads like flags of victory—they were free. Remy was dragging behind painfully slowly, like he was pulling a cartload of mud. He was such a contrast to the other little fourth graders, who seemed so carefree, so happy to be out of school and going home. He was the last one on, and the driver slammed the doors as the bus lurched forward. Mrs. Gregory worried about Remy. He was so different from the others in her class, so unhappy, and he took his learning problems much more seriously than the other children. The others had a hard time learning, too, but seemed to manage, and certainly they seemed to forget it all when the bell rang. Not Remy. He agonized over every mistake and failing. She just couldn't figure out what to do for Remy that would be different and help him more. She had spent many nights puzzling over what to do for Remy. After musing about it, she decided there wasn't much to do that she had not tried. Remy did have a doctor. Maybe he eventually would find a way to help the boy.

Remy got off the bus in front of his house and was glad to see his mom and dad were not home yet. He ran inside quickly to get some of his favorite things: one of each of his marbles, his coins from Germany that his parents brought back from their last vacation, his E.T. eraser, and a little Swiss army knife. He stuffed them all into his pocket. He took off his shirt, which was still damp from the tears and saliva, and put on his favorite old, soft sweatshirt. "Going to ride my bike, Nance," he shouted at his sister as he ran for the back door.

"Better be back here when Mom and Dad get home! You know they want you here doing your homework by the time they're home from work. Hear me, Remy? You better be here, little creep. I always get in trouble if you're not here when they get home.

"Yeah, I hear you." Remy lifted the garage door and shot out on his bike, off to his favorite place. He finally felt good, riding with the breeze in his face. He could hardly wait to get there. He rode up on the cliff overlooking the creek and got off his bike. He took in a deep breath to smell the woods and the water below and sat down on the edge of the cliff to just feel, and smell, and listen to the sounds of this most beautiful place.

Remy reached in his pocket and took out all of his best things. He spread them out on the ground and picked up each one carefully. He rubbed them with his hands and studied them. They were all his lucky things. He felt very good having them. He thought about his day at school and all the other days like this one, so terrible he never wanted to go back. He couldn't do anything there, no matter how nice Mrs. Gregory was. She was the best teacher he had ever had, but she couldn't help. He started to cry again, this time softly—quiet tears like when Uncle John died. They said Uncle John was much happier now—in a long, long sleep, and nothing could ever hurt him again.

With his finger, he drew a little house in the dirt and put each of his favorite things in one of the rooms. Then he scooped up more dirt and pushed and patted it into the shape of a wall around the house. From the side of the path he picked a flower and planted it in front of what was supposed to be the yard. Off to the side, he moved the dirt around until it looked like a cemetery, and with his finger he wrote "UJ" for "Uncle John." Then he picked another flower to put on his uncle's grave.

Remy stood up and walked around his creation, reflecting on the details of his work. He smiled. He liked it—it had all good things. Not one thing was wrong, and he did it by himself. He marveled at how well he could do things up here in his favorite place. He wished he could stay here forever. He mulled over his drawing in the dirt again, and decided something needed to be added. With his finger he drew another grave next to Uncle John's and wrote his name on it. He walked around and around his drawing, scrutinizing every part of it. Then he jumped in the air with a feeling of satisfaction. All his wonderful, favorite things, finally in the right place, the way they should be.

Remy looked up to see the sun setting and realized he was probably late again. Mom and Dad would be home now and angry that he was not in his room doing his homework. Nance would be mad because they would scold her for letting him go out. He looked down at the creek below and took another deep breath so he could smell the woods again, then jumped on his bike and circled around to head down the path. He rode down to the big pine tree and circled his bike around again. The pedaling started, very hard and very fast. He was going as fast as he could, maneuvering his bike away from his dirt drawing and all of his favorite things. With no noise or cry whatsoever, Remy grabbed his handlebars tightly and went over the cliff.

....

From Remy's story we know that he is about 9 years old because he is a fourth grader. Remy certainly has some of the characteristics of a depressed and suicidal child. One outstanding feature is how hard he is on himself. His teacher recognizes that Remy is different, but she really does not know how to help the child. She is very good at trying to minimize the seriousness of his perceived failings. "This work is not so important. If it doesn't get done today, then tomorrow, or sometime when you are able to do it. Everybody can't know everything. I'll help you with your work." But Remy needs more than his teacher can provide. He has a doctor, but we do not know if it is the family doctor, a pediatrician, or a psychiatrist. Presumably it is not a psychiatrist, who would not tell the boy that things will get better when he is able to learn. Are the parents applying too much pressure? Probably so. The story hints that this is the case. Remy could be helped if all the adults concerned were working toward the same goal, but that doesn't seem to be the case for Remy. The teacher is on the right track, but she cannot do it alone.

It is no longer a rare occurrence for young children to kill themselves, if it ever was as rare as once thought. It is the eighth leading cause of death among children from 5 to 15 years of age (Bernhardt & Praeger, 1985). Suicide is a subject that even today remains cloaked in superstition and misunderstanding. It becomes particularly alarming to observe steadily rising suicide rates and realize that it ranks as one of the major causes of death among youths. The leading researchers and clinicians are definite that, among adolescents, the third leading cause of death is suicide (Paluszny, Davenport, & Kim, 1991). There are many people, however, who still do not believe that children Remy's age or younger could possibly even think of, let alone commit, suicide.

The actual figures for suicide are probably much higher than the statistics indicate. It is believed that the number of suicides and suicide attempts is underestimated by 30% or more. This is partly attributed to the stigma attached to suicide. Many deaths are reported falsely to protect the families, and criteria used by coroners to establish death by suicide vary by region, which also contributes to the problem of uncounted suicides. Certain physicians openly admit that they never record a child death as suicide, regardless of the age and even if a suicide note was left, because they do not want to stigmatize the parents or add to their grief and guilt (Lester, 1990; Rosenthal & Rosenthal, 1984; Teri, 1982b).

Remy's age is not nearly as young as that of some reported suicides and suicide attempts. There are studies of preschool children, as young as 3 years old, attempting suicide. The children stab themselves, hang themselves, run in front of cars, jump from high places, drink poisonous fluids, and try to overdose on medicines commonly found around the house. Most people think that these incidents are accidents, but Rosenthal and Rosenthal (1984) have evidence that these acts are intentional.

Of all suicide attempts in the United States, 12% are made by adolescents. According to Hillard (1983), estimates comparing the ratio of attempts to completed suicides range from 5:1 to 100:1, with figures indicating that females are more likely to attempt suicide (2:1) whereas males are more likely to complete suicide (2:1). One explanation that has been suggested to account for this difference is that our society is generally more tolerant of emotional expression and failure in females than in males. Since an incompleted suicide by a male would only tend to aggravate his existing problems, sure death becomes the preferred option. Parents and peers often presume that a person will not attempt suicide unless he or she is ashamed of something or is seriously ill mentally (Rich, Sherman, & Fowler, 1990). The pressure of feelings of shame becomes a powerful force for the young, who already feel alienated and misunderstood.

The method used in committing suicide may be a factor in explaining why more males than females commit suicide. Males primarily use firearms, which is a more violent means than other methods and seldom leaves any chance for survival. Females frequently use poisons, which are slower acting, thereby increasing the chance for discovery and intervention. Some researchers allude to social training as the reason for this choice: boys grow up playing with toy guns and have the freedom, if not the expectation, to be more aggressive. Males are more familiar with firearms. It is more common for them to have had some experience with guns, such as on hunting trips with their fathers. In these cases, there is easy access to firearms since they may be available in the home. Females typically do not receive training in the use of firearms, nor do they typically go on hunting trips. Vendors of firearms will sell guns to boys without question if they appear to be old enough and sometimes even if they are not of legal age. A girl might receive more attention and questioning if she attempted to buy a gun, which may discourage a suicide-prone female from making the purchase.

The female, on the other hand, may be making an appeal for help and tends to face less of a humiliation in surviving a suicide attempt than the male because of a greater acceptance of the emotional side of her nature.

It has been shown that fewer than 10% of those attempting but failing to commit suicide later kill themselves, and that many who succeed in committing suicide do so on their first attempt (Seiden, 1969). Actually, no one has adequately explained why the two sexes choose the different methods that they do.

A high percentage of suicide-prone adolescents come from unstable and disorganized homes in which there is a lack of sympathy for and understanding of feelings of insecurity, frustration, depression, and being unwanted and alone (Zinner, 1987). Rosenthal and Rosenthal (1984) found that, among suicide-prone preschoolers, a high percentage are unwanted, abused, or neglected. These preschoolers also felt detached, lonely, and isolated, and saw themselves as "bad."

It is important to be aware that almost all the research on suicidal behavior is retrospective, which leads to underreporting. It is fairly well accepted that in cases of suicide, death certificates may be altered to protect survivors, or out of embarrassment and shame, the survivors may deliberately conceal the true method of death.

Self-destructive acts among youth have interested clinicians and researchers for some time. Many one-car accidents, accidents in the home, unnecessary heroism, and serious accident-proneness may be a part of suicidal behavior that is not recognized. It should also be noted that, just as suicides are frequently misreported, many attempted suicides go unreported to physicians or to any agency that could make them part of an official record (Bernhardt & Praeger, 1985).

Generally, the people closest to a suicide victim do not understand why it happened. Family and friends are often unaware of the depth of feelings of despair experienced by the victim. As perceptive as she is, even Remy's teacher does not realize how distraught and depressed he really is as she says to him, "Nobody wants to die, Remy. You shouldn't say that kind of thing." Remy's despair becomes even deeper as he realizes that no one understands. The most difficult suicides to understand are those committed by children and adolescents. Notes left by people who commit suicide contain phrases like "Nobody cares or loves me," "I'm awful and unlovable," and "It hurts so much I want to die" (Draper, 1976).

What is it that makes life so unbearable and not worth living? The message communicated in these notes is one of extreme depression. The act of suicide is really a symptom with many causes, and depression is obviously a major component.

Depression

A simple, general definition of depression is that it is an affective condition characterized by sadness and withdrawal. Depression can be a normal phenomenon. According to Renshaw (1974):

> At different growth phases, from infancy to adolescence [and to old age] "depressive equivalents" occur. Normal mourning, appropriate sorrow and sadness, demoralization, dejection at defeat and frustration are all to be differentiated from clinical depression. They are usually closely time-related to environmental stress, transient in nature, and acceptable to the person as "normal" discomfort. They rarely produce the sustained signs and symptoms of severe depression; nor is there an element of self-blame. (p. 487)

Even though some researchers report that there are environmental or situational factors that depress a youth to the point of suicide, it seems to me that this is an unsatisfactory explanation. Everyone, as Renshaw pointed out, is subjected to unpleasant and even tragic life events, but we do not all kill ourselves. It must be assumed, then, that suicide victims suffer from clinical depression.

Hinsie and Campbell (1974) noted that a good overall definition of depression does not exist because there are many types. Depression can be differentiated as psychotic or neurotic, and each of these can be subdivided into types. These types of depression have definitions, antecedents, manifestations, and treatments. Most psychological states with subcategories overlap to some degree, and depression is one of these states, but there are distinguishing features of each type that allow them to be discussed separately.

Children present a unique problem in that they consistently underestimate their symptoms and rate themselves as less depressed than others rate them (French & Berlin, 1979; Kazdin, French, & Unis, 1983). Malmquist (1983) was skeptical that children can be accurately diagnosed as depressed. He believed that for the largest number of children there is diagnostic confusion and uncertainty because the children have not reached the level of major symptomatic disturbance witnessed in adults. Malmquist asserted that symptom lists are, for the most part, only borrowed from adult symptom lists.

There is wide disagreement with this view of Malmquist's, and most researchers and experts agree that there is a clear, clinical phenomenon of childhood depression that is identifiable and can be diagnosed (Carlson & Cantwell, 1979; Cytryn, McKnew, & Bunney, 1980; Leon, Kendall, & Garber, 1980; Poznanski, 1982; Teri, 1982a).

There are several classifications of childhood depression. All warrant considerable attention because they are believed to be explanations for suicidal behavior in children.

Types Of Depression

In 1946 Spitz wrote a classic article on anaclitic depression, also termed the "deprivation syndrome." Anaclitic depression may develop in a normal infant after loss of the mother when there is no provision for a substitute. If the depression is deep-seated enough it leads to such irreversible symptoms as signs of organic brain disease with malnutrition and anemia. Spitz observed that depression due to deprivation of the person on whom the infant has become dependent is characterized by a period of misery followed by loss of interest in the environment. The motherless infant lacks adaptive mechanisms and loses even the capacity for such reflex adaptations as sucking, grabbing, or pushing away.

Bowlby (1951) observed the development of an "affectionless psyche" after maternal deprivation. The infants he studied became inert, forlorn, and disinterested in their surroundings and in other people. Initially they protested actively, but finally became apathetic, showing decreased physical and mental activity, and rejecting all adults. This infant–child depression involves such symptoms as apathy, listlessness, inactivity, failure to thrive, and poor development.

To minimize the devastating effects of this kind of deprivation, both Bowlby and Spitz believed that treatment is highly dependent on timing and on the genuineness of a new mother substitute. If a new substitute who is genuinely warm and caring cannot be found, they believe the child will become emotionally debilitated for life.

It is possible that if maternal deprivation is experienced in infancy, the symptoms can be carried on into childhood and adolescence. Perhaps some mothers who are rejecting, abusing, or emotionally and cognitively unavailable because of mental illness create the same result. In such cases there would be no mother substitute because the real mother is physically present, but the child experiences the deprivation just the same. This premise is in accord with the work of Rosenthal and Rosenthal (1984), who studied suicide and suicide proneness in preschoolers and found that many of them had been abused and neglected.

In Danny's story from Chapter 3, his youngest sibling, Jason, who is 4 years old, has been without his mother perhaps since his birth and throughout critical stages of development. Physically she is with him, but because of her mental illness, emotionally and cognitively she is unavailable. Jason could be suffering from this type of depression.

Reactive depression. Reactive depression is attributed to some form of trauma or loss that is frequently accompanied by feelings of guilt for past failure or transgressions. The loss of a parent does not necessarily mean that an affective disorder, such as depression, will develop; however, an unsatisfactory parent–child relationship is an extremely important factor. Abrahams and Whitlock (1969) believed that a poor parent–child relationship has the most significance in terms of the development of the ultimate form of an affective disorder. Others have found that low self-esteem is the most important factor in depression (Leon et al., 1980; Teri, 1982a).

In the section on sexual abuse, it was noted that some girls attempt or commit suicide as a result of incest. Depression was cited as a major characteristic of children who had been physically and sexually abused. Indeed, these are poor parent–child relationships; frequently, as a result of the incest, a parent is lost. In fact, the mothers who do not stop the incest or who contribute to it directly were probably never emotionally available to their children in the first place. Damaged self-esteem is a common denominator of children who have suffered all the types of abuse. Stacy, Irma, and Chuy from earlier chapters fit this category of depression. Guilt is another common feature of children who are sexually abused because they blame themselves for whatever family conflict results from an incestuous relationship. All the forms of abuse, which we now know are more common than formerly believed, could well be the cause of reactive depression in many children and adolescents, with suicide being the ultimate escape or atonement in the mind of the child for "badness."

Acute depressive reaction. Acute depressive reaction frequently is characterized by a masked depressed mood, progressive withdrawal, lack of appetite, school failure, sleep disturbance, sadness, and verbal expressions indicating hopelessness and despair. The onset of the depression generally occurs after some traumatic event such as the loss of a loved one. Assuming that the relationship with the loved one was healthy, the prognosis for recovery from this type of depression is very good (Cytryn & McKnew, 1972, 1974; Friedman & Doyal, 1974; Hollan, 1970; Lesse, 1974; Phillips, 1968).

This type of depression is very straightforward and what we would expect to see in Geneva (see Chapter 3). Since Danny has lost his mother through mental illness and we cannot know what kind of relationship he had with her before the onset of her illness, his is a unique situation. It is a case of ongoing loss and a poor relationship. His depression may not have a very good prognosis, and it would not be surprising if he later attempted suicide.

Chronic depressive reaction. The chronic depressive reaction is generally more extreme and includes making suicidal threats. Some features of this type are the presence of depressed mood and behavior, including suicidal ideation very early in childhood, repeated separations from important maternal figures starting in infancy, and the presence of chronic depression in the mother. This type of depression does not have an immediate precipitating event; rather, there are periodic, recurring experiences that are emotionally depriving. Several studies show a high incidence of maternal depression associated with a child suffering from this type of depression (Cytryn & McKnew, 1972, 1974; Waldron, Shrier, Stone, & Tobin, 1975).

This type of depression is a good match for the children in Danny's story. Danny's mother is suffering from a serious mental illness (probably manic-depressive, and we get a brief glimpse of Danny's siblings and how they are reacting: Annie, who almost constantly sits and rocks and sings to herself, and Jason, who screams in frustration from the abandonment he feels. All three children are undoubtedly depressed. Jason's may be a different (anaclitic) depression from the depression of the two older children.

Masked depression. Masked depression is the most common form of depression seen in children. The term indicates that behind a psychosomatic disorder, such as ulcers, or various behavioral patterns, such as hyperactivity, there is a severe depression that eventually becomes overt. Usually the depression comes to the surface spontaneously under certain circumstances (French & Berlin, 1979; Lesse, 1974).

Behavioral characteristics of this syndrome can take the form of antisocial acts, explosive sexual behavior, compulsive eating or not eating, compulsive work patterns, accident proneness, and, finally, suicidal behavior. Alcohol and drug abuse, school phobia and failure, and delinquency are considered forms of masked depression. Anger resulting from emotional abandonment or from an extremely hostile and punitive environment is common in this type of depression. Some children feel extreme anger over their situation but are afraid to act out their anger directly for fear of losing their parents. Other children feel terrified while constantly being reminded of how grateful they should be, which sometimes leads to passive aggressive behavior. Others act out their deep feelings directly (Forrest, 1983).

Two of the stories from earlier chapters might serve as examples here: Lisa and Stacy. Lisa is antisocial, and what is sad is that important people in her life miss the depression and focus on her surface behavior. She is failing in school, undoubtedly she is using drugs or alcohol, and she is on her way to acting out sexually if she hasn't done so already. She is running away with her boyfriend Torry, who has already been in trouble for delinquent activities. She feels emotionally abandoned. Her mother has been trying to arrange for her to live with her estranged father, who apparently does not want the child either. Lisa is quite aware that her stepfather doesn't want her. Somewhere in the story is the idea that the home environment is hostile. School is certainly punitive, but Lisa presents a tough outside appearance to hide her feelings. She will go where she thinks she can find love. She needs it desperately; something must offset her depression. If the alternative she has chosen does not work out, and undoubtedly it will not, this adolescent is a likely suicide victim.

Stacy's behavior is different, but she is also younger. Perhaps some of her absentmindedness and accidents are passive aggressive ways of reacting to her emotionally abusing mother. She is constantly reminded of how grateful she should be to have her mother, and there are threats of abandonment. She does not act out directly, but she can retaliate against her mother with behavior that is most annoying and troublesome. Stacy is deprived of her mother's and father's love, and undoubtedly she feels constantly terrified that at any moment she could be tossed aside for good. She does not recognize these dynamics consciously, She just feels and responds in the only way in which she is capable at the moment. As an outcome, suicide would not be surprising.

Endogenous depression. Endogenous depression, as the term implies, is thought to be genetically or innately determined. This label is used with reference to infants and children, as well as adults, when precipitating factors are not clear or definite. It is believed to exist, to some degree, throughout the life of the children, giving them the appearance of lacking self-confidence and being cognitively retarded (Halligan, 1983; Ossofsky, 1974).

Although this depression may reach psychotic or suicidal proportions, remissions do occur. Brumback and Staton (1983) proposed an interesting theory regarding this type of depression and the learning disabilities seen in children. These authors speculated that right-hemispheric cognitive dysfunction shares a common pathophysiology with childhood endogenous depression. They also believed that this type of depression exists in as much as 2% of the elementary school-age population.

Remy could fit into this category of depression. Certainly there is pressure in his home, perhaps more than he can handle. He has, as the story leads us to understand, severe learning problems. Why? Brumback and Staton may have an answer as to why he has such severe emotional reactions to his problems. The brain dysfunction that creates the cognitive difficulties may also be creating depression. This makes sense; other children, many of them, have learning problems and yet do not kill themselves. The question can also be asked whether Remy has severe learning problems because of his depression. There is no real indication in the story that he has had an unusually traumatic or morbid home life with his family. The parents do not appear to be that different from thousands of others who have children with learning problems. They want him to study, to improve. Doing homework after school is really not a harsh or unreasonable expectation for most children. If Remy's depression is of this type, and let's say it is, then medications rather than homework, understanding and leeway rather than pressure, might have prevented his suicide.

Development and Depression

The stages in the depression process are described as fantasy, verbal expression, mood, and behavior (Cytryn et al., 1980; Cytryn & McKnew, 1974).

In the fantasy stage the expression of depression is through dreams, play, and other indirect outlets. There are common themes in depressive fantasies that include mistreatment, being obstructed and seeking revenge, criticism, loss and abandonment, self-injury, death, and suicide.

Verbal expressions are a more direct way of ventilating depression. These include expressions of hopelessness, helplessness, and guilt, and self-deprecating comments about feeling unattractive, worthless, stupid, and unloved, as well as a preoccupation with committing suicide.

Examples of mood and behavioral manifestations are psychomotor retardation, crying and sadness, too much or too little sleeping, too much or too little eating, and masked signs, such as school failure, hyperactivity, aggressiveness, delinquency, and psychophysiological symptoms (ulcers, asthma, and other disorders).

There appears to be a predictable sequence of events in the gradual recession of depressive symptoms. First, the depressive mood and behavior disappear, often followed by disappearance of the verbal expressions. The fantasy material is usually the last to go.

It is important to understand depression as it relates to a child's age and level of development. French and Berlin (1979) believed that children are not able to express feelings of sadness and depression in quite the same way as adults. They are not cognitively as sophisticated and mature and therefore use more primitive and concrete forms of self-expression. Furthermore, they are not able to test reality as well as adults and so use defenses such as denial, projection, avoidance, and magical thinking to ward off feelings (French & Berlin, 1979). This certainly may be true of some children, but it is not true of all. Although the material on Remy was presented in story form, it is representative of reality. Many children react to their depressed feelings exactly as Remy did, and he usually could have been more explicit about how he felt.

Approaching the subject from a developmental point of view does make the differences that exist among children more understandable. For instance, an infant's life consists mainly of eating and sleeping. Infants have not acquired the ability to verbalize and have not experienced the world, and so there is little to draw on for fantasizing. They do not have the ability to retain and then discharge depressive affect but are nonetheless vulnerable to emotional flooding, so they respond to their depression through their only available means: sleeping and eating disorders (Evans, Reinhart, & Succop, 1980).

Preschoolers and school-age children have made many advances in cognitive, verbal, and motor abilities, and therefore are better able to communicate feelings and problems. Because they are young and usually more motor oriented, much of their affect is expressed through behavior. Because they have had more experiences with the world they are able to fantasize, but because their conscience is not well developed it is often harsh and punitive. They still are not able to test reality in a logical way, which keeps some of the depressive process at the fantasy level. Researchers have shown that some preschoolers often manifest depression through night terrors, enuresis, and encopresis. The older school-age child may become more outwardly aggressive, anxious, and antisocial (Kazdin et al., 1983; Poznanski, 1982; Wolff, 1971).

Adolescents have the ability to test reality and do not need or use fantasy so much. They seldom use such defenses as denial, projection, and magical thinking. Their better-developed conscience exacerbates their guilt feelings and low self-esteem so that depression becomes more overt (Glaser, 1967; Teri, 1982b).

Emotional and intellectual deprivation in small children can lead to cognitive retardation and depression. For older children, behavior problems, delinquency, school phobia, tantrums, truancy, disobedience, running away, and self-destructiveness are frequent indicators of depression. These children are often referred for their learning problems, with little, if any, attention given to their underlying emotional conflicts. These situations lead to greater feelings of worthlessness and guilt, resulting in even greater failures. Other important signs that should catch our attention include obvious depressed affect, inability to have fun (anhedonia), low self-esteem, social withdrawal, fatigue, answering questions in monotonic one- or two-word sentences, crying, and suicide attempts (Leon et al., 1980; Poznanski, 1982; Toolan, 1962).

There are others (Burks & Harrison, 1962) who view antisocial, impulsive, and aggressive behavior in children as a means of avoiding feelings of depression. Situations that seem to stimulate depressive feelings and elicit aggressive behavior are seen when a child's adequacy and fantasized omnipotence are threatened by reality. This means that the child feels threatened by the possibility of receiving and returning positive feelings from adults, which forces the child to recognize his or her lack of autonomy and need for affection.

French and Berlin (1979) speculated that aggression and violence are temporary escapes from depression. It is believed that, in some instances, aggression is a way of avoiding schizophrenic withdrawal.

Teri (1982b) found that youths who were more assertive were also more depressed. She believed that since children are not expected to be assertive they are negatively reinforced for such behavior, resulting in their feeling rejected, isolated, helpless, and unable to influence their own environment. Characteristically, those who were more depressed also had more difficulties in other areas of their lives. The youths in this study felt awkwardness and discomfort about their bodies, dissatisfaction with recent body changes, and feelings of ugliness, weakness, and helplessness. Negative self-concept was associated with pubescent physical changes, and more females scored higher on depression than males.

Teri's study is not only interesting but also extremely important. Perhaps her findings can lead to a better understanding of anorexia nervosa, which is predominantly a female disorder in which young girls can literally starve themselves to death. If we focus on pubescent physiological changes and low self-esteem, then Teri's study does offer insight into why more females than males attempt suicide.

Most investigators agree that although personality characteristics and level of intelligence do not directly relate to depression and suicide, they may act as stimulators in children facing problems that seem overwhelming and unsolvable. Overall, suicidal children and adolescents have been found to be more emotionally unstable, shy, prone to guilt, and tense. Adolescents in particular demonstrated more anger, aggression, anxiety, withdrawal, and weak interpersonal relationships with family and peers. In addition, they had greater sexual conflicts, more frequent academic failure, and poorer physical health (Cantor, 1976; Halligan, 1983; Hillard, 1983; Kocourkova & Konecny, 1973; Korella, 1972; Teri, 1982a).

A number of experts believe that suicide rarely occurs among people who are psychiatrically well; clinical depression is a necessary component. Some research indicates that mental illness is a precondition for self-destruction rather than a reaction to specific stressful circumstances. According to certain authorities, motivations and circumstances are important, but no matter what the precipitating events were there always existed an ongoing psychiatric illness (French & Berlin, 1979; Weiner, 1970).

A good case for this position was made in a study by Weiner (1970) in which he found that 67% of hospitalized, mentally ill adolescents had communicated desires and plans to commit suicide. This information was compared with that from a group of adolescents who were considered emotionally disturbed but not seriously enough to be hospitalized. Within the latter group, only 13% had expressed some kind of suicidal intent.

These ideas are strongly supported by other research. For instance, earlier studies showed that schizophrenia was the main factor in suicide among adolescents (Glaser, 1967; Toolan, 1962). The typical suicide-prone youths were withdrawn and delusional, spending a great deal of time fantasizing about how others had slighted them in some way. These youths did not have the problems seen in the less severely disturbed, such as physical complaints, sleeping and eating disorders, and anxiety. Weiner also argued that adolescent suicide is not simply the result of impulsive behavior but is the final solution or end result of a long mental illness. The adolescent who commits suicide does so after other attempts to achieve balance, such as running away or rebelling, have failed.

There are a number of precipitating events that are common across studies of mental illness and suicide. The most common precipitating event is an argument with parents. The second most common factor is parental conflict with the suicide victim's girlfriend, boyfriend, or spouse. Other common precipitators include extreme embarrassment over school failure, lost self-esteem, and separation from significant persons.

The link between depression and suicide is obvious, which is why the two topics are treated together in this chapter. Depression appears as a symptom resulting from all the different childhood crises presented in this book. As demonstrated in the section on types of depression, each of the children in the vignettes throughout this text could represent some category of depression. With the exception of endogenous depression, all the other types of depression can be explained by external life events. Situations fraught with tragedy and crises can create depression. Although I do believe that people do not kill themselves unless they are beset with clinical depression in the first place, some serious precipitating event also must occur. This precipitating event would explain why other people who are clinically depressed do not commit suicide. Clinical depression and life crises together are probably the precursors to suicide.

Psychiatrists today recognize the importance of the information that can be obtained from school personnel. In fact, they deem such information necessary in determining the type of treatment appropriate for depressed children. This information becomes of paramount concern if the physician is considering the use of certain medications. The discovery of certain antidepressant drugs offers more hope for the treatment of major depressions. Children who have well-defined melancholia respond to pharmacotherapy as successfully as some adults. Although the FDA has not approved the use of antidepressants for children under the age of 12, the final decision is left to the physician and the parents. Consequently, because of the success that many psychiatrists believe they have had with these new drugs, they are being used with more frequency than ever before (Koplan, 1983).

Suicide

Suicide in Children

To understand the motives for suicidal thoughts in children, it is important to know how they conceptualize death. Children's thinking about death was discussed in greater detail in Chapter 3. Some of those main ideas appear again in this chapter but presented this time from the perspective of how young children can be capable of suicide.

Frequently, suicidal behavior in children is impulsive and pre-cipitated by events that seem like small problems to adults. Younger children cannot appreciate the dangers involved as clearly as older children or adolescents, and they therefore make no provisions for a rescue when they attempt something drastic. Suicide occurs in the young because often they are not fully aware of their own mortality. Although they are believed to have some concept of death, generally children view it as temporary, reversible, and gradual. Some chil-dren frequently equate death with running away or escaping from an unbearable situation (Bernhardt & Praeger, 1985; Rosenthal & Rosenthal, 1984; Schuyler, 1973; Saffer, 1986; Schaffer, 1974).

It has been suggested that children who have repeated acci-dents show self-destruction that is on a continuum with suicide. Several studies reveal that suicidal adolescents showed some form of early childhood self-destructive behavior between the ages of 6 and 13. These children had a history of problems that peaked just prior to self-destructive behavior (Renshaw, 1974; Shrut, 1962; Toolan, 1962).

A more realistic understanding of death usually emerges devel-opmentally with chronological age, but it is not until about the age of 9 that the child realizes the finality and irreversibility of death. However, in one interesting study (McIntire & Angle, 1971) 16% of the subjects, 17 and 18 years old, openly admitted to the fantasy of reversibility of death. These findings suggest that not only young children but also some adolescents may regard death in an unreal-istic way.

Very young children are more limited than adolescents in their knowledge of possible methods of committing suicide. For this age group there is no distinct pattern other than an impulsive quality that emerges in the young child. Running into traffic, drowning, hanging, jumping from high places, electrocution, or poisoning are all methods that children are able to use with minimal planning and little difficulty. Some child mental-health workers believe these "accidents" are actually suicides in more cases than people realize, perhaps as many as 30% or more (French, Steward, & Morrison, 1979).

Rosenthal and Rosenthal (1984) compared preschoolers who had seriously injured themselves or attempted to do so with preschoolers who had diagnosed emotional problems but had not tried to injure themselves. The results showed that the preschoolers who were suicidal had higher rates of running away, directed their aggression inwards, and showed no negativism. The nonsuicidal children showed aggression toward others, unmanageable behavior, hyperactivity, and a very negative attitude.

More than half of the suicidal preschoolers had mothers who were depressed or abused alcohol or drugs. Also, these children had one or more relatives who had attempted suicide. Rosenthal and Rosenthal found that these children, for the most part, were rejected, neglected, and abused. Because of their abuse, they had a very harsh way of treating themselves. They saw themselves as "bad" and so treated themselves as their parents treated them. Finally, the authors determined four causes for suicidal behavior in these young children: (1) escape, (2) rectification of an unbearable life situation, (3) self-punishment, and (4) reunion with a central nurturant figure.

The Rosenthal and Rosenthal work is extremely important for several reasons. The authors have shown that very young children do have suicidal tendencies, and they are probably the first to demonstrate that loss and abuse can have even more severe immediate consequences than earlier researchers have believed. They have effectively countered the idea that all childhood accidents are really accidental.

Suicide in Adolescents

In the past, adolescent suicide was neglected, and only recently with the rapid rise in the rate at which young people kill themselves has there been a resurgence of interest. Some researchers speculate that the problem was ignored because it created too much guilt in the adults who were morally and legally responsible for an adolescent; they preferred to attribute the deaths to accidental causes rather than voluntary annihilation. Another reason discussed is each person's own fear of death. The adolescent is representative of life, beauty, hope, and the future. Death among youth may have been too anxiety-provoking for many adults (Saffer, 1986).

Typically, adolescence is a stage fraught with extreme emotional stresses, making it very difficult to distinguish actual clinical depression from the usual ups and downs of teenagers. The risk of suicide appears to be the greatest between the ages of 15 and 25, which is attributed to an increase in impulsive behavior along with an increase in availability of information and in the physical capability to self-destruct (Lester, 1990).

In 1983, in a suburb in Texas, six adolescents committed suicide over a period of just 6 months (Kraft, 1983). The reasons given were guilt over the death of a friend, the pressures of school, unsuccessful romances, distress over another's suicide, and a forbidden love affair that led to a double suicide. The suicides received a great deal of publicity, which prompted one parent of a suicide victim to say, "When one child does it, it sparks the idea in another." A family therapist in this town was quoted as saying, "One of the most important things in adolescence is joining, and whenever there is a series of suicides it's almost as if they figure they can join the way out."

These are the reasons they gave for why those youths decided to kill themselves, but they are hardly causes or explanations. Thousands of adolescents experience broken romances, sometimes several a year. Most are under some kind of school-related pressure, and some may feel responsibility and guilt when a friend is killed. The majority of youths, however, do not kill themselves when faced with these circumstances. To imply that knowing someone else has committed suicide prompts others to do likewise is, at the very least, an oversimplification. At the most, it is almost like equating it with fads. Selecting such oversimplified reasons to explain suicide is a way of trying to avoid the problem. If it can be brushed off as imitation and just something that some teenagers will do, then no one has to feel responsible for the mental health work that should have been done with these youths. It is as if they believe that you cannot do any more about imitation suicide than you can about adolescents who imitate the style of dress and jargon of their favorite rock stars.

Warning Signs

Statistics indicate that child and adolescent suicides occur more frequently in late spring and early summer, and most often at home between 3:00 p.m. and midnight. These facts might be related to the previous information about the link between suicide, poor family relationships, and school failure. A late spring or early summer suicide could be the conclusion to a real or perceived school failure. Also, this is the time when children have fewer support systems available. Peers, teachers, and counselors are generally unavailable when school dismisses for the summer vacation.

The times during the day when suicide incidents are highest are after school hours; this might be attributed partly to the fact that this is when children are with their parents. It is a logical time for the family disagreements that often precede suicide. Suicidal behavior, it seems, is based on chronic crisis, as the youths become more and more depressed and socially isolated (Paluszny, Davenport, & Kim, 1991).

Unlike adults, children are more likely to attempt suicide than to complete the act. Suicide may be a gesture signaling a request for help when the children do not know how to ask for it. According to most researchers, suicide seldom occurs without some kind of warning, either verbal or behavioral (French & Berlin, 1979; Hillard, 1983; Poznanski, 1982; Teri, 1982b).

There are several behavioral indicators of suicide, such as a change from extroversion to introversion, a change from aggressive and angry behavior to overly solicitous and ingratiating behavior, a change from passivity to hyperactivity, silliness and showing-off behavior, and a gradual preoccupation with and obsessive thoughts about death. Adolescents attempt to counteract depressive suicidal behavior by the excessive use of drugs and alcohol; changes in appetite by refusing to eat (anorexia nervosa) or overeating (as in bulimia); changes in sleep patterns, such as insomnia or excessive sleeping; and antisocial acts such as stealing or sexual promiscuity (Carlson & Cantwell, 1979; Carter & Duncan, 1984; Jalali, Jalali, Crocetti, & Turner, 1981; Kagan & Squires, 1984; Leon et al., 1980; Piazza, Rollins, & Lewis, 1983; Renshaw, 1974; Teri, 1982b).

The most important behavioral predictors of suicide are thought to be psychiatric illness or depression, characterized by fatigue, restlessness, increased worrying about bodily functions, and an inability to concentrate (Halligan, 1983; Weiner, 1970). Three important features for predicting suicide are depressive syndrome, inability to communicate and relate to others, and a history of self-destructive accidents or suicide attempts (Poznanski, 1982).

Glaser (1959) suggested four types of suicidal communications that are diagnostic warning signs. The first is "just talk," which often goes unheeded and even unnoticed. The second is a gesture, such as putting a knife to the throat, which can lead to more serious attempts if it does not effect the desired change. The third is the threat. The fourth and most serious is the attempt itself, which Glaser felt indicates the need for immediate and complete psychiatric evaluation. This evaluation should include consideration of the depth of the conflict within the child, the inner resources of the child to handle the conflict, the outer resources available to the child, and a realistic appraisal of the stressful circumstances leading up to the episode.

Some researchers make no distinction between threats and attempts but consider both equally serious. In the majority of cases, suicide was considered well in advance by emotionally unstable children, and the intent was communicated to someone who could have helped (Halligan, 1983; Poznanski, 1982; Teri, 1982b; Zinner, 1987).

Several studies show that over 80% of suicidal adolescents express their intentions to their parents, and over 15% have talked to teachers, counselors, or doctors about their feelings. Obviously, it is extremely important—even critical—for school professionals to become more aware of and sensitive to verbal threats and other warning signs (Cytryn et al., 1980; Forrest, 1983; McBrien, 1983; McIntire & Angle, 1971).

Factors Related to Suicide in Youth

There are several approaches that researchers take in trying to understand why youths kill themselves. Following are the factors given the most credence as explanations for suicidal behavior. None of them explains why some children choose to end their lives. They are, however, patterns that have been found in children who have committed or attempted suicide. Although they may not be the actual causes, they can serve as additional warning signs to alert us so that some preventive action can be taken.

There are a number of theories about suicide that are extensive and complex, each one a treatise in itself. Basically, they include the major theoretical positions taken to explain any type of abnormal behavior. For the reader interested in theory, there are a number of books written entirely about suicide that have an extensive coverage of the theoretical aspects. The focus of this book is to stay at the practical level as much as possible.

Environmental factors. School adjustment is one variable related to self-destructive behavior. Extremely poor academic performance has been noted in a majority of adolescents attempting suicide. In a number of cases, suicidal youths were not attending school, and some were not even enrolled. In many cases, suicidal adolescents see the school as socially repressive, making them feel demeaned by continually treating them like children (Smith, 1976). In a related study, Wright (1982) found that adolescents who were not permitted to date until later than most teens ("late" in this study and by today's standards being 16 years old and older) used drugs and had suicidal thoughts more frequently than their peers who were allowed to date at younger ages. These suicide-prone adolescents felt like they were being treated like children, that their mothers were overly strict, and that they were being socially repressed by their parents. Overall, they were more unsure of themselves, were more dependent, and had poorer relationships with their mothers.

McCranie and Bass (1984) found that suicide-prone adolescents experienced two different kinds of depression that characterized them as follows: (1) the anaclitic, dependent person and (2) the introjective, self-critical person with guilt feelings. Those who scored highest on anaclitic dependency had mothers who dominated the family and maintained an overly firm and rigid control, particularly over their daughters. Those who scored highest on introjective self-criticism indicated that both parents used stricter controls and inconsistent affection. In both types there were elements of rejection, lack of affection, and much stricter control over the adolescents, leaving them feeling helpless and like failures.

There is a high incidence of suicide attempts among college students, usually occurring during the first 6 weeks of the first academic term (Craig & Senter, 1972; Hendrickson & Cameron, 1975; Miller, 1975; Wolfe & Cotler, 1973). The transition from high school to college is difficult for most adolescents and seems to be impossible for some, which may be related to the findings in the studies by Wright (1982) and McCranie and Bass (1984). The students have just left one environment where they felt they were treated like children, overprotected, oversupervised, and greatly restricted, only to enter a new environment that is impersonal and leaves them feeling isolated and lost. College usually brings the first break with the family, as the adolescents are suddenly thrust into an unstructured, hectic, and demanding environment. Where only a short time ago they felt oversupervised, they now feel alienated and believe that no one cares. It is thought that under these new pressures, some adolescents react with suicide attempts.

If this is so, the schools should be looking into ways in which they can assist youths toward developing a more internal locus of control—a personality dimension that is considered to be highly desirable, for a number of reasons, for all children. Overly dependent children of all ages should come to attention early on for special help from counselors and others in the schools who can aid them in developing in a healthier way.

Other structures within the environment make the future look devastatingly bleak to some children in minority groups. The suicide rates are high among black and Puerto Rican adolescents, although not as high as among whites. Native Americans show a suicide rate that far exceeds the national average, and while the suicide rate for Hispanic youths is not equal to that of whites, that rate has risen by 42% over the last 8 years (Pedigo, 1983). In addition, Hispanic and black children commit suicide at younger ages than do children belonging to other groups (Loya, 1977). Cultural conflicts that intensify as the child grows older are thought to be one of the major problems and reasons for suicide among minority groups.

For all minority groups, it is speculated that the urbanization process is the primary factor in suicide. These youths are thought to experience a feeling of having no control over their own lives because of lower socioeconomic status, social disorganization, cultural conflicts, and breakdown of the family structure, all of which compound feelings of alienation and low self-worth (Babow & Rowe, 1990; Loya, 1977; May & Dizmang, 1977; Pedigo, 1983; Schneer, Perlstein, & Brozovsky, 1975).

Sociological factors. A variety of sociological studies indicate that suicidal adolescents appear to live in alienated environments. These youths come from broken homes and ruined families, and they generally have poor relationships with adults. For instance, several studies showed that half of the adolescents who committed suicide had lost one parent before the age of 14 from either separation, divorce, abandonment, or death (Adam, Lohrenz, & Harper, 1973; Adams-Greenly & Moynihan, 1983; Corder, Page, & Corder, 1974; Duche, 1976; Roberts & Maddax, 1982; Sojleva, 1975; Walker, 1983; Wallerstein, 1983; White, 1974).

Even in families with both parents living, there were other outstanding problems, such as a mentally ill parent, a parent who had attempted suicide, or a parent who was an alcoholic (Corder et al., 1974; Duche, 1976; Walker, 1983; Williams & Lyons, 1976). These studies cite the father as the major figure in the problem. There seem to be two general types of fathers of suicidal children: (1) fathers who are involved but who are strict, rigid disciplinarians, overtly hostile toward their children; and (2) fathers who are habituated to gambling and alcohol and who have occasional outbursts of violence. Overall, the fathers in the second group are basically ineffectual, irresponsible, and unconcerned about their families (White, 1974). This is the flip side of the studies in which the dominant parent influencing suicide was the mother (McCranie & Bass, 1984; Wright, 1982).

Parental rejection, at the conscious or unconscious level, is felt by the child. Even though the parents' efforts to be rid of the child are covert, they do not go entirely unnoticed. Instead, suicidal children are poignantly aware of their parents' feelings about them. It is hypothesized that these children, because of rejection, turn their anger inward and attempt to fulfill the parents' wishes by committing suicide (Evoy, 1983; Sabbath, 1972).

Parent–child role reversal is considered to be another important element in the suicidal behavior of some adolescents (Kreider & Motto, 1974). Unresolved dependency needs of a parent inevitably come into conflict with the dependency and independent needs of the adolescent, as pointed out in Chapter 4. As a result, the adolescent may feel anxiety, frustration, and hostility toward the parent but remain unable to express those feelings for fear of losing the parent and whatever nurturing the parent does provide. The adolescent's feelings develop into suicidal desires. When children are very young, they often become self-abusive and then turn to suicide when they reach adolescence. It is well known and widely accepted that abused children blame themselves for everything that goes wrong and view self-destruction as a punishment that they deserve (Babow & Babow, 1974; Cataldo & Harris, 1982; Edelson, Taubman, & Lovass, 1983; Justice & Justice, 1976; Rosenthal & Rosenthal, 1984).

In a very interesting study, Hill (1970) found that parents of suicidal adolescents had the least ability to be empathic; parents of nonsuicidal but emotionally disturbed adolescents had moderate empathic ability; and the parents of well-adjusted adolescents had the most empathic ability. It seems not only desirable but critical that parents be able to understand and communicate with their children, or if not the parents then some significant person such as a teacher or counselor. The importance of empathic adult models who can create an atmosphere that will greatly minimize suicide potential in adolescents was emphasized by Konopka (1983). Her results showed overwhelmingly that the most influential people in the lives of children and adolescents were parents, grandparents, and teachers.

Psychological factors. The adolescent at risk for carrying out suicide has been described as feeling rage because of a sense of hopelessness, helplessness, insecurity, and uncertainty. These feelings are thought to be associated with the anxiety and crises created by changes in libido as the adolescents search for new relationships (Condini & Constantini, 1974; Duncan, 1977). There is a dramatic increase in reported suicides near the age and onset of puberty, suggesting that strong sexual drives, along with the physical and social changes taking place, create adjustment problems that are just too overwhelming (Miller, 1975; Teri, 1982b). The suicidal adolescent has been described as calling on defenses that ward off depression stemming from disappointments related to libidinal impulses (Haim, 1974). While there is some logic to this theory, it does not seem as reasonable as theories pertaining to biochemical changes during adolescence that potentiate the development of different disorders—most notably, depression (Halligan, 1983; Ossofsky, 1974).

The individual constitution has been cited as a factor in suicide. Some adolescents are thought to be more susceptible to committing suicide because of a hypersensitive and suggestible nature (Miller, 1975). Hypersensitive youths attempt suicide for a variety of reasons: from anger and the attempt to manipulate, as a cry for help during a crisis when they are experiencing emotional disintegration, and as a desire to join a deceased loved one (Ross, 1970; Schuyler, 1973). It is possible that this is an outgrowth of anaclitic or endogenous depression.

Regarding anger, suicidal behavior is seen as a punishment or threat that is intended to provoke guilt and remorse in a closely related person and as an attempt to punish the parents (Otto, 1972). Lester (1990) reported that approximately 65% of suicide attempts are manipulative maneuvers designed to control or punish others. Manipulation has two purposes: to prevent another person from leaving and dissolving a relationship, and to capture another's affection and attention. Manipulative attempters make their attempts repeatedly because they are so effective (Otto, 1972). As an example, when one 15-year-old girl was asked why she had tried to commit suicide, she replied, "I wanted to see how many of my friends would come to see me at the hospital." This could be one explanation for the high proportion of adolescent suicide attempts that are unsuccessful.

We must be very careful, however, to avoid minimizing any suicide attempt even if it is known to be manipulative. Many adults are tempted to ignore youths who are being manipulative. A deliberate attempt to capture someone's attention by such drastic means is indicative of a most disturbed child who needs attention and help; that child should not be ignored. Nor should the child who is ready with a simplistic answer like the one quoted above, to the question of why he or she attempted suicide, be ignored. That child is concerned with deeper problems than how many friends will visit in the hospital. Sometimes a quick and simple answer is an attempt to put people off, allowing the child to try again and perhaps the next time be successful.

Emotional disintegration is among the reasons cited for the adolescent's tendency to resort to dramatic action. Many adolescents think and fantasize about death as the solution to all their problems. A few, it seems, dwell too long on the subject and succumb to the temptation to cross the line between thought and action. Suicide-prone adolescents are frequently grieving over some type of loss, ranging from a loss of face or of ideals to the loss of love or of a person (Haim, 1974; Schuyler, 1973).

Miller (1975) theorized that with the loss of a parent, the child experiences a sense of lowered self-esteem and feels abandoned. The stress placed on the entire family at the time of a death may change the living parent to such a degree that the child feels that he or she has lost love from the living parent as well. Feelings of guilt become even more exacerbated as the child begins to feel hate that becomes aggression turned inward, followed by depression, antisocial acts, accident proneness, and finally, suicide (Zinner, 1987).

Substance Abuse and Altered States

Substance abuse is a topic that is important to discuss in this section since many suicides are thought to be the result of deliberate drug overdoses rather than accidents. Jalali and colleagues (1981) proposed a comprehensive approach to the understanding of adolescent drug use. They categorized users into three groups. The experimental user may try once or twice out of curiosity but rarely becomes a compulsive user. The situational (sometimes referred to as recreational) user uses drugs and alcohol in a party spirit in the company of peers. The compulsive user is seeking relief from boredom, anxiety, sadness, and anhedonia (the inability to experience pleasure, as is seen in depression). These youths are seen as clearly disturbed, with disturbed family and individual dynamics. It is thought that they are using substances for relief and to cope with low self-image.

Distress levels have been found to be higher than average in female drug users, who experience more anxiety and lowered self-esteem. Their attitude, "I feel, therefore I am," is seen in self-destructive individuals showing extreme psychopathology. The use of alcohol appears to be associated more with identification with and the repetition of family patterns (Hochman & Brill, 1973; Pedigo, 1983; Rollins & Holden, 1972).

Curbrksak (1972) noted that instead of trying to find pleasure through relationships with others, children are turning to artificial means to relax and feel good. This may not always mean drugs and alcohol. A provocative study by Burgess and Hazelwood (1983) revealed that there are 500 to 1,000 adolescent deaths annually that are referred to as autoerotic asphyxial deaths, which means death due to solo sexual practice to create euphoria through the use of injurious agents. Such deaths are always classified as accidents by medical examiners, and Burgess and Hazelwood classified them in the same way. It is not unreasonable, however, to raise the possibility that some of these deaths are suicides, like deaths resulting from drug use. According to Burgess and Hazelwood, deaths from sexual practice have a devastating impact on families; they are apparently more disturbing than other types of death. If consideration is given to anger at loved ones as one major feature in some suicides, then autoerotic asphyxial suicide seems all the more plausible.

Children of Substance Abusers

It is a well known fact that children and adolescents commit suicide while they themselves are under the influence of drugs and alcohol. However, youths growing up in homes where there is substance abuse are at greater risk for being abused, abusing drugs or alcohol themselves, and for becoming depressed. Growing up with the inconsistency and unavailability of parents who are drunk or drugged has an extremely damaging effect on the self-esteem of those children (Towers, 1989). There is a high incidence of suicide among adolescents who are extremely depressed due to growing up in homes where one or both parents are incapacitated by drugs or alcohol (Berkowitz & Perkins, 1988; Perkins & Berkowitz, 1991). This section discusses this issue.

There are at least 15 million school-age children in the United States who have at least one parent who is a substance abuser. There is a strong indication that children of substance-abusing parents are at a greater risk for becoming substance abusers themselves. In many cases, but not all, a genetic link is a factor (Perkins & Berkowitz, 1991). Other studies have shown that children who have parents who are substance abusers have more positive expectations of the effects of drugs and alcohol and are more likely to use them regularly and become addicted themselves (McGue, Pickens, & Svikis, 1992; Sher, Walitzer, Wood, & Brent, 1991).

Children who grow up in homes where there is substance abuse are at greater risk for neglect and physical, sexual, and emotional abuse. Aside from abuse, there are other damaging consequences. All of these children grow up feeling fearful, guilty, and shameful. Many are depressed, suicidal, angry, anxious, and shy; they have a number of physical complaints (e.g., headaches, stomachaches), and they are frequently absent from school and, when in school, have difficulty concentrating, thus becoming failures or stressed-out overachievers (Robinson, 1989). Substance abuse negatively affects every aspect of a child's life (Campbell, 1988).

Younger children are likely to experience more damage because they do not get the consistent parenting that is necessary for them to develop in ways needed to be successful in school. During the elementary school-age years, teachers can assist these children tremendously by giving them the attention they miss at home and helping them build self-esteem. Adolescents especially need help in learning how to make good decisions and develop good peer relationships. There are a number of characteristics that teachers need to be aware of to help identify the youths who come from homes where there is substance abuse or where the student is abusing substances:

- inability to concentrate
- chronic absenteeism
- poor grades and/or neglect of homework
- poor scores on standardized tests not related to IQ or learning disabilities
- uncooperative and quarrelsome
- sudden behavior changes
- shy and withdrawn
- compulsive behaviors
- chronic health problems
- signs of neglect and abuse
- low self-esteem
- anger, anxiety, and/or depression
- poor coping skills
- unreasonably fearful
- difficulty adjusting to change

(Berkowitz & Perkins, 1988; Goodman, 1987; Perkins & Berkowitz, 1991)

Once a teacher has identified these students, help then can be provided by a supportive classroom environment, consistent discipline, a structure that is maintained, and assignments that build positive self-esteem. The worst kind of classroom environment for students like these is one that is constantly changing and where students decide their own curriculum and classroom rules. Those types of classrooms work for certain kinds of students but not for students who are under the influence or come from homes where their models are consistently under the influence.

The schools have become a prime location for the sale of drugs and alcohol to children (Vrcan, 1988). The average age for boys to first try drugs is 11; and for girls it is 13 (Greenbaum, Garrison, James, & Stephens, 1989). Growing up in poverty and in environments of poverty increases the likelihood of substance abuse, and schools in poverty-stricken areas become the marketplace for gangs drug dealings. The school grounds become the turf for violence, fear, and the sale and use of alcohol, drugs, and weapons.

CRITICAL CONSIDERATIONS

Some researchers believe that the mass media, which gives high visibility to drugs, violence, and aggression, creates an atmosphere in which destruction can more easily occur (Garner, 1975). Others speculate that societal crisis events, such as war, unemployment, political scandals, and social and material deprivation, are partially responsible for rising suicide rates (Boor, 1976; Robertson & Cochrane, 1976).

It is natural for people to look at the external events occurring around them when a crisis as devastating as suicide of the young suddenly draws attention. What needs to be remembered is that child and adolescent suicide is not a new phenomenon. In the past, people did not talk about it as much as they do today; nor was it reported or recorded as suicide. It may be that suicide has not increased but the numbers are finally being recorded accurately. There is no way of knowing how many deaths recorded in the past as accidents were actually suicides. The rate of suicide may not be rising—only the willingness to face the situation so that the number of these tragedies can be decreased.

No single cause or factor predisposes a child to suicide. Instead, there are many elements in the process leading to suicide. Suicidal behavior is a complex symptom with multiple determinants interacting in both predictable and unpredictable ways.

If there is one single factor more important than others to which suicide in children and adolescents can be attributed, it is the devaluation of children. Most suicides are preventable. If children acquire and maintain a positive self-image, effective decision-making skills and coping strategies, and appreciation of their own cultural background as well as the cultural backgrounds of others, the likelihood of suicide is diminished. Teachers can be trained to recognize the warning signs of youth suicide, identify the at-risk students, assess their needs, and make appropriate referrals.

Some students may be more likely than other students to commit suicide. There is no simple cause and effect explanation for suicide. Two students may experience the same crisis, and while one goes on functioning, the other may commit suicide. There are some factors, however, that may be indicators of high risk. Depending on the child's level of self-esteem, social and problem-solving skills, and ability to cope with loss and failure, the following conditions may increase a child's level of risk for suicide:

- victim of some form of abuse
- alcohol or drug abuse
- parents' marital conflict or divorce
- family history of suicide (particularly a parent)
- depression
- death of a relative or close friend
- chronic illness
- situations resulting from poverty (homelessness)
- pregnancy
- sexual identity crisis (Gay youth are at higher risk)
- experienced some kind of extreme humiliation
- involved in gangs and/or delinquent activity

These are situations that may result in feelings of hopelessness, worthlessness, despair, rejection, and depression. Signals that students are having difficulty coping are: substance abuse, crying episodes, sleep disturbances, mood swings, inability to concentrate, excessive irritability, aggressive outbursts, talk about death, lack of energy, withdrawal from family and friends, change in appetite, running away, or giving away prized possessions.

PREVENTION AND HELP

There are two aspects to prevention. One is global and has to do with prevention of the tragic situations that are damaging to children. It is no accident that suicide is the last crisis presented in this book and follows the chapters on separation, divorce, loss, and child abuse. These crises appear over and over again in the background of suicidal children. If we can somehow mend the broken spirits of children and help them through such crises, we may be able to prevent what appears to be their sequela in so many cases: suicide.

The second aspect of prevention is more specific. It is preventing the act of suicide itself once a child or adolescent has reached the stage of desperation.

Our greatest potential for doing anything about suicide at any age is prevention, and success in prevention depends largely on prediction, which in turn depends on a thorough knowledge and understanding of the factors contributing to the crisis.

Unfortunately, the most significant indication that a youth will commit suicide is a prior attempt. It is unfortunate because an attempt means that there has been failure in helping a child through other crises. We find ourselves, then, with a child in the most desperate condition a person can be in: preferring death to life. Since suicide attempts are the only really dependable predictors, every attempt must be taken seriously and every effort must be made to ensure that the youth receives help. Prevention of suicide involves the early identification of those at high risk.

In addition to prior attempts or threats, there are other important clues to recognizing what may be suicidal intent among youth that can make prediction possible and so prevent a suicide. Among the warning signs, the following seem to be the most predictive.

1. withdrawal
2. a change in physical appearance, such as extreme weight loss or gain
3. physical complaints
4. a significant mood change from depression to euphoria
5. preoccupation, daydreaming, and isolation
6. a change for the worse in academic performance
7. inability to concentrate
8. obsessions with trivial matters

9. accident proneness

10. lack of peer interaction

11. crying or an appearance of sadness

12. constant fatigue

Psychological testing has been useful in screening potential suicides, but there is no instrument capable of predicting suicide with any degree of accuracy. Projective personality tests are especially sensitive to depression and self-destructive thinking; however, if administered long before the youth becomes suicidal they are not effective in predicting self-destruction. Prediction of an actual suicide is complicated by the fact that some children who have made the decision to commit suicide appear more relaxed and less disturbed than ever before. Apparently, less ambivalence, followed by a sense of relief, influences test results so that the child does not appear to be self-destructive (Schecter & Sternlof, 1970). For example, Remy seemed calm and serene following a tremendous emotional upheaval. His thought processes concerning his Uncle John and death are apparent; while he does not explicitly think of suicide in the same way that an adolescent or an adult might, in some place in his subconscious he has the idea of ending his life.

School professionals should be especially alert to children who have been diagnosed as depressed. If the child shows a change of mood and if he or she has not received treatment for depression or has not been in treatment very long, then the school professionals should switch from alert to alarm. It is very important to contact the child's therapist at this point to determine if antidepressant medications could be responsible for the mood change and to exchange information with the therapist, who should also be told about the mood change. Communication among professionals is essential and critical.

An encouraging development in the field is the growth of suicide-prevention centers. Their objectives are to provide help either by direct personal contact or on an emergency telephone basis. Hotlines are used extensively in these centers, manned by volunteers who have been trained in handling phone calls from potentially suicidal people. They act both as active listeners and as sources for referral for various problems. Most major cities have hotlines or suicide-prevention centers, and school professionals should be familiar with them. These hotlines will receive calls and advise others as how to best handle a potential suicide. They can be very helpful to teachers, counselors, and social workers who may not know just what to do for a particular child suspected of being suicidal. School professionals would do well to visit one of these centers for information before they are faced with a crisis situation.

Notable efforts have been made to define the suicidal personality, especially as it relates to children and adolescents. The literature suggests that only when you view the total history of a child are you able to intelligently consider a high-risk situation. While a complete history would be ideal, it probably is not necessary. We may make mistakes and consider children to be high risks when they are not, but it is better to err in that direction than in the opposite direction. Generally, we have access to only a very limited portion of a child's history. The alternative is that we become more sensitive and responsive to subtle as well as obvious signs of stress in children and adolescents.

School professionals can play a very important role in preventing childhood suicide, if for no other reason than that children are required to attend school. Children can isolate themselves from all other people, but sustained contact with people in the school is unavoidable. This situation puts school professionals in an excellent position to intervene and help. Teachers, counselors, and social workers involved as a team can provide very effective help for a child. They cannot sit around waiting until a suicidal youth can get an appointment to see a therapist. Although not technically a therapist, each person on the team of school professionals has skills that can be used effectively in therapy.

Although the seriousness and complexity of working with suicidal youths should not be oversimplified, we mental health professionals should avoid the mind-set that the situation is so complex and so intricate that any little thing we might do or say could tip the scales and push a child into suicide. We should not be so intimidated that we become impotent and helpless in the face of a crisis, nor should we just sit by, waiting it out until the youth can receive more expert treatment. Remember that suicide-prevention centers are staffed with volunteers, most of whom are not trained mental-health professionals but who have been trained in some skills that enable them to cope with this most serious crisis, and that these volunteers show more successes than failures in preventing suicide.

Some professional groups are very adamant in their preaching that counselors, teachers, and social workers should not try to be therapists, but perhaps this is more a territorial posture than a professional attitude. The possibility of suicide is a life-threatening situation, and the children threatened need all the help they can get—and they need it immediately. Physicians have recognized that some life-threatening situations cannot wait until the patient arrives at the hospital to receive expert treatment. As a result, they have encouraged the training of emergency medical technicians, and they have provided information to the layman on how to keep patients alive until they can receive full treatment. The situation is comparable to the case of suicide.

In the direction of prevention, efforts must be made to work with the children who are survivors of others who have committed suicide. Generally, those left behind are overwhelmed with feelings of guilt, as well as grief, mourning, and bewilderment. These feelings reinforce the plea for more mental health programs in the schools, whether those programs are carried on in the educational curriculum or through direct intervention and involvement of all school professionals. Both approaches seem not only necessary but highly preferable to the alternative of suicide.

A Team Approach
in the Schools

This book was written as an odyssey through some of the experiences children live with day to day. At any time, you could have put the book down and made a speedy return to your reality; and now, at the conclusion of this last chapter, the odyssey, for you, is ended. For the children it continues. For some readers, this is perhaps the beginning of a long and sustained interest in helping the children who are caught in the series of woes described. If you are one of them, there are things you will need in order to succeed in your endeavor, in addition to knowledge about some of the problems you will confront in your attempts to help these children.

Your Needs

The word *team* implies that there is more than one person working for the betterment of the children described in this book. The same letters in this word can also form the acronym T.E.A.M. (To Each A Mentor). This adds more to the concept of a team than a group of people working together to facilitate for children. The problems described throughout this text are complex problems; they are painful not only to the children who live with them but also to those who work with the children. If professionals get involved in earnest and attempt to tackle these problems alone, they can be overwhelming. If they become overwhelming, they become burdensome, and because we are only human, our inclination then is to give up, or give less. No one can do this work alone without suffering the consequences in some form. Those who do not give up or give less, and who continue working in a vacuum, pay in terms of their own mental health and probably in other ways too.

One of the first rules learned by those in the helping professions is that their own mental health must come first. If that sounds callous, particularly in light of the suffering of the children you have just read about in this book, remember that you can be of no good to anyone if you are not yourself a healthy person. Each one of us working with these stressful situations needs a mentor, someone we can turn to and trust to provide help and wise advice when needed. Working with a team creates a natural framework for the members to be mentors to each other. This is one important side to functioning as a team. There are also other practicalities to consider.

Certainly each professional, on an individual basis, can be helpful to these children. However, one individual's help will not be as comprehensive or as effective as it could be if he or she were working with a team of professionals, pooling their expertise and efforts toward the same goals for children who are in the midst of crises. The use of the word *team* here goes beyond the obvious, as when three people might be involved in assisting the same child: a teacher, a counselor, and a social worker collaborating as a team. This is the usual situation in the schools, but seldom do the professionals communicate with each other except over minor details.

An attitude of cooperation among professionals has the most chance for success. It is, in fact, absolutely essential that traditional feelings of protecting your own turf be put away for good. No worker has mastered every function or technique known to his or her particular profession. Most school professionals have overlapping skills in some areas and unique skills in others. This makes the team approach all the more logical and powerful. If some phases of counseling get duplicated, the lesson is reinforced. If some remedial teaching or extra help with academics gets doubled, good. If parental contact gets increased, that also is good. If any of the things a child needs to survive and function overlap, all the better. There really is no place for petty jealousies when children are in such desperate need for all the help they can get.

The purpose of communication and teamwork is not to discern if services are overlapping. Rather, these factors are extremely important for finding out what is missing, what the child needs, and what information one team member has that could be helpful to everyone in reaching the goals set for the child. They also ensure that each person has a mentor when one is needed.

This team approach is necessary for prevention as well as for treatment during and after the fact. A team of trained and skilled professionals will be able to help grieving children resolve their losses before deeper problems occur and become entrenched. The team will identify those children being abused and neglected, and it will intervene, not only to stop the abuse but also to help the children learn how to cope with what has happened to them and to offset as much of the long-term damage as possible. The team also will spot those youths who are in so much despair that they are in danger of killing themselves and work with them to provide the incentive to go on living. For now, we can expect at the least to have teams that can alleviate some of the pain that accompanies these tragedies that keep surfacing with apparently greater frequency.

Finally, the concept of the team is not limited to the few professionals we work with in one isolated environment. It also refers to the entire community of various mental health professionals everywhere. We all have common interests that can only be protected, improved, or expanded if we are working as a team. Here, the concept of a team is being used in a much broader societal context. There already are many individuals who recognize this need and are trying to effect some change, but there still are many who are not.

We need each other for many reasons. Those in the helping professions know that if our work is going to be truly lasting and meaningful, we need to deal with even more than the immediate stress and pain that a child is experiencing. There are also all the dangers and hazards awaiting these children in the future because they have been damaged and their potential impeded, perhaps permanently. There are the current, ongoing destructive practices that compound the problems for the children and inhibit the effectiveness of the professionals. There are the voids, omissions, obstructions, and deliberate destruction of some of the necessary programs and resources needed for the delivery of optimal services. There are the negative attitudes of some groups who would keep professionals from doing what they know will benefit children. The sections that follow, which discuss these problems in greater detail, perhaps give more focus to the need for a professional team to carry on the preventive work that must be done.

What Is Preventing Prevention?

Dangers and Hazards in the Child's Future

Few professionals have worked with these children without worrying about what was in store for them in the future. We recognize that we have provided some help, perhaps even saved a life, but we also know that many of these children bear some permanent scars, and we often feel helpless to prevent what we know the children will suffer later as a result of their earlier experiences. Some of these children will continue to need special services when they become older, but there is no real way of ensuring that they will receive that help. We cannot even be sure, if they move to another locale, they will continue to receive the services they need in their new schools.

These are difficult realities to live with when we invest so much of ourselves in the rectification of children's lives. Although it is personally troubling to us, it is also a national problem that requires some forceful influence from all who have a vested interest in mental health. The need for consistency in the immediate period and over the long run means that the same necessary services are guaranteed for a child for as long as needed and not just for the amount of time allotted by an artificial schedule; that they receive what they need from one school to the next, from one district to another, and from state to state; and that just because a youth reaches a particular age, all help is not discontinued.

Current Practices

In 1985 corporal punishment was still being used to discipline children in both the home and the schools. Children have few rights in this country that are upheld by law. In 1975 the Supreme Court ruled, over the objection of parents, that it is constitutionally permissible for the school to punish by corporal means. They ruled again, in 1977, that harsh punishment does not violate the Eighth Amendment (cruel and unusual punishment), since this amendment pertains only to persons convicted of crimes and does not apply to corporal punishment in the schools. In other words, adult criminals in prisons are protected, by constitutional law, from corporal punishment, while children are not protected from such treatment.

The 1977 decision reaffirmed that corporal punishment can be used in the schools to enforce discipline. Then, in 1980, the Supreme Court recognized the substantive due process rights of children in school settings; however, it added that it must be proved that the person who used excessive force with a child did it with malice (Levy, 1983). In 1984, in a town in Tennessee, the majority of parents along with a county board of education backed a teacher who spanked, by her admission, at least 25 students for such things as returning books late, sitting sideways in their seats, and failing to bring pencils to class. And yet we are called a child-centered society!

Consider for a moment that we have in our schools children in emotional pain because their parents are divorcing, because they have lost a parent through death and have not resolved their grief, because they have a parent who is mentally ill, or because they are abused. Consider that there are children in our schools who are depressed and contemplating suicide. In each chapter of this book, symptoms or behaviors were described that children manifest as a result of each of these crises. Most of these behaviors are the same no matter what the crisis, and many of the behaviors are ones that are generally targeted for corporal punishment. If abused children do misbehave in school, should they be abused further in the school setting?

Instead of being offered a therapeutic environment, children in crises are given physical punishment when they bring their problems to school. School is a place where children need to have experiences and find role models that teach them how to be better human beings, and where they need to be provided with the necessary psychonutrients that foster growth and positive mental health. School is a place where children need to find adults who are positive facilitators. Instead, some of the practices engaged in and condoned by law could make the schools the final annihilator. Every child deserves the right to a terror-free environment in the school, if not possible in the home.

It will take a tremendous amount of effort and an inordinately long time before the Supreme Court decisions can be reversed, particularly if a majority of parents or professionals do not oppose corporal punishment. Until that comes about, if it does, it is the task of professionals in the school system to try to educate colleagues about the dangers and destructiveness of corporal punishment.

Of course there are youths who misbehave, and not only because they are in the midst of crisis. But that misbehavior does not excuse the use of corporal and excessive force as a disciplinary measure. Our society preaches the abhorrence of violence and force in other societies and yet uses it regularly in its schools. Part of the purpose of the internal educational process is to show others how to discipline in ways that do not involve physical punishment. Hyman and Fina (1983) found that the elimination of corporal punishment did not have a negative effect on school discipline, that corporal punishment did not benefit the cause of education, that teachers who were not spanked as children did not hit children (a strong case for role modeling), and that most cases of corporal punishment were perpetrated against poor and minority children. Poor children, who have the highest incidence of physical neglect, and minority children, who have the highest incidence of low self-esteem, are being asked to pay the highest price for variables beyond their control.

In a school in Texas in 1984, some building administrators wanted to suspend an adolescent girl because she had attempted suicide. A few of her teachers fought to keep her in school, and they succeeded. But what does this say about the level of sensitivity, understanding, concern, and logic of some of the professionals to whom our youth is entrusted? It speaks highly for those teachers, but it makes us shudder to think of what could have happened if the teachers had not won and the girl had been suspended and her support system taken away. She would probably today be among the statistics of youthful suicide.

There are some school districts that use detentions and year-long suspensions freely and excessively. Some youths are suspended for a whole year after being tardy a certain number of times or not having their pencils or books. Are some of these neglected and abused children, whose parents detain them at home for whatever the reason or do not help them get to school on time or do not buy them pencils? There are children who are, in fact, trying to cope with just that kind of circumstance. And the school tosses them out, taking away their sanctuary and their opportunities to learn and to be with adults and peers who care and depriving them of needed resources and a support system. Are some of these children the ones who are preoccupied with the loss of someone dear to them, who are depressed, who want to die? Indeed, some of them are the ones undergoing those crises and the school dumps them out. When professionals have tried to advocate for some children in these circumstances, they have been told that rules are rules. More of us need to pull together as a team, like those teachers who fought to keep the suicidal girl in school, to eliminate these inhumane practices.

Voids, Omissions, Obstructions, Destructions, and Negative Attitudes

Morse (1978) explained some of the reasons why we have not advanced far in terms of prevention in the schools. He gave several reasons:

1. There is no one person responsible or accountable for emotional development as there is for academic development.

2. Prevention receives no attention when there are serious and pressing problems looming before us that require services.

3. Prevention requires change in social organizations on a grand scale, which costs money, and when there is a budget crunch in education, such change receives low priority.

4. Parents have begun to fear professionals and the potentials of labeling, and they believe that the affective side of the child is the parents' business and not the business of the schools.

5. The results of prevention are difficult to prove, making it even harder to have prevention funded when those approving the funds are accountability-minded.

6. There is not enough money to meet all needs, the competition for resources is fierce, and quality preventive programs are expensive.

The whole area of prevention and preventive programs is a void in the school system and in society. Morse cited the reasons why prevention is neglected, but those reasons are also the excuses that systems use to avoid what they do not want to deal with or pay for. These reasons need to be examined one by one.

No one person is responsible for or accountable for emotional development. This is partly an omission and partly an obstruction. What are the criteria used to evaluate counselors? Their training prepared them for the work of emotional and affective development, but they are not evaluated along that dimension. This is omission. In many schools throughout the nation, counselors are allowed little time to attend to counseling matters. They are hired as counselors for youths, but instead are put to clerking tasks: scheduling, unloading boxes, and distributing books. This is obstruction.

Many districts throughout the nation do not even have counselors in the elementary schools. Most people recognize the importance of early intervention, and yet the critical age group served in the schools goes without counseling services. If you recall from the chapters on divorce and loss, young children were the most vulnerable to developing serious problems in reaction to these crises. Most abuse is administered to younger and smaller children unable to protect themselves. If children received the help they need when they are very young, perhaps we would not see statistics that point to suicide as the second leading cause of death in adolescents. Children in the elementary schools are at the ages when counseling could have the most positive impact in terms of prevention. This is a serious void.

Not just one person, however, should be held accountable and solely responsible for the total emotional development of youths. Children grow and develop and become what and who they are as a result of the input of many. One person may teach a child how to draw letters, but many people are involved in teaching him or her how to draw conclusions about values, feelings, and subsequent behavior. One person alone cannot be held accountable for the reparation of children like those described in this book; there are too many facets to the crises that these children face.

Prevention receives no attention because of serious and pressing problems that demand services. What could be more serious and more pressing than having children in our schools who want to kill themselves or children living in homes in which the adults want to kill them? Many people hold that the most pressing task is teaching children how to read; that task is the responsibility of the schools, whereas the emotional side is not. This is the type of negative attitude that creates omissions. Some children are not motivated to learn how to read or are unable to learn because they are trying to cope with severe emotional crises.

The problem can be looked at in the broader social context as well. Programs that were once funded have been dropped in favor of money for defense. This is a destruction. Monies that had, at one time, been allocated for social programs and research have been diverted into military budgets. Although it is not known for certain whether child abuse and suicide among the young are on the increase, research has shown that factors such as poverty, unemployment, and lack of access to essential services are, at the very least, involved in creating the type of environment in which such abuse and suicide occur with more frequency.

Prevention requires change in social organizations on a grand scale. This involves social organizations at all levels: families, schools, communities, professions, and local, state, and federal governments. It is an attitude problem. Systems—and all the aforementioned are systems—rarely want very much to change, especially if the cost is going to be high. They are basically entrophic, more eager to use their energy in maintaining the status quo than in making changes. All of these systems need to be shown why it is important to change, whether the potential benefits are greater if they do change, and how to change. Transmitting that knowledge will take a lot of educating, and it will take a lot of influence to enforce the desired alterations. It will not come about through the work of just a few people or even one entire professional organization. It will take a team of organizations.

Professional organizations like the American Association for Counseling and Development, the American Psychological Association, and the Council for Exceptional Children provide newsletters and journals, but rarely do they refer to each other's work, let alone join forces to fight for their common interests. They all seem to cloister themselves with their own kind. Perhaps they too are entrophic to internal change; maybe also they do not respect each other enough. Professionals on the front line, out there in the schools, often work successfully as a team. The reality of their situation brings or forces them together. But in the upper echelons of their leadership this is not happening, and they are cheating themselves in terms of the power they could have and the goals they could accomplish if they coalesced as a team. Consequently, these professional organizations are cheating their beneficiaries out of all that expertise and the difference that that expertise could make.

Fear of professionals and the belief that the affective development of children is the parents' business. If parents do indeed fear professionals, it is no wonder. The professionals have done little else (at least in special education) for over a decade but tell the parents and others how they have been doing everything wrong, have damaged children with labeling, have no real understanding of emotions and affect, just behavior, and have, after all these years, accomplished very little.

What nonsense! Special educators have been responsible, at least in part, for seeing that children who were once excluded are now included, for teaching children to read and understand the ordinary curriculum, for helping youths who were once nonfunctional to become functioning human beings who are better prepared for life, and for helping children whose emotions and behavior were out of control to become happier, better adjusted, and better able to join their peers in the mainstream. These improvements occurred because the children were appropriately labeled so that they could receive those special services. What people forget is that the children were labeled, in cruel ways, by peers and others long before they came to the attention of any professional. If it takes a label, and it does, to get the money to buy special services that children need in order to cope and survive, then professionals would be glad to label them all. Many of these children in crises are never labeled because they do not fit the exact criteria for any category and therefore are not eligible for special attention and special services. Perhaps a new label needs to be coined to include them. At the present time, when a counselor knows a child is in trouble and needs help, if that child has not been labeled for special education the counselor is not even allowed to talk to the child.

Recently, I talked with a counselor who had just testified in a sexual abuse case. The mother in this case (a case of incest) did not believe her child and was extremely furious with the counselor for reporting and testifying. The little girl was not permitted to talk with the counselor anymore; without parental permission, a counselor cannot talk to a child. So, after this most devastating experience of first being sexually abused, then going through legal proceedings, followed by being treated with rejection and hostility by her mother, this young child was left on her own with no support system. Rules like those are destructive obstructions and voids.

There are deeper problems in this area as well. Humanism has become a dirty word to some people. Humanistic and affective education have, at times, been used interchangeably, and not necessarily incorrectly so. To emphasize the emotional life of children, to care about their feelings, and to work with them in the other important areas of life along with the usual academic curriculum—these are critical functions in the education and development of children. But because some groups have equated the word humanistic with something contradictory to their religion, they have been responsible for eliminating such programs from many schools. This is destruction.

The results of prevention are difficult to prove. You cannot prove something you never do, of course. But certainly at least two of the crises in this book are prime candidates for proving that prevention programs can be effective: a look at the statistics showing less abuse and fewer suicides would show their effectiveness. Lack of prevention and treatment programs in all our schools for children in crises is a serious omission. We should be able to substantiate success in other crises areas as well as abuse and suicide. Remember the overlapping symptoms and behaviors that have been mentioned many times in this book? Improvement in diminishing these symptoms is as good a proof of success as any other claims of success made in the educational process now or in the past.

As with the other areas, this area has a broader component as well. It seems more and more true that lawyers are running this country, and often contrary to common sense. During the summer of 1984, a child molester was set free on the basis of an argument that he was not allowed to face his accuser and that this restriction violated his constitutional rights. In the past, most child molesters were set free because children were too traumatized to appear in court, answer lawyers' questions, and face the terrifying person who had perpetrated the whole situation in the first place. Then people began to think of reasonable, sensitive, humane, and logical ways to deal with this problem: to make videotaped recordings of a child's testimony, to allow an adult to give the child's testimony, and to have a child therapist determine whether certain questions might be emotionally harmful and therefore could not be asked. These are innovative ideas, and they are preventive in that more child molesters would be convicted and removed from society, and also because if a potential child molester knew that conviction was certain, that knowledge might be a deterrent. All of these strategies for protecting the sexually abused child are in jeopardy right now as lawyers presumably worry over the right of a child molester to face his or her accuser.

Quality preventive programs are expensive. This is a negative attitude. Quality programs can be put together with the help of many professionals already available in the schools. This may require some reorganization and prioritizing, a little creative thinking, and perhaps more money—maybe as much as is required for a new gymnasium or maybe only as little as is required to hire one additional counselor or a few clerks.

The problem runs deeper, but where is there a better place to put our money? Continued questioning has gotten us nowhere in this not-so-child-centered society. The National Committee for Prevention of Child Abuse has reported that the financial cost of these problems to society is enormous. And this committee is addressing only the issue of child abuse, not suicide or any of the other results of untreated childhood crises. Many of the results are the same for all crises: failure, lost potential, delinquency, and physical and mental illness. Our greatest natural resource, our children, is being sacrificed.

If large-scale preventive work had been done, society would not be facing these issues that are confronting it so forcefully and on such a large scale. Prevention is an ideal that is more penetrating and profound than the accomplishments that teams working in the schools have been equipped to attain.

The subject of prevention leads back to an earlier statement in this book referring to the team in a broader context—that of the whole community of various mental health professionals everywhere effecting change within the societal system. The broader context means programs in the schools to prepare children as much as possible for significant losses: a curriculum for education about death. A few really advanced schools have such programs, but they are in the minority. The program should include research and services: prevention of mental illness and good, free care to all who need the help. They also should include a curriculum for sex education: elimination of the factors that incite adults to abuse children in all sorts of ways and preventive programs in the schools to teach children how to avoid sexual abuse and what to do if they encounter it. Again, a few schools have instituted this type of program, but they are few in number. If society could find a cure for the major affective disorder of depression, perhaps there would be little or no suicide. But that cure cannot be found so long as funding for mental health research remains meager in comparison to the money spent on research for other diseases.

So, what can we do right now? What alternatives are available to use in the present to serve children?

A REGENERATION OF INTERVENTIONS

There are no quick and snappy answers, no materials, no recipes, no formulas for "death kits" that can take people step by step through methods for working with these crises. This section is entitled a regeneration because what will be discussed is not really new. It is quite rare for something original and innovative to be created at just the moment when it is needed most.

What follows are program concepts that people have continued to practice without much acclaim, although the programs have always been successful and effective. They have not received enough attention in the past but are now resurfacing in different parts of the country because their merit has been proved. They are not expensive programs; they use already available resources, and since they do not necessarily depend on external or additional funding they are sometimes referred to as a self-help type of intervention. This kind of intervention is worthy of being used with more variety and on a larger scale. In this section of the chapter, three models that are basically self-help programs are discussed.

The need for a book like this was not just the author's overnight brainstorm. Nor was the book conceived in response to all the publicity recently given to some of these crises, and to abuse in particular. The idea for the book began during weekly meetings held with graduate students who were involved in field-raining experiences. The purpose of those meetings was to give the students time together in a group to share the exciting things they were doing for children and the facts that they were learning and to discuss problems they were encountering as they worked with children for the first time. The usual problems surfaced, like how to make a child stop doing so much of this and start doing more of that; but then some very serious problems began to surface more frequently, and those problems constitute the crises described in this book.

The first of these serious problems emerged when one of the students arrived at the meeting in great distress. She told her fellow graduate students that a 10-year-old in her group had hanged himself. Except for a few consoling remarks, the response was a long silence. The subject of child suicide had never come up in the practicum seminars before this, nor were lectures given on childhood suicide; there was nothing available in textbooks. Occasionally, a student would write a research paper on suicide and make a few references to adolescent suicide, but nothing had been written on young children killing themselves. Even adolescent suicide seemed pretty far removed from what these students might be expected to experience as professionals. I asked the student a few questions about the child at the time, but I really had nothing more to offer than consolation. I did not have all the answers then and still do not. It was at this point that the group started to function as a team. The graduate students wanted to ask more questions about other children who acted "different" and to try to understand whether the behaviors they were encountering were indicative of potential suicides. They provided each other with answers and emotional support. They were no longer just a group of practicum students sharing time together. Before the end of that year, all the crises described in this book had been brought before the group, which had become a team. That was quite a year!

The Team Approach

Teams do not just fall together naturally. Groups do, but not teams. It took an experience that was of critical importance to everyone before the group of practicum students reached the turning point and shifted from being just a group to being a team. Different people at different times became the pivotal member. This is the way it should be, and it is the way it happens if people are operating as a team and not just a group. It is true that these students all had the same profession in common, but their common profession did not make a difference. Teams are formed by people from different backgrounds once they are in the schools together. The team's membership becomes interdisciplinary and also can include others who are not trained professionals per se.

The team might consist of only two people or several, and at any one time can include any combination of a counselor, special education teacher, regular education teacher, social worker, nurse, principal, assistant principal, speech therapist, school psychologist, clinical psychologist, physician, parent, or another student. In actuality, however, a team generally consists of a counselor, a social worker, and at least one teacher, usually a special education teacher; this would constitute a core team. The questions most frequently asked about this approach are: (a) How does, or can, this work? (b) Where are these people supposed to find the time? (c) What does it cost?

In Naisbitt's book *Megatrends* (1984), he talked about what he called "bellwether states." These are the states where trends start; other states follow suit. Naisbitt stressed that trends are not fads; trends last, whereas fads do not. Trends start from the bottom (a grass roots movement) and fads start from the top (institutional hierarchies). Self-help programs are trends. One of the bellwether states he mentioned is Colorado. In that state, the team approach is functioning very well, so it will be used as a model to answer the questions that people have about how a team can operate.

How does, or can, this work? Yes, it can work and is working very well. For example, in one junior high school in Boulder, Colorado, there are monthly meetings on a particular day for each of the seventh-, eighth-, and ninth-grade staffs. These meetings are held during the last period; this is nonteaching time, but all staff are required to remain in the building anyway. The building administrator supports the team-approach concept by requiring these meetings and requiring that they be attended by at least one counselor; one representative teacher from each department at each grade level, including coaches and physical education staff; one special education teacher; one of the administrators; and, when possible, other specialists, such as a speech therapist. Parents may come, and many who feel their children are having problems do come voluntarily to bring their child to the attention of the staff.

Typically, these meetings are coordinated by the counselor, and at this time any staff (team) member can bring to attention a child who is having problems. This provides the opportunity for staff members to communicate whatever information they have concerning that child. Depending on the information that derives from these meetings, a child may be designated for further observation, referred for some special service such as a counselor, or perhaps asked to join one of the school's ongoing peer group meetings, like the children's divorce group. If a child is having real difficulties, a smaller team (the core team) is chosen from this larger team to give intensive time and help according to the child's particular needs. This core team may decide to recruit to supplement their efforts the skills of a psychologist, physician, or some other specialist, and if necessary, involve an outside agency (as in cases of suspected abuse or neglect). The counselor usually continues as the coordinator for the core team.

Where are these people supposed to get the time? One of the keys to the success of this team approach is the support and encouragement of the administrative staff in this school. Scheduling has been creatively arranged so that the last working hour of the day is a non–student-contact period. The youths have left school, and unless one of these special meetings is taking place, this hour is used for parent conferences and other responsibilities of the faculty. Planning hours are still in the faculty's schedule. Since all faculty members in the district are required to be in their buildings at the same hours, this does not add an extra hour to their workday; it is simply a difference in scheduling and one of the ways the building administrator has decided that time will be used.

The types of tasks that counselors are required to perform in some districts do not exist in the Colorado school. A secretary is provided for the counselors, and although the counselors advise students with their schedules, their secretaries and the assistant principal also help with the scheduling process. Special education teachers advise students in their classes about their schedules. After the advisement period, the counselors are free to counsel and to run special peer group sessions—work in the realm of emotional development.

This school does not have a morale problem. No one on the teams feels overburdened or required to do more than he or she is paid for. In fact, morale is high because all people in the school feel they are valuable members of a team doing important work. If these professionals did not already start with the attitude that there is more to do in education than just teach a subject, that attitude develops as they become more humanistically involved with their students' total development and well-being.

This is a faculty whose members seem to like and respect one another because they have common vested interests and know that everyone is involved in efforts that go beyond the ordinary expectations in most schools. They depend on each other for support and know that the other team members can be relied on to provide help when problems become weighty—to each a mentor.

What does it cost? It costs nothing! The program takes no extra internal or external funding. Again, the importance of leadership with creativity, ingenuity, common sense, and a humanistic side comes into focus. The cost is not in dollars but in a small amount of time invested to serve the interests of the schools' children in a fuller and richer way.

The School Liaison Approach

What happens when a caring professional is stuck in a district in which this type of scheduling is not allowed or there is no support for this kind of program? That is a question frequently asked by concerned teachers, counselors, social workers, and administrators who would like very much to practice the type of team approach just described but are restricted from doing so. There are two answers to the question, one concerned with the long run and one concerned with the present.

For the long run, these professionals need to work together to convince those who have the power and final say-so that programs for children with mental health needs are not just desirable but essential and critical. Together, the professionals and those in power can constitute a lobbying group. And don't forget the role of parents in the process. Concerned and energetic parents are a powerful force to reckon with. Highlighted here are the logic and necessity of having the various professional groups forgo their territorial inclinations and work as a team.

The school professional is in a position, or more accurately, the child is in a position, such that something must be done immediately; they cannot wait until people have decided that there may be some truth in their words. The school liaison model might be another choice under these circumstances. In schools with restrictive schedules, people working within a group with the same child are not able to interact with each other as frequently or as comprehensively as in the team approach previously described. Someone is needed who will coordinate the internal and external operations, communicate the activities and progress to each person involved in a child's intervention program, ascertain any other needs the child might have, and appraise the effectiveness of these efforts.

When this model is operating, what usually happens is that the liaison person is self-appointed. In other words it falls naturally, by acquiescence, to the one who knows the most about and, for whatever the reasons or circumstances, has taken the greatest interest in a particular child. The school liaison person is not likely to be a teacher, not because teachers are incapable or unskilled but because they are tied to schedules of direct student contact for the entire day, with the exception of a planning period. Some teachers have, however, assumed this role when it was evident that others would not, as in the example given earlier in which teachers took the initiative to fight to keep a suicidal adolescent in school when others wanted the youth expelled. These teachers worked on this problem during their planning periods and lunch breaks, as well as after school. But it is unreasonable to impose such demanding sacrifices on any teacher or to expect them to be able to maintain that level of work overload for extended periods without endangering their own mental or physical health.

A number of school personnel are not as bound to a schedule as teachers are; this would include counselors, social workers, diagnosticians, and assistant principals. Any one of these professionals is a likely candidate to be the school liaison person, not because he or she is not busy enough but because there is more flexibility in the jobs of these school professionals. Their schedules are not as restricted, whereas every minute of each school period is, for a teacher, preempted by a classroom of students who have exclusive rights to that time.

This model also works without additional cost to a district, but it requires even more careful planning. The liaison model must give the strictest attention to insuring that participation is full rather than piecemeal and that there are no breakdowns in communication. This model takes more contributions of time; there are always things to be done. The professionals involved often feel that duties sitting on the back burner, as they should be, are less important, but nevertheless those nagging responsibilities remain, waiting for attention. The greatest weakness of this model is the loss of an opportunity for professionals to have mentors of their own; but this is a model born of necessity rather than an expression of the ideal.

The Peer Counseling Approach

Another bellwether state identified by Naisbitt (1984) is California, which recently enacted a law to provide for the development in the schools of programs for the prevention of youth suicide. In July of 1984, two demonstration programs were scheduled to start in Los Angeles and San Mateo counties. These were areas where strong suicide-prevention centers already existed; however, since the suicide rate appeared to have doubled over the previous 20 years, and childhood suicide consequently received widespread publicity, California decided that more needed to be done.

The intention of California's school mental health program is to make youths aware of the association between suicide and substance abuse, to teach students to recognize the signs of suicidal tendencies, to provide awareness of suicide-prevention services; and to develop information materials for youths, parents, and teachers. Folkenberg (1984) quoted a consultant from the Los Angeles Suicide Prevention Center who said that most suicidal plans are discussed with peers but not parents, teachers, or doctors. The consultant's words have the ring of truth; it is difficult to believe that not one of the adolescents in that Texas suburb where many recent suicides have been reported talked to a friend or peer about his or her feelings before committing the act of suicide.

The idea of peer counseling, peer help, peer tutoring, and peer participation in the alleviation of many problems is not new. It has been around for some time and in most instances has been successful (Hamburg & Varenhorst, 1972; Lippitt & Eiseman, 1969; Rioch, 1971; Varenhorst, 1969; Vriend, 1969). The use of peer groups as an additional mental health support system recently has gained momentum, particularly among divorce groups and drug and alcohol abuse groups. This is another example of the regeneration of an intervention approach to meet current pressing needs.

More recently, Siegel and Griffer (1983) studied the ability of adolescents to identify peers who were suffering from depression. They asked 12- to 18-year-old youths to describe the characteristics of depressed adolescents: what they thought, how they spent their free time, and what they were like. These youths described their depressed peers as being social isolates: not interacting with friends or siblings; spending much time alone; daydreaming; crying frequently; acting moody, angry, rejected, unpleasant, bored, restless, and lonely; and being involved in substance abuse. They thought the causes stemmed from trouble with their intimate relations, trouble with the law, money problems, and family problems. Those youths had pretty good diagnostic skills!

Anyone who knows adolescents understands that the most powerful influence in their lives is their peer group. It is not uncommon for adolescents to exclude adults from their world to some degree because they feel at odds with older generations. This is a natural stage and is normal behavior during this phase of development. Besides the fact that mental health resources and personnel are inadequate, many young people are opposed to becoming involved in counseling; they feel that it is socially stigmatizing. Since they like to be almost exclusively with each other, where they feel freer to share their most intimate problems and secrets, the logical conclusion is to engage young people in the process of doing mental health work with their peers.

Another obvious reason for this approach is that schools are constantly confronted with these problems—even though the schools are not the cause—and have a significant influence on the socialization process of children. Over the years, the public has expected the schools to assume more and more responsibility for a number of societal ills. Drug abuse is one notable example. Even though there is disagreement, with the rise in teenage pregnancies many people believe that the schools should also be responsible for sex education. This may be another excellent approach to handling the crises that confront the schools and to meeting the needs of many children in desperate circumstances. Of course, there is a deeper philosophical conviction behind the idea of meeting the needs of children, which is the belief that we should help each other wherever possible, and learning to do that is something that starts early in our lives. There is the added benefit that helping can be healing (Morgan, 1983). Others (Hamburg & Varenhorst, 1972) also have found that students who provided considerable help to another derived significant benefits themselves. Peer counseling was particularly beneficial to students who themselves felt lonely and tended toward isolation.

The same questions that are asked about the other approaches are asked about the peer counseling and help programs, with even greater skepticism and with quite a bit of fear. In this case, the skepticism and fear are healthy. They can be dealt with, however, by responding to the three major questions asked about any self-help program.

How does, or can, this work? Yes, it does work, and quite successfully. There is considerable proof of the efficacy of peer counseling and help as viable mental health approaches (Hamburg & Varenhorst, 1972; Lippitt & Eiseman, 1969; Rioch, 1971). This approach is not something to be jumped into lightly, however; it requires considerable planning, monitoring, and ongoing evaluation.

It should be understood at the outset that peer counseling does not completely replace adult counselors or the possible need for involvement of some outside mental health professionals. However, when peer counseling functions effectively, it does minimize the necessity for higher levels of professional help. Obviously, in very serious cases, it would be dangerous and extremely irresponsible to allow mental health problems to remain entirely at the peer level. There will always be some youths who require treatment from a highly specialized professional. Even when less serious problems are being managed through peer counseling, the program operates under the ongoing supervision and direction of trained professionals in the schools.

Before a program like this can be implemented, it is crucial to ensure acceptance and support from the school hierarchy and the community (parents). This would require permission from the superintendent of schools, who would probably need approval from the school board, approval from the director of pupil personnel services, and support from the district Parent Teachers Association (PTA), which represents parents.

The functions of peer counseling programs can range from merely identifying and referring students who need intensive help and leading established groups for special kinds of problems to individual counseling. Ideally, peer counselors should represent different developmental ages and stages as well as different racial and ethnic groups.

Stringent requirements must be established for determining who can be a peer counselor to avoid the danger of entrusting others to students who are themselves so disturbed they could cause more harm than good, meaning primarily students with psychotic disturbances. It does not exclude the larger population of students experiencing the types of problems that have been discussed in this book. Those who might be experiencing their own aftereffects of divorce, loss, or abuse or who might be depressed and potentially suicidal should not necessarily be restricted from participation. Some of the most effective peer counseling groups consist entirely, with the exception of a professional mental health worker, of youths who share the same problem (e.g., drug self-help groups, divorce groups, and now suicide prevention self-help groups). These youths are able to understand, at a personal level, the experiences and feelings of their peers. They have been in similar circumstances and made the same responses, and they have discovered the hard way the ineffectiveness of certain ways of coping with their problems. They have many insights to share with their peers, whereas others who have never gone through the same things often cannot relate to such experiences.

Effectiveness in peer counseling comes from two directions: one is the sharing of similar problems with other members of a group, and the other is the perspective or help that can be attained through talking individually with someone your own age who is not caught up in similar circumstances, who is functioning well, and who can think clearly about the problems. The advantages of the first direction, offered by the peer group counseling process, has already been discussed.

The second direction in a peer counseling program, help in gaining perspective, makes different requirements of the participants. The major characteristics or behavioral evidence that a youth is suited to this type of peer counseling are positive personal traits, some talent for counseling, a strong sense of responsibility, and a high degree of commitment.

In implementing a peer counseling program, a bunch of children are not just put together and then allowed to talk. There must be some training sessions prior to implementation. The training sessions should be conducted in small groups with the school mental health professionals. The first part of training needs to focus on the ability to identify the signs or symptoms of individuals in crisis, particularly those individuals who are in severe distress and are potentially suicidal. Peer counselors need to be able to discern the types of problems that require immediate referral to a professionally trained person. These training sessions offer information that includes facts about certain types of problems, information about causes and effects of certain types of problems and misunderstandings associated with such problems, and help in determining the particular areas in which peers can be most helpful. Later training sessions will deal with actual counseling techniques such as using the facets of communication and being active listeners. This type of training can be done through a variety of methods: role playing, group discussion of some of their own problems with their supervisor and other peer counselors, using commercially available materials geared toward development of the ability to make decisions and the clarification of values, and discussions based on prepared stories (like the ones in this book) or case studies that illustrate the types of problems that require their help.

Where will these people find the time? In a truly committed system, this program could become one that carries credit hours for the peer counselors. Peer counseling is as worthy and important a learning activity as some of the students' elective courses, and it also can provide prevocational work for some students. If a district selects this option, then additional time is not required of the staff, even the professionals, since the counseling would be part of their responsibilities as counselors. The program would require unburdening counselors of some of the nonprofessional tasks they now are required to do.

Another alternative is to ensure that this program is given at least the same respect as other extracurricular activities. Extracurricular activities are activities that students do on non-school time anyway. For the professional staff, this program could substitute for other extracurricular activities that they might be required to supervise. It is an activity that is certainly as deserving of additional remuneration as coaching. Of course, there are always students and staff who will volunteer their free time to prepare and work on a project like this. Ideally, though, they should be reimbursed for their time.

What does it cost? Initially, there might be some cost in training materials, but those can be nominal. There should be some funding for consultation services from psychiatrists, whose advice could be needed from time to time; however, in some places where these peer programs are functioning and have been maintained, the schools have had little trouble in finding a few psychiatrists who will volunteer their services for this cause. As in the other approaches, it could be more a matter of commitment, caring, and creative management and organization than a matter of money.

Pro-Bono Counseling

One of the most innovative and proactive approaches to children who are at risk is the El Paso Children's Pro-Bono Project (S. Jacobson, personal communication, July, 1993). Some mental health counselors and psychologists in the greater El Paso region are volunteering time to work with youths who are experiencing or could experience mental health problems. These youths are first identified in their schools by school counselors as students who may need but do not yet qualify for counseling services in the schools. The school counselor refers them to Pro-Bono therapists who accept them as clients if their families do not qualify for assistance from a social service agency. The target population of the Pro-Bono project are families who cannot afford therapy but still make too much money to qualify for public assistance. The Denver Pro-Bono Project (Denver Mental Health Association, 1992) is aimed not only at children but also adults. The basic philosophy is the same as El Paso's: to get services to those who otherwise would go without the assistance that they need.

The El Paso Project has very much of a preventative thrust. Any child known to the school counselor to be is at risk may actually receive therapeutic assistance before deeper problems develop. These two projects are exemplary models that could be implemented in any city or town. The costs for Pro-Bono projects is very minimal because all of the actual services are being provided to the clients free of charge. Small stipends are needed to fund someone to coordinate these projects and to purchase some clerical and evaluation services.

CONCLUSIONS

No one should attempt to make these powerful crisis situations a lone struggle. The necessity of working with a team of people, from the standpoint of both practicality and your own mental health, was emphasized in the beginning of this chapter. The problems we face as professionals and as a society dictate that we learn to work together, to use one another's expertise, to trust and depend upon one another, to give some of ourselves to each other, and to give away some of our treasured skills we have been trying to hoard. There is no way that we are going to be successful in our attempts to help children if energies, talents, and information are not pooled. Success in major prevention efforts will never come about until the entire community of professionals, from the bottom up, learns the value of being a team of mental health professionals and not just a team of counselors, a team of teachers, a team of social workers, or a team of psychologists.

Spending time with the content of these chapters can be a most distressing experience indeed. When all the factors are taken into consideration, the work left to be done in helping these children seems almost insurmountable. But the outlook looks brighter when we learn about the many others who have found efficacious ways to provide services to children in need. Each of the intervention approaches has as its basis the concept of working with teams in one way or another. These approaches are tried and proved models now working in different schools throughout districts across the nation. They are unimpeded by such burdens as unavailable professional resources, lack of time, and not enough money in the budget.

These are healthy self-help models that do require commitment, leadership, flexibility, creativity, common sense, and the willingness to change. But it should be heartening to know that there are front-line professionals and eager, altruistic youths who are already busy at the task of implementing this work. The message of this book is the commitment to understanding not ignorance, cooperation not competition, possibilities not impossibilities, successes not failures, energy not inertia, and hope not despair.

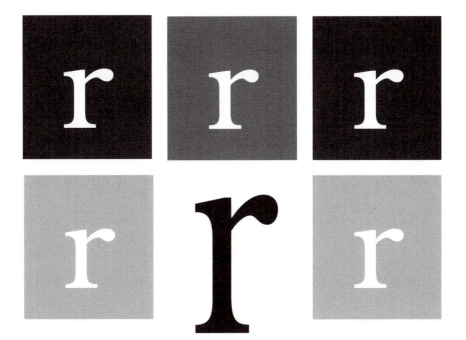

References

Abrahams, M. J., & Whitlock, F. A. (1969). Childhood experience and depression. *British Journal of Psychiatry, 115,* 883–888.

Abrams, J. C., & Kaslow, F. (1976). Learning disability and family dynamics. *Journal of Clinical Child Psychology, 1,* 35–41.

Ackerman, N. W. (1966). *Treating the troubled family.* New York: Basic Books.

Adam, K., Lohrenz, J., & Harper, P. (1973). Suicidal ideation and parental loss: A preliminary research report. *Canadian Psychiatric Association Journal, 18*(2), 95–100.

Adams-Greenly, M., & Moynihan, R. (1983). Helping the children of fatally ill parents. *American Journal of Orthopsychiatry, 53*(2), 219–229.

Adams-Tucker, C. (1982). Proximate effects of sexual abuse in childhood: A report of 18 children. *American Journal of Psychiatry, 139*(10), 1252–1256.

Alexander, I., & Alderstein, A. (1958). Affective responses to the concept of death in a population of children and early adolescents. In R. Fulton (Ed.), *Death and identity.* Baltimore: Charles Press.

Alperstein, G., Rappaport, C., & Flanigan, J. M. (1988). Health problems of homeless children in New York City. *American Journal of Public Health, 78,* 1232–1233.

Amato, P. R. (1987). Family processes in one-parent, stepparent, and intact families: The child's point of view. *Journal of Marriage and the Family, 49,* 327–337.

American School Counselor Association. (1983). American school counselor association position statement on child abuse/neglect. *The ASCA Counselor, 20*(4), 1–2.

Anderson, L. M., & Shafer, G. (1979). The character-disordered family: A community treatment model for family sexual abuse. *American Journal of Orthopsychiatry, 49*(8), 436–445.

Andofer, J. C. (1984). Affective pattern recognition and schizophrenia. *Journal of Clinical Psychology, 40*(2), 403–409.

Anthony, E. J., & Koupernik, C. (1974). *The child in his family: Children at psychiatric risk.* New York: John Wiley and Sons.

Anthony, S. (1972). *The discovery of death in childhood and after.* New York: Basic Books.

Athey, J. L. (1991). HIV infection and homeless adolescents. *Child Welfare, 70*(5), 517–528.

Linn-Benton Education Service Digest. (1991). *At risk youth in crisis: A handbook for collaboration between schools and social services.* Albany, OR: Author.

Babow, I., & Babow, R. (1974). The world of the abused child: A phenomenological report. *Life Threatening Behavior, 4*(1), 33–42.

Babow, I., & Rowe, R. (1990). A suicidal adolescent's sleeping beauty syndrome: Cessation orientations toward dying, sleep, and drugs. *Adolescence, 25,* 791–798.

Bakan, P. (1971). *Slaughter of the innocents.* San Francisco: Jossey-Bass.

Barclay, A., & Cusumano, P. (1967). Father absence, cross sex identity, and field dependent behavior in male adolescents. *Child Development, 38,* 243–250.

Baron, M. A., Byar, R. L., & Sheaff, P. J. (1970). Neurological manifestations of the battered child syndrome. *Pediatrics, 45,* 1023–1024.

Bass, C. (1975). Matchmaker–matchmaker: Older child adoption failures. *Child Welfare, 14*, 505–511.

Bauer, W., & Bauer, J. L. (1982). Adolescent schizophrenia. *Adolescence, 17*(67), 685–693.

Bayrakal, S., & Kope, T. M. (1990). Dysfunction in the single-parent and only-child family. *Adolescence, 25*(97), 1–7.

Beardslee, W., Bemporad, J., Keller, M., & Klerman, G. (1983). Children of parents with major affective disorders: A review. *American Journal of Psychiatry, 140*(7), 825–832.

Beauchamp, N. (1974). The young child's perception of death. *Dissertation Abstracts International, 35*(6-A), 3288A–3289A.

Beck, I. (1988, September 12). Help teen-agers keep ties with divorced parents. *The El Paso Times*, p. D3.

Belcher, V. B. (1983). History need not repeat itself: Make children aware of child abuse through literature. *The School Counselor, 31*(1), 44–48.

Bender, L., & Blau, A. (1937). Sex relations of children with adults. *American Journal of Orthopsychiatry, 7*, 500–518.

Bender, L., & Grugett, A. E. (1952). A follow-up report on children who had atypical sexual experiences. *American Journal of Orthopsychiatry, 22*, 828–837.

Bendiksen, R., & Fulton, R. (1976). Death and the child: An anterospective test of the childhood bereavement and later behavior disorder hypothesis. In R. Fulton (Ed.), *Death and identity*. Baltimore: Charles Press.

Berkowitz, A., & Perkins, H. W. (1988). Personality characteristics of children and alcoholics. *Journal of Consulting and Clinical Psychology, 56*(2), 206–209.

Bernhardt, G. R., & Praeger, S. G. (1985). Preventing child suicide: The elementary school death education puppet show. *Journal of Counseling and Development, 63*(1), 311–312.

Bertman, S. (1974). Death education in the face of taboo. In E. Grollman (Ed.), *Concerning death*. Boston: Beacon Press.

Bertoia, J., & Allan, J. (1988, October). School management of the bereaved child. *Elementary School Guidance & Counseling, 23*, 30–38.

Biller, H. B. (1969). Father absence, maternal encouragement, and sex role development in kindergarten-age boys. *Child Development, 40*, 539–546.

Biller, H. B. (1971). *Father, child, and sex role*. Washington, DC: Heath Company.

Biller, H., & Bahm, R. (1971). Father absence, perceived maternal behavior, and masculinity of self-concept among junior high boys. *Developmental Psychology, 4*, 178–181.

Biller, H., & Borstelmann, L. (1967). Masculine development: An integrative review. *Merrill–Palmer Quarterly, 13*, 253–294.

Birtchnell, J. (1969). The possible consequences of early parent death. *British Journal of Medical Psychiatry, 42*, 1–12.

Blanchard, R., & Biller, H. (1971). Father availability and academic performance among third grade boys. *Developmental Psychology, 4*, 301–305.

Bloch, D., Silber, E., & Perry, S. (1956). Some factors in the emotional reaction of children to disaster. *American Journal of Psychiatry, 113*, 416–422.

Boor, M. (1976). Relationship of internal–external control and United States suicide rates: 1966–1973. *Journal of Clinical Psychology, 32*(4), 795–799.

Boszormenyi-Nagy, I., & Spark, G. (1973). *Invisible loyalties.* Hagerstown, MD: Harper & Row.

Bowlby, J. (1951). Maternal care and mental health. *World Health Organization Monograph, Series* (No. 2).

Bowlby, J. (1960). Grief and mourning in infancy and early childhood. *Psychoanalytic Study of the Child, 15,* 9–52.

Bowlby, J. (1984). Violence in the family as a disorder of the attachment and caregiving system. *The American Journal of Psychoanalysis, 144*(1), 9–25.

Brant, R. S. T., & Tisza, V. B. (1977). The sexually misused child. *American Journal of Orthopsychiatry, 1,* 80–90.

Brendtro, L. K., Brokenleg, M., & Bockern, S. V. (1990). *Reclaiming youth at risk.* Bloomington, IN: National Education Service.

Briggs, F., & Lehmann, K. (1989). Significance of children's drawings in cases of sexual abuse. *Early Child Development and Care, 47,* 131–137.

Brumback, R., & Staton, R. (1983). Learning disability and childhood depression. *American Journal of Orthopsychiatry, 53*(2), 289–334.

Brunnquell, D., Crichton, L., & Egeland, B. (1981). Maternal personality and attitudes of disturbances of child rearing. *American Journal of Orthopsychiatry, 51*(4), 680–691.

Burgess, A. W., & Hazelwood, R. (1983). Autoerotic asphyxial deaths and social network response. *American Journal of Orthopsychiatry, 53*(1), 166–170.

Burgess, R., & Conger, R. (1978). Family interaction in abusive, neglectful, and normal families. *Child Development, 49,* 1163–1173.

Burks, C., & Harrison, D. (1962). Aggressive behavior as a means of avoiding depression. *American Journal of Orthopsychiatry, 32*(3), 416–422.

Campbell, J. D. (1988, March). Children of alcoholics. *Learning,* 45–48.

Cantor, D. (1979). Divorce: A view from the children. *Journal of Divorce, 2,* 357–361.

Cantor, P. (1976). Personality characteristics found among youthful female suicide attempters. *Journal of Abnormal Psychology, 85*(3), 324–329.

Cantrell, V. L., & Prinz, R. J. (1985). Multiple perspectives of rejected, neglected, and accepted children: Relation between sociometric status and behavioral characteristics. *Journal of Consulting and Clinical Psychology, 53*(6), 884–889.

Carlson, G., & Cantwell, D. (1979). A survey of depressive symptoms in a child and adolescent psychiatric population. *Journal of American Academy of Child Psychiatry, 18*(4), 587–599.

Carter, J. A., & Duncan, P. A. (1984). Binge-eating and vomiting: A survey of a high school population. *Psychology in the Schools, 21*(2), 198–203.

Cary, W., Lipton, W., & Myers, R. (1975). Temperament in adopted and foster babies. *Child Welfare, 53,* 352–359.

Cataldo, M., & Harris, J. (1982). The biological basis for self-injury in the mentally retarded. *Analysis and Intervention in Developmental Disabilities, 2,* 21–39.

Chang, P., & Deinard, A. (1982). Single-father caretakers: Demographic characteristics and adjustment processes. *American Journal of Orthopsychiatry, 52*(2), 236–243.

Childers, P., & Wimmer, M. (1971). The concept of death in early childhood. *Child Development, 42*(4), 1299–1301.

Chiriboga, D. A., & Catron, L. S. (1991). *Divorce.* New York NY University Press.

Clay, J. W. (1990). Working with lesbian and gay parents and their children. *Young Children, 18*, 31–35.

Clay, J. W. (1991, April). Respecting and supporting gay and lesbian parents. *The Education Digest*, 51–57.

Cohen, J. A., & Mannarino, A. P. (1988). Psychological symptoms in sexually abused girls. *Child Abuse & Neglect, 14*, 571–577.

Cohler, B., Grunebaum, H., Weiss, J., Gamer, E., & Gallant, D. (1977). Disturbance of attention among schizophrenic, depressed, and well mothers and their young children. *Journal of Child Psychology and Psychiatry, 18*, 115–135.

Colletta, N. (1979). The impact of divorce: Father absence on poverty. *Journal of Divorce, 3*, 27–35.

Condini, A., & Constantini, M. (1974). Psychodynamic considerations regarding suicidal tendency of the adolescent. *Psychological Abstracts, 51*, No. 7746.

Corder, B., Page, P., & Corder, R. (1974). Parental history, family communication and interaction patterns in adolescent suicide. *Family Therapy, 1*(3), 285–290.

Court, J. (1974). Characteristics of parents and children. In J. Carter (Ed.), *The maltreated child*. London: Priory Press.

Craig, L., & Senter, R. (1972). Student thoughts about suicide. *Psychological Record, 22*, 355–358.

Crase, D. R., & Crase, D. (1989). Single-child families and death. *Childhood Education, 14*, 153–156.

Criville, A. (1990). Child physical and sexual abuse: The roles of sadism and sexuality. *Child Abuse & Neglect, 14*, 121–127.

Crumbley, F., & Blumenthal, R. (1973). Children's reactions to temporary loss of the father. *American Journal of Psychiatry, 130*, 778–782.

Cunningham, L., Remi, J., Loftus, R., & Edwards, J. (1975). Studies of adoptees from psychiatrically disturbed biological parents: Psychiatric conditions in childhood and adolescence. *British Journal of Psychiatry, 47*, 534–549.

Curbrksak, C. (1972). Sociologists in India and USA. In P. Blachly (Ed.), *Progress in drug abuse*. Springfield, IL: Charles C. Thomas.

Cytryn, L., & McKnew, D. H. (1972). Proposed classification of childhood depression. *American Journal of Psychiatry, 129*(2), 149–154.

Cytryn, L., & McKnew, D. H. (1974). Factors influencing the changing clinical expression of the depressive process in children. *American Journal of Psychiatry, 131*, 879–881.

Cytryn, L., McKnew, D., & Bunney, W. (1980). Diagnosis of depression in children: A reassessment. *American Journal of Psychiatry, 137*, 22–25.

Cytryn, L., McKnew, D., Zahn-Waxler, C., Radke-Yarrow, M., Gaensbauer, T., Harmon, R., & Lamour, M. (1984). A developmental view of affective disturbances in the children of affectively ill parents. *American Journal of Psychiatry, 141*(2), 219–221.

Dail, P. W. (1990). The psychosocial context of homeless mothers with young children: Program and policy implications. *Child Welfare, 69*, 291–308.

Daniel, J. H., Hampton, R. L., & Newberger, E. H. (1983). Child abuse and accidents in black families: A controlled comparative study. *American Journal of Orthopsychiatry, 53*(4), 645–653.

Davoren, E. (1974). The role of the social worker. In R. E. Helfer & C. H. Kempe (Eds.), *The battered child* (2nd ed.). Chicago: University of Chicago Press.

Davidowitz, E. (1989). "Die mother, father, brother:" The true story of a boy who vowed to do the devil's dirty work. *Redbook, 172,* 132–134.

De Francis, V. (1969). *Child victims of sex crimes.* Denver, CO: The American Humane Association, Children's Division.

De John, A. R. (1982). Sexual abuse of children: Sex, race and age dependent variations. *American Journal of Diseases of Children, 136*(2), 129–134.

Dean, D. (1979). Emotional abuse of children. *Children Today, 6*(4), 18–20.

Deblinger, E., McLeer, S. V., Atkins, M. S., Ralphe, D., & Edna, F. (1989). Post-traumatic stress in sexually abused, physically abused, and nonabused children. *Child Abuse & Neglect, 13,* 403–408.

Delisle, R. S., & McNamee, A. S. (1981). Children's perceptions of death: A look at the appropriateness of selected picture books. *Death Education, 5,* 1–13.

Delsordo, J. D. (1974). Protective casework for abused children. In J. Leavitt (Ed.), *The battered child: Selected readings.* Fresno, CA: General Learning Press.

Demo, D. H., & Acock, A. C. (1988). The impact of divorce on children. *Journal of Marriage and the Family, 50,* 619–648.

Derdeyn, A. P., & Scott, E. (1984). Joint custody: A critical analysis and appraisal. *American Journal of Orthopsychiatry, 54*(2), 199–209.

Devlin, P. K., & Cowan, G. A. (1985). Homophobia, perceived fathering, and male intimate relationships. *Journal of Personality Assessment, 49*(5), 467–473.

Dlugokinski, E. (1977). A developmental approach of coping with divorce. *Journal of Clinical Child Psychology, 6*(12), 27–30.

Dollinger, S. J. (1982). On the varieties of childhood sleep disturbance. *Journal of Clinical Child Psychology, 11,* 107–115.

Dominic, K., & Schlesinger, B. (1980). Weekend fathers: Family shadows. *Journal of Divorce, 3,* 241–247.

Draper, E. (1976). A developmental theory of suicide. *Comprehensive Psychiatry, 17,* 63–77.

Duche, D. (1976). Attempts at suicide by adolescents. *Psychological Abstracts, 56,* Abstract No. 4232.

Duncan, J. (1977). The immediate management of suicide attempts in children and adolescents: Psychological aspects. *Journal of Family Practice, 4*(1), 77–80.

Edelson, S., Taubman, M., & Lovass, O. (1983). Some social contexts of self-destructive behavior. *Journal of Abnormal Child Psychology, 11*(2), 299–312.

Eiduson, B., & Livermore, J. (1975). Complications in therapy with adopted children. *American Journal of Orthopsychiatry, 4,* 534–539.

Einbender, A. J., & Friedrich, W. N. (1989). Psychological functioning and behavior of sexually abused girls. *Journal of Consulting and Clinical Psychology, 57*(1), 155–157.

Elizur, E., & Kaffman, M. (1983). Factors influencing the severity of childhood bereavement reactions. *American Journal of Orthopsychiatry, 53*(4), 393–415.

Ellerstein, N. S., & Canavan, J. W. (1980). Sexual abuse of boys. *American Journal of Diseases of Children, 134*(3), 255–257.

Ellison, E. (1983). Issues concerning parental harmony and children's psychosocial adjustment. *American Journal of Orthopsychiatry, 53*(1), 304–309.

Elmer, E. (1967). *Children in jeopardy.* Pittsburgh, PA: University of Pittsburgh Press.

Emery, R. E. (1989). Family violence. *American Psychologist, 44*(2), 321–327.

Erikson, E. H. (1968). *Identity, youth, and crisis.* New York: Norton.

Evans, S., Reinhart, J., & Succop, R. (1980). Failure to thrive: A study of 45 children and their families. In S. Harrison & J. McDermott (Eds.), *New directions in childhood psychopathology.* New York: International Universities Press.

Evoy, J. J. (1983). *The rejected.* University Park, PA: Pennsylvania State University Press.

Fallon, M. T. (1976). Fear of death in young adolescents: A study of the relationships between fear of death and selected anxiety, personality and intelligence variables. *Dissertation Abstracts International, 36*(9-A), 5941A–5942A.

Felner, R., Ginter, M., Boike, M., & Cowan, E. (1981). Parental death or divorce and the school adjustment of young children. *American Journal of Community Psychology, 9,* 181–191.

Felner, R., Strolberg, A., & Cowen, E. (1975). Crisis events and school mental health referral patterns of young children. *Journal of Consulting and Clinical Psychology, 43,* 305–310.

Fine, S. (1986). Divorce: Cultural factors and kinship factors in the adjustment of children. *Child Psychiatry and Human Development, 27*(2), 121–127.

Folkenberg, J. (1984, April). To be or not to be: Preventive legislation. *Psychology Today,* p. 9.

Fontana, V. J., & Schneider, C. (1978). Help for abusing parents. In L. E. Arnold (Ed.), *Helping parents help their children.* New York: Brunner/Mazel.

Foreman, S., & Seligman, L. (1983). Adolescent abuse. *The School Counselor, 31*(1), 17–25.

Formanek, R. (1974). When children ask about death. *Elementary School Journal, 75,* 92–97.

Forrest, D. V. (1983). Depression: Information and interventions for school counselors. *The School Counselor, 30*(4), 269–279.

Fox, L. S. (1991). Baby boom parents and homosexuality: Continued challenge for college health educators. *Journal of American College Health, 40,* 141–143.

Fox, S. J., Barnett, R. J., Davies, M., & Bird, H. (1990). Psychopathology and developmental delay in homeless children: A pilot study. *Journal of the American Academy of Child and Adolescent Psychiatry, 29,* 732–735.

Franson, J. (1988, October). When tragedy comes to school. *NASSP Bulletin,* p.p. 88–94.

Fredlund, D. J. (1977). Children and death from the school setting viewpoint. *The Journal of School Health,* 533–537.

French, A., & Berlin, I. (1979). *Depression in children and adolescents.* New York: Human Sciences Press.

French, A., Steward, M., & Morrison, T. (1979). A longitudinal study of two depressed, self-destructive latency-age boys: A six year and four year follow-up. In A. French & I. Berlin (Eds.), *Depression in children and adolescents.* New York: Human Sciences Press.

Freud, A. (1956). *Indications of child analysis and other papers.* New York: International Universities Press.

Freud, S. (1950). Family romances. In *Collected papers* (Vol. 5). London: Hogarth Press.

Freud, S. (1954). *The origins of psychoanalysis, letters to Wilhelm Fliess, drafts and notes.* Letter No. 69. New York: Basic Books. Original work published 1897.

Friedman, R. J., & Doyal, G. T. (1974). Depression in children: Some observations for the school psychologist. *Psychology in the Schools, 11,* 19–23.

Fry, P., & Trifiletti, R. (1983). An exploration of the adolescents' perspective: Perceptions of major stress dimensions in the single parent family. *Journal of Psychiatric Treatment and Evaluation, 5,* 101–111.

Furman, E. (1974). *A child's parent dies.* New Haven, CT: Yale University Press.

Gaensbauer, T., Harmon, R., Cytryn, L., & McKnew, D. (1984). Social and affective development in infants with a manic-depressive parent. *Journal of Psychiatry, 141*(2), 223–228.

Galdston, P. (1974). Observations on children who have been physically abused by their parents. In J. Leavitt (Ed.), *The battered child: Selected readings.* Fresno, CA: General Learning Press.

Gallagher, U. (1971). Adoption resources for black children. *Children, 18,* 49–53.

Gannett, N. S. (1986, January 12). Study: Children of divorce suffer financially. *El Paso Times,* p. A12.

Garbarino, J., & Garbarino, A. C. (1984). *Emotional maltreatment of children.* National Committee for Prevention of Child Abuse.

Garbarino, J., & Gilliam, G. (1980). *Understanding abusive families.* Lexington, MA: Lexington Books.

Garner, H. (1975). An adolescent suicide, the mass media and the educator. *Adolescence, 10*(38), 241–246.

German, D. E., Habenicht, D., & Futcher, W. G. (1990). Psychological profile of the female adolescent incest victim. *Child Abuse & Neglect, 14,* 429–438.

Giarretto, H. (1982). A comprehensive child sexual abuse treatment program. *Child Abuse and Neglect: The International Journal, 6*(3), 263–278.

Gigeroff, A. K. (1968). *Sexual deviation in the criminal law: Pedophilic offenses.* Toronto, Ontario: University of Toronto Press.

Gil, D. G. (1976). Primary prevention of child abuse: A philosophical and political issue. *Pediatric Psychology, 1*(2), 54–57.

Glaser, K. (1967). Masked depression in children and adolescents. *American Journal of Psychotherapy, 21*(4), 565–574.

Gleser, G., Green, B., & Winget, C. (1981). *Prolonged psychosocial effects of disaster: A Study of Buffalo Creek.* New York: Academic Press.

Goodman, R. W. (1987). Adult children of alcoholics. *Journal of Counseling and Development, 66,* 162–163.

Goodman, R., Silberstein, R., & Mandell, W. (1963). Adopted children brought to a child psychiatric clinic. *Archives of General Psychiatry, 9,* 451–456.

Gordy, P. L. (1983). Group work that supports adult victims of childhood incest. *Social Casework, 64*(5), 300–307.

Grayson, H. T. (1967). Psychosexual conflict in adolescent girls who experienced early parental loss by death. *Dissertation Abstracts International, 28*(5-B), 2136.

Greenbaum, S., Garrison, R., James, B., & Stephens, R. (1989). *School bullying and victimization.* National School Safety Center Resource Paper. Malibu, CA: Pepperdine University Press.

Greenberg, L. I. (1975). Therapeutic grief work with children. *Social Casework, 56,* 396–403.

Greene, B. L. (1965). *The psychotherapies of marital disharmony.* New York: Free Press.

Greene, N. D. (1974). Identifying the battered or molested child. In J. Leavitt (Ed.), *The battered child: Selected readings.* Fresno, CA: General Learning Press.

Greenwald, E., Leitenberg, H., Cado, S., & Tarran, M. (1990). Childhood sexual abuse: Long-term effects on psychological and sexual functioning in a nonclinical and nonstudent sample of adult women. *Child Abuse & Neglect, 14,* 503–513.

Grollman, E. A. (1974). *Concerning death.* Boston: Beacon Press.

Grollman, E., & Grollman, S. (1977). How to tell children about divorce. *Journal of Clinical Child Psychology, 6*(2), 35–38.

Grow, L., & Shapiro, D. (1975). Adoption of black children by white parents. *Child Welfare, 14,* 57–59.

Haim, A. (1974). *Adolescent suicide.* New York: International Universities Press.

Halligan, F. G. (1983). Reactive depression and chronic illness: Counseling patients and their families. *The Personnel and Guidance Journal, 61*(7), 401–406.

Hamburg, B. A., & Varenhorst, B. B. (1972). Peer counseling in the secondary schools: A community mental health project for youth. *American Journal of Orthopsychiatry, 42*(4), 566–581.

Hammond, J. (1979). Children of divorce: A study of self-concept, academic achievement, and values. *Elementary School Journal, 80,* 55–62.

Handford, H. A., Mattison, R., Humphrey, F. J., & McLaughlin, R. E. (1986). Depressive syndrome in children entering a residential school subsequent to parent death, divorce, or separation. *Journal of the American Academy of Child Psychiatry, 25*(3), 409–414.

Hansen, Y. (1973). Development of the concept of death: Cognitive aspects. *Dissertation Abstracts International, 34*(2-B), 853.

Hare, J., & Koepke, L. A. (1990). Susanne and her two mothers. *Day Care and Education, 18*(2), 20–21.

Hendrickson, S., & Cameron, C. (1975). Student suicide and college administrators: A perceptual gap. *Journal of Higher Education, 46*(3), 349–354.

Henning, J., & Oldham, J. (1977). Children of divorce: Legal and psychological crises. *Journal of Clinical Child Psychology, 6*(2), 55–59.

Hersch, P. (1988, January). Coming of age on city streets. *Psychology Today,* p.p. 28–37.

Hetherington, E., & Deur, J. (1971). Effect of father absence on child development. *Young Children, 26*(4), 233–248.

Hill, M. (1970). Suicidal behavior in adolescents and its relationship to the lack of parental empathy. *Dissertation Abstracts International, 31*(1-A), 472.

Hillard, J. R. (1983). Emergency management of the suicidal patient. In J. I. Walker (Ed.), *Psychiatric emergencies.* Philadelphia: J. B. Lippincott.

Hinsie, L. E., & Campbell, R. J. (1974). *Psychiatric dictionary* (4th ed.). New York: Oxford University Press.

Hochman, J., & Brill, N. (1973). Chronic marijuana use and psychosocial adaptation. *American Journal of Psychiatry, 130*(1), 132–140.

Hoeffer, B. (1981). Children's acquisition of sex role behavior in lesbian-mother families. *American Journal of Orthopsychiatry, 51*(2), 536–543.

Hofling, C., & Joy, M. (1974). Favorable responses to the loss of a significant figure: A preliminary report. *Bulletin of the Menninger Clinic, 38,* 527–537.

Hollan, T. H. (1970). Poor school performance as a symptom of masked depression in children and adolescents. *American Journal of Psychotherapy, 24*(1), 258–263.

Howing, P. T., Wodarski, J. S., Kurtz, P. D., & Gaudin, J. M. (1990). The empirical base for the implementation of social skills training with maltreated children. *Social Work, 35*(5), 244–248.

Hunt, P., & Baird, M. (1990). Children of sex rings. *Child Welfare, 69*(3), 195–207.

Hyman, I. A., & Fina, A. (1983). The national center for the study of corporal punishment and alternatives in the schools: Moving from policy formation to implementation. *Journal of Clinical Child Psychology, 12*(3), 257–260.

Jalali, B., Jalali, M., Crocetti, G., & Turner, F. (1981). Adolescents and drug use: Toward a more comprehensive approach. *American Journal of Orthopsychiatry, 51*(1), 120–130.

James, H. (1975). *The little victims: How America treats its children.* New York: David McKay.

Jauch, C. (1977). The one–parent family. *Journal of Clinical Child Psychology, 6*(2), 30–35.

Johnson, B., & Morse, H. (1968, March). *The battered child: A study of children with inflicted injuries.* Denver, CO: Denver Department of Welfare.

The Joint Commission of Mental Health of Children. (1970). *Crisis in child mental health: Challenge for the 1970's.* New York: Harper & Row.

Jones, J. G. (1982). Sexual abuse of children: Current concepts. *American Journal of Diseases of Children, 136*(2), 142–146.

Junewicz, W. J. (1983). A protective posture toward emotional neglect and abuse. *Child Welfare, 6*(3), 243–252.

Justice, B., & Justice, R. (1976). *The abusing family.* New York: Human Sciences Press.

Kagan, M. M., & Squires, R. L. (1984). Eating disorders among adolescents: Patterns and prevalence. *Adolescence, 19*(2), 73–84.

Kalter, N., & Rembar, J. (1981). The significance of a child's age at the time of parental divorce. *American Journal of Orthopsychiatry, 51*(1), 85–100.

Kastenbaum, R. (1974). Childhood: The kingdom where creatures die. *Journal of Clinical Child Psychology, 3*(2), 14–17.

Kastenbaum, R., & Aisenberg, R. (1972). *The psychology of death.* New York: Springer Publishing.

Katz, L. (1974). Adoption: Some guidelines. *Child Welfare, 53,* 180–188.

Kavanagh, C. (1982). Emotional abuse and mental injury: A critique of the concepts and a recommendation for practice. *Journal of the American Academy of Child Psychiatry, 21*(2), 171–177.

Kazdin, A., French, A., & Unis, A. (1983). Child, mother, and father evaluations of depression in psychiatric inpatient children. *Journal of Abnormal Child Psychology, 11*(2), 167–180.

Kelly, J., & Wallerstein, J. (1977). Part–time parent, part–time child: Visiting after divorce. Journal of Clinical Child Psychology, 6 (2), 51–55.

Kempe, C. H., Silverman, F. N., Steele, B. F., Droegemueller, W., & Silver, H. K. (1962). The battered child syndrome. *Journal of the American Medical Association, 181,* 17–24.

Kempe, R., & Kempe, C. H. (1976). Assessing family pathology. In R. Helfer & C. Kempe (Eds.), *Child abuse and neglect.* Cambridge, MA: Ballinger.

Kent, J. T. (1976). A follow–up study of abused children. *Journal of Pediatric Psychology, 1*(2), 25–31.

Khan, M. (1983). Sexual abuse of younger children. *Clinical Pediatrics, 22*(5), 269–272.

Kinard, E. M. (1979). The psychological consequences of abuse for the child. *Journal of Social Issues, 35*(2), 82–100.

Kinsey, A., Martin, C., Pomeroy, W., & Gebhard, P. (1953). *Sexual behavior in the human female.* Philadelphia: W.B. Saunders.

Kliman, G. (1968). *Psychological emergencies of childhood.* New York: Grune & Stratton.

Kline, D., & Christiansen, J. (1975). *Educational and psychological problems of abused children.* Logan: Utah State University. (ERIC Document Reproduction Service No. ED 121 041)

Koch, M. (1980). Sexual abuse in children. *Adolescence, 15*(59), 643–649.

Kocourkova, J., & Konecny, R. (1973). Characteristics of the personality of adolescent studies. *Psychological Abstracts, 49,* Abstract No. 11421.

Konopka, G. (1983). Adolescent suicide. *Exceptional Children, 49*(5), 390–394.

Koocher, G. P. (1974a). Conversations with children about death: Ethical considerations in research. *Journal of Clinical Child Psychology, 3*(2), 19–21.

Koocher, G. P. (1974b). Talking with children about death. *American Journal of Orthopsychiatry, 44,* 404–411.

Koplan, C. R. (1983). Pediatric psychopharmacology. In E. Bassuk, S. Schoonover, & A. Gelenberg (Eds.), *The practitioner's guide to psychoactive drugs.* New York: Plenum Medical Book.

Korella, K. (1972). Teen–age suicidal gestures: A study of suicidal behavior among high school students. *Dissertation Abstracts International, 32* (9-A), 5039A.

Kraft, S. (1983, October 10). Teen suicide. Plans: What happened in Eden? *The El Paso Times,* pp. 1C, 4C.

Kreider, D., & Motto, J. (1974). Parent–child role reversal and suicide states in adolescence. *Adolescence, 9*(35), 365–370.

Kübler–Ross, E. (1969). *On death and dying.* New York: Macmillan.

Kurdek, L. (1981). An integrative perspective on children's divorce adjustment. *American Psychologist, 36,* 856–866.

Kurdek, L. A., & Sinclair, R. J. (1988). Adjustment of young adolescents in two–parent nuclear, stepfather, and mother–custody families. *Journal of Consulting and Clinical Psychology, 56*(1), 91–96.

Kurtz, P. D., Kurtz, G. L., & Jarvis, S. V. (1991). Problems of maltreated runaway youth. *Adolescence, 26*(103), 543–555.

Lampl–de Groot, J. (1976). Mourning in a six year–old girl. *The Psychoanalytic Study of the Child, 31,* 273–281.

Leahey, M. (1984). Findings from research on divorce: Implications for professionals' skill development. *American Journal of Orthopsychiatry, 54*(2), 298–317.

Leon, G. R., Kendall, P. C., & Garber, J. (1980). Depression in children: Parent, teacher and child perspectives. *Journal of Abnormal Child Psychology, 8*(2), 221–235.

Lesse, S. (1974). Depression masked by acting–out behavior patterns. *American Journal of Psychotherapy, 28*(2), 352–361.

Lester, D. (1990). Ecological correlates of adolescent attempted suicide. *Adolescence, 25*, 383–485.

Levy, E. F. (1992). Strengthening the coping resources of lesbian families. *The Journal of Contemporary Human Services*, January, 23–31.

Levy, E. R. L. (1983). The child's right to corporal integrity in the school setting: A right without a remedy under the constitution. *Journal of Clinical Child Psychology, 12*(3), 261–265.

Levy–Shiff, R. (1982). The effects of father absence on young children in mother–headed families. *Child Development, 53*, 1400–1405.

Lidz, T., & Bloth, S. (1983). Critique of the Danish–American studies of the biological and adoptive relatives of adoptees who became schizophrenic. *American Journal of Psychiatry, 140*(40), 426–435.

Lippitt, P., & Eiseman, J. (1969). *Cross–age helping program.* Ann Arbor: The University of Michigan, (Center for Research in Utilization of Scientific Knowledge).

Livingood, A. B., & Daen, P. (1983). The depressed mother as a source of stimulation for her infant. *Journal of Clinical Psychology, 39*(3), 118–122.

Lloyd, R. (1976). *For love or money: Boy prostitution in America.* New York: Vanguard Press.

Lomas, P. (1967). *The predicament of the family.* New York: International Universities Press.

Long, K. (1983). The experience of repeated and traumatic loss among Crow Indian children. *American Journal of Orthopsychiatry, 53*(1), 56–67.

Lourie, I., & Stefano, L. (1978). On defining emotional abuse. In M. Lauderdale, R. Anderson, & S. Cramer (Eds.), *Child abuse and neglect: Issues on innovation and implementation* (Vol. 1) (DHEW Publication No. OHDS 78–30147, pp. 201–208). Washington, DC: U.S. Department of Health, Education, and Welfare.

Loya, F. (1977). *Suicidal rates among Chicano youths in Denver, Colorado: A statistical and cultural comparison.* Unpublished manuscript, Denver General Hospital, Denver.

Lystad, M. H. (1975). Violence at home: A review of the literature. *American Journal of Orthopsychiatry, 45*(3), 328–345.

MacIntyre, J. E. (1976). Adolescence, identity, and foster family care. *Children, 17*, 213–217.

Mahler, M. S. (1968). *On human symbiosis and the vicissitudes of individuation.* New York: International Universities Press.

Mahon, E., & Simpson, D. (1977). The painted guinea pig. *The Psychoanalytic Study of the Child, 32*, 283–303.

Maisch, H. (1972). *Incest.* New York: Stein & Day.

Malmquist, D. P. (1983). Major depression in childhood: Why don't we know more? *American Journal of Orthopsychiatry, 53*(2), 262–268.

Marino, C., & McCowan, R. (1976). The effects of parent absence on children. *Child Study Journal, 6*(3), 19–27.

Martin, H.P. (1976). *The abused child.* Cambridge, MA: Ballinger.

Martin, H. P., & Beezley, P. (1974). Prevention and consequences of child abuse. *Journal of Operational Psychiatry, 6,* 68–77.

Martin, H. P., & Rodeheffer, M. A. (1976). The psychological impact of abuse on children. *Pediatric Psychology, 1*(2), 12–16.

Masterson, J. F. (1976). Physical abuse of children—an agency study. In *Protecting the battered child.* Denver, CO: American Humane Association, Children's Division.

May, P., & Dizmang, L. (1977). Suicide and the American Indian. *Psychological Abstracts, 57,* Abstract No. 3588.

McBrien, E. J. (1983). Are you thinking of killing yourself? Confronting students' suicidal thoughts. *The School Counselor, 31*(1), 75–82.

McCranie, E. W., & Bass, J. D. (1984). Childhood family antecedents of dependency and self–criticism: Implications for depression. *Journal of Abnormal Psychology, 93*(1), 3–8.

McGord, J. (1962). Some effects of paternal absence on male children. *Journal of Abnormal and Social Psychology, 64,* 361–369.

McGue, M., Pickens, R. W., & Svikis, D. S. (1992). Sex and age effects on the inheritance of alcohol problems: A twin study. *Journal of Abnormal Psychology, 101* (1), 3–17.

McIntire, M., & Angel, C. (1971). Suicide as seen in poison control centers. *Pediatrics, 48*(1), 914.

McIntire, M., Angel, C., & Strumpler, L. (1972). The concept of death in midwestern children and youth. *American Journal of Diseases of Children, 123,* 527–532.

McKeever, P. (1983). Siblings of chronically ill children: A literature review with implications for research and practice. *American Journal of Orthopsychiatry, 53* (2), 209–217.

McWhinnie, A. (1967). *Adopted children and how they grow up.* London: Routledge and Kegan Paul.

Melear, J. (1972). Children's conceptions of death. *Dissertation Abstracts International, 33*(2-B), 919B.

Merrill, E.J. (1975). Physical abuse of children—an agency study. In *Protecting the battered child.* Denver, CO: American Humane Association, Children's Division.

Meyer, J. (1975). *Death and neurosis.* New York: International Universities Press.

Miller, J. (1975). Suicide and adolescence. *Adolescence, 10*(37), 11–22.

Milne, A. M., Myers, D. E., Rosenthal, A. S., & Ginsburg, A. (1986). Single parents, working mothers, and the educational achievement of school children. *Sociology of Education, 59,* 125–139.

Mitchell, M. E. (1967). *The child's attitude to death.* New York: Shocken Books.

Money, J. (1982). Child abuse: Growth failure, I.Q. deficit, and learning disability. *Journal of Learning Disabilities, 15*(10), 579–582.

Montare, A., & Boone, S. (1980). Aggression and paternal absence: Racial–ethnic differences among inner–city boys. *Journal of Genetic Psychology, 137,* 223–232.

Morgan, S. R. (1976). The battered child in the classroom. *Journal of Pediatric Psychology, 1*(2), 47–49.

Morgan, S. R. (1979). Psychoeducational profile of emotionally disturbed abused children. *Journal of Clinical Child Psychology, 8*(1), 3–6.

Morgan, S. R. (1983). Development of empathy in emotionally disturbed children. *Journal of Humanistic Education and Development, 22*(2), 70–79.

Morgan, S. R. (1984). Counseling with teachers on the sexual acting–out of disturbed children. *Psychology in the Schools, 21*(2), 234–243.

Morgan, S. R. (1985). *Children in crises.* Austin, TX: PRO-ED.

Moriarty, D. (1967). *The loss of loved ones.* Springfield, IL: Charles C. Thomas.

Morse, C. W., Sahler, O. J. Z., & Friedman, S. B. (1970). A three year follow–up study of abused and neglected children. *American Journal of Disabled Children, 120,* 437–446.

Morse, W. C. (1978). Children and youth with socio-emotional impairments: Implications for prevention in the public schools. In S. J. Apter (Ed.), *Focus on prevention* (Special Education Series, Publications in Education). Syracuse, NY: Syracuse University School of Education.

Mosley, P. (1974). Selected child beliefs about death: Toward the development of instruments to measure the source of these beliefs. *Dissertation Abstracts International, 35*(6-A), 3577A.

Moss, S. Z., & Moss, M. S. (1984). Threat to place a child. *American Journal of Orthopsychiatry, 54*(1), 168–173.

Mrazek, P. B. (1980). Sexual abuse of children. *Journal of Child Psychology and Psychiatry, 21*(1), 91–95.

Nagera, H. (1970). Children's reactions to the death of important objects: A developmental approach. *Psychoanalytic Study of the Child, 25,* 360–400.

Naisbitt, J. (1984). *Megatrends: Ten new directions transforming our lives.* New York: Warner Books.

National Center on Child Abuse and Neglect. (1991). *Family violence: An overview.* Washington, DC: Author.

National Committee for Prevention of Child Abuse. (1983). *It shouldn't hurt to be a child.* Chicago: Author.

Neilson, J. (1972). Placing older children in adoptive homes. *Children Today, 27,* 7–13.

Neilson, J. (1976). Tayari: Black homes for black children. *Child Welfare, 55,* 41–50.

Nelson, R., & Peterson, W. (1975). Challenging the last great taboo: Death. *School Counselor, 22*(5), 353–361.

Oates, R. K. (1989). The consequences of child abuse and neglect. *Early Child Development and Care, 42,* 57–69.

O'Brien, J. M., Goodenow, C., & Espin, O. (1991). Adolescents' reactions to the death of a peer. *Adolescence, 26*(102), 431–440.

Offord, D., Apponte, J., & Cross, L. (1969). Adopted children. *Archives of General Psychiatry, 20,* 110–116.

Orbach, I., Gross, Y., Glaubman, H., & Berman, D. (1985). Children's perceptions of death in humans and animals as a function of age, anxiety and cognitive ability. *Journal of Child Psychology and Psychiatry, 26*(3), 453–463.

Orr, D.P. (1980). Management of childhood sexual abuse. *Journal of Family Practice, 11*(7), 1057–1064.

Orvaschel, H., Weissman, M., & Kidd, K. (1980). Children and depression. *Journal of Affective Disorders, 2,* 1–16.

Orvaschel, H., Weissman, M., Padian, N., & Lowe, T. (1981). Assessing psychopathology in children of psychiatrically disturbed parents. *Journal of the American Academy of Child Psychiatry, 20,* 112–122.

Ossofsky, H. J. (1974). Endogenous depression in infancy and childhood. *Comprehensive Psychiatry, 15,* 19–25.

Otto, M. L. (1984). Child abuse: Group treatment for parents. *The Personnel and Guidance Journal, 62*(6), 336–338.

Otto, U. (1972). Suicidal behavior in childhood and adolescence. In J. Waldenstrom, T. Larson, & N. Ljungstedt (Eds.), *Suicides and attempted suicides.* Stockholm: Nordiska.

Ounsted, C., Oppenheimer, R., & Lindsay, J. (1974). Aspects of bonding failure: The psychopathology and psychotherapeutic treatment of families of battered children. *Developmental Medical Child Neurology, 16,* 447–456.

Palombo, J. (1981). Parent loss and childhood bereavement: Some theoretical considerations. *Clinical Social Work Journal, 1,* 3–33.

Paluszny, M., Davenport, C., & Kim, W. J. (1991). Suicide attempts and ideation: Adolescents evaluated on a pediatric ward. *Adolescence, 26*(10), 209–215.

Parish, T. S. (1981). Concordance of children's descriptions of themselves and their parents as a function of intact versus divorced families. *Journal of Psychology, 107,* 199–201.

Pattison, E. M. (1976). The fatal myth of death in the family. *American Journal of Psychiatry, 133*(6), 674–678.

Pattison, E. M. (1977). *The experience of dying.* Englewood Cliffs, NJ: Prentice–Hall.

Peck, R. (1966). The development of the concept of death in selected male children: An experimental investigation of the development of the concept of death in selected children from the point of no concept to the point where a fully developed concept is attained with an investigation of some factors which may affect the course of concept development. *Dissertation Abstracts Interntaional, 27*(4-B), 1294B.

Pecot, M. G. (1970). When the parents are divorced. *Childhood Education, 46,* 294–295.

Pedigo, J. (1983). Finding the meaning of Native American substance abuse: Implications for community prevention. *The Personnel and Guidance Journal, 61*(5), 273–277.

Perkins, H. W., & Berkowitz, A. D. (1991). Collegiate COAs and alcohol abuse: Problem drinking in relation to assessments of parent and grandparent alcoholism. *Journal of Counseling and Development, 69*(1), 237–240.

Perry, R. W. (1979). Detecting psychopathological reactions to natural disaster: A methodological note. *Social Behavior and Personality, 7,* 173–177.

Perry, S. E., Silber, E., & Bloch, D. A. (1956). *The child and his family in disaster: A study of the 1953 Vicksburg tornado.* Committee on Disaster Studies, Monograph No. 5. Washington, DC: National Academy of Sciences–National Research Council.

Peters, J. J. (1976). Children who are victims of sexual assault and the psychology of the offenders. *American Journal of Psychotherapy, 30,* 398–421.

Peterson, K. D. (1989, February12). Does a split have lasting effects? *USA Today,* p. 9.

Phillips, G. N. (1968). Problem behavior in the elementary school. *Child Development, 39,* 895–903.

Piazza, E., Rollins, N., & Lewis, F. (1983). Measuring severity and change in anorexia nervosa. *Adolescence, 18*(70), 293–305.

Powell, G. F., Brasel, J. A., & Blizzard, R. M. (1967a). Emotional deprivation and growth retardation simulating idiopathic hypopituitarism: 1. Clinical evaluation of the syndrome. *New England Journal of Medicine, 276,* 1271–1278.

Powell, G. F., Brasel, J. A., & Blizzard, R. M. (1967b). Emotional deprivation and growth retardation simulating idiopathic hypopituitarism: 2. Endocrinologic evaluation of the syndrome. *New England Journal of Medicine, 276,* 1279–1283.

Powell, R. E. (1987). Homosexual behavior and the school counselor. *The School Counselor, 34*(1), 202–208.

Poznanski, E. D. (1982). The clinical phenomenology of childhood depression. *American Journal of Orthopsychiatry, 52*(2), 308–313.

Raphael, B., Cubis, J., Dunne, M., Lewin, T., & Kelly, B. (1990). The impact of parental loss on adolescents' psychosocial characteristics. *Adolescence, 25*(99), 689–699.

Rapoport, J. L., & Ismond, D. R. (1984). *DSM-III training guide for diagnosis of childhood disorders.* New York: Brunner/Mazel.

Reinhard, D. (1977). The reaction of adolescent boys and girls to the divorce of the parents. *Journal of Clinical Child Psychology, 6*(2), 21–24.

Reinhold, T. (1988). Life without a father. *Woman's World Journal,* 6–7.

Reiss, A. J. (1964). The social integration of queers and peers. In H. S. Becker (Ed.), *The other side.* New York: The Free Press.

Renshaw, D. C. (1974). Suicide and depression in children. *Journal of School Health, 44,* 487–489.

Rescoria, L., Parker, R., & Stolley, P. (1991). Ability, achievement, and adjustment in homeless children. *American Journal of Orthopsychiatry, 61,* 210–219.

Rich, C. L., Sherman, M., & Fowler, R. C. (1990). San Diego suicide study: The adolescents. *Adolescence, 25*(100), 855–865.

Rioche, M. (1971). *Pilot project in training mental health counselors (follow up).* (Public Health Service Publication No. 1254). Washington, DC: U.S. Printing Office.

Ritual Abuse Task Force. (1986, September). *Ritual abuse.* Symposium conducted at the meeting of the Colorado/Wyoming Detective Association, Fort Collins, Colorado.

Ritual Abuse Task Force. (1989, September). *Ritual abuse.* Symposium conducted at the meeting of the Los Angeles County Commission for Women, Los Angeles.

Roberts, M., & Maddax, J. (1982). A psychosocial conceptualization of nonorganic failure to thrive. *Journal of Clinical Child Psychology, 11*(3), 216–227.

Robertson, A., & Cochrane, R. (1976). Attempted suicide and cultural change: An empirical investigation. *Human Relations, 29*(9), 863–883.

Robertson, J. J. (1986). Mental disorder among homeless persons in the United States: An overview of recent empirical literature. *Administration in Mental Health, 14*(1), 14–27.

Robinson, B. E. (1989). *Working with children of alcoholics.* Boston: Lexington Books.

Rochlin, G. (1967). How younger children view death and themselves. In E. Grollman (Ed.), *Explaining death to children.* Boston: Beacon Press.

Rogers, R. (1969). The adolescent and the hidden parent. *Comprehensive Psychiatry, 10,* 296–301.

Rohner, R. (1975). *They love me, they love me not: A worldwide study of the effects of parental acceptance and rejection.* New Haven, CT: Human Relations Area File Press.

Rollins, J., & Holden, R. (1972). Adolescent drug use and alienation syndrome. *Journal of Drug Education, 2,* 249–261.

Rolston, R. H. (1971). The effect of prior physical abuse on the expression of overt and fantasy aggressive behavior in children. *Dissertation Abstracts International, 32,* 2453B–3086B. (University Microfilms No. 71–29, 389).

Rosen, R. (1977). Children of divorce: What they feel about access and other aspects of the divorce experience. *Journal of Clinical Child Psychology, 6*(2), 24–27.

Rosenthal, P., & Rosenthal, S. (1984). Suicidal behavior by pre–school children. *American Journal of Psychiatry, 141*(4), 520–524.

Ross, M. (1970). Death at an early age. *Canada's Mental Health, 18*(6), 7–10.

Roy, C., & Fuqua, D. (1983). Social support systems and academic performance of single–parent students. *The School Counselor, 30*(3), 183–192.

Russell, S. C., & Williams, E. U. (1988). Homeless handicapped children: A special education perspective. *Children's Environments Quarterly, 5*(1), 3–7.

Ryker, M. J. (1971). Six selected factors influencing educational achievement of children from broken homes. *Education, 91,* 200–211.

Sabbath, J. (1972). The role of the parents in adolescent suicidal behavior. *Psychological Abstracts, 47,* Abstract No. 7453.

Saffer, J. B. (1986). Group therapy with friends of an adolescent suicide. *Adolescence, 21*(83), 743–745.

Sandgrund, A., Gaines, R., & Green, A. (1974). Child abuse and mental retardation: A problem of cause and effect. *American Journal of Mental Deficiency, 79,* 327–330.

Santrock, J. W. (1972). Relation of type and onset of father absence to cognitive development. *Child Development, 43,* 455–469.

Santrock, J. W., & Warshak, R. A. (1979). Father custody and social development in boys and girls. *Journal of Social Issues, 35*(4), 112–125.

Schaffer, D. (1974). Suicide in childhood and early adolescence. *Journal of Child Psychology and Psychiatry, 15,* 275–291.

Schecter, M. (1960). Observations on adopted children. *Archives of General Psychiatry, 3,* 21–32.

Schecter, M., Carlson, P., Simmons, J., & Work, H. (1964). Emotional problems in the adoptee. *Archives of General Psychiatry, 10,* 109–118.

Schecter, M., & Sternlof, R. (1970). Suicide in adolescents. *Postgraduate Medicine, 47,* 220–223.

Schmitt, B.O. (1975, November–December). What teachers need to know about child abuse and neglect. *Childhood Education, 52,* 58–62.

Schneer, K., Perlstein, A., & Brozovsky, M. (1975). Hospitalized suicidal adolescents: Two generations. *Journal of the American Academy of Child Psychiatry, 14*(2), 268–280.

Schoepfer, A. E. (1975). Legal implications in connection with physical abuse of children. In *Protecting the battered child*. Denver, CO: American Humane Association, Children's Division.

Schultz, L. G., & Jones, P. (1983). Sexual abuse of children: Issues for social service and health professionals. *Child Welfare, 62*(2), 99–108.

Schuyler, D. (1973). When was the last time you took a suicidal child to lunch? *Journal of School Health, 43*(8), 504–506.

Scott, J. P., & Senay, E. C. (1973). *Separation and depression*. Washington, DC: American Association for the Advancement of Science.

Segal, J., & Yahraes, H. (1978). *A child's journey: Forces that shape the lives of our young*. New York: McGraw-Hill.

Seiden, R. (1969). *Suicide among youth*. PHS Publication No. 1971. Washington, DC: U.S. Government Printing Office.

Shah, C. P. (1982). Sexual abuse of children. *Annals of Emergency Medicine, 11*(1), 41–46.

Shamray, J. A. (1980). A perspective on childhood sexual abuse. *Social Work, 25* (2), 128–131.

Sheehy, G. (1984, July 29). When a child is abused: Are you ready to listen? *The El Paso Times Parade*, p.p. 4–6.

Sher, K. J., Walitzer, K. S., Wood, P. K., & Brent, E. E. (1991). Characteristics of children of alcoholics: Putative risk factors, substance use and abuse, and psychopathology. *Journal of Abnormal Psychology, 100*(4), 427–448.

Sherman, A., & Lepak, L. (1986, October). Children's perceptions of the divorce process. *Elementary School Guidance & Counseling, 26*, p.p. 29–36.

Shoor, M., & Speed, M. (1963). Death, delinquency and the mourning process. In R. Fulton (Ed.), (1976). *Death and identity*. Baltimore: Charles Press.

Shrut, A. (1962). Suicidal adolescents and children. *Journal of the American Medical Association, 188*, 1103–1107.

Siegel, L. J., & Griffer, N. J. (1983). Adolescents' concepts of depression among their peers. *Adolescence, 18*(72), 965–973.

Silvern, S. B., & Yawkey, T. D. (1974). *Divorce: Some effects on and teaching strategies for young children*. Unpublished manuscript, University of Wisconsin, Division of Early Childhood Education, Madison.

Simon, N., & Senturia, A. (1966). Adoption and psychiatric illness. *American Journal of Psychiatry, 122*, 858–868.

Smith, B. K. (1988). Neglect wears many faces. *Academic Therapy, 24*(1), 37–42.

Smith, D. (1976). Adolescent suicide: A problem for teachers. *Phi Delta Kappan, 57*, 539–542.

Smith, T. E. (1990). Parental separation and the academic self–concepts of adolescents: An effort to solve the puzzle of separation effects. *Journal of Marriage and the Family, 52*, 107–117.

Soeffing, M. (1975). Abused children are exceptional children. *Exceptional Children, 42*, 126–135.

Sojleva, M. (1975). Psychological examination of adolescents with suicidal attempts. *Psychological Abstracts, 54*, Abstract No. 5549.

Solkoff, N. (1981). Children survivors of the Nazi holocaust: A critical review of the literature. *American Journal of Orthopsychiatry, 51*(1), 29–40.

Somerville, R. (1971). Death education as a part of family life education: Using imaginative literature for insights into family crisis. *The Family Coordinator, 20,* 209–224.

Sorenson, G. P. (1991). Sexual abuse in schools: Reported court cases from 1987–1990. *Educational Administration Quarterly, 27*(4), 460–480.

Sorosky, A. D. (1977). The psychological effects of divorce on adolescents. *Adolescence, 50*(45), 71–74.

Sorosky, A., Baran, A., & Pannor, R. (1975). Identity conflicts in adoptees. *American Journal of Orthopsychiatry, 45,* 18–27.

Spinetta, J. J., & Rigler, D. (1972). The child–abusing parent: A psychological review. *Psychological Bulletin, 77*(4), 296–304.

Spitz, R. A. (1946). Anaclitic depression. *The psychoanalytic study of the child* (Vol. II). New York: International Universities Press.

Steacy, A., & Bethune, B. (1989). Questions of satanism: Tales of ritual abuse are common. *Maclean's, 102,* 62.

Steele, B., & Pollock, C. (1974). A psychiatric study of parents who abuse infants and small children. In R. Helfer & C. Kempe (Eds.), *The battered child* (2nd ed., opp. 89–133). Chicago: University of Chicago Press.

Steinberg, L. (1987). Single parents, stepparents, and the susceptibility of adolescents to antisocial peer pressure. *Child Development, 58,* 269–275.

Steinberg, L. D., Catalano, R., & Dooley, D. (1982). Economic antecedents of child abuse and neglect. *Child Development, 52*(3), 975–985.

Steiner, G. (1966). Children's concepts of life and death: A developmental study (Doctoral dissertation, University of Oklahoma). *Dissertation Abstracts International, 26*(2-B), 1164B.

Stoenner, H. (1976). Child sexual abuse seen growing in the United States. In *Plain talk about child abuse.* Denver, CO: American Humane Association, Children's Division.

Stover, D. (1992, May). The at–risk students schools continue to ignore. *The Education Digest,* p.p. 37–40.

Straker, G., & Johnson, R. S. (1981). Aggression, emotional maladjustment, and empathy in the abused child. *Behavioral Disorders, 17*(6), 762–765.

Stratford, L. (1991). *Satan's underground: The extraordinary story of one woman's escape.* Gretna, LA: Pelican Publishing.

Sugar, M. (1970). Children of divorce. *Pediatrics, 46*(4), 82–88.

Summit, R., & Kryso, J. (1978). Sexual abuse of children: A clinical spectrum. *American Journal of Orthopsychiatry, 48*(2), 237–251.

Swain, H. L. (1976). The concept of death in children (Doctoral dissertation, University of Oklahoma). *Dissertation Abstracts International, 37*(2-A), 898–899.

Swift, C. (1979). The prevention of sexual child abuse: Focus on the perpetrator. *Journal of Clinical Child Psychology, 8*(2), 133–136.

Tallmer, M. (1974). Factors influencing children's conception of death. *Journal of Clinical Child Psychology, 3*(2), 11–14.

Tec, L., & Gordon, S. (1967). The adopted child's adaptation to adolescence. *American Journal of Orthopsychiatry, 37,* 402.

Tennant, C., Bebbington, P. R., & Hurry, J. (1980). Parental death in childhood and risk of adult depressive disorders: A review. *Psychological Medicine, 10*(2), 289–299.

Terestman, N. (1980). Mood quality and intensity in nursery school children as predictors of behavior disorders. *American Journal of Orthopsychiatry, 50*(1), 18–32.

Teri, L. (1982a). The use of the Beck Depression Inventory with adolescents. *Journal of Abnormal Child Psychology, 10*(2), 277–284.

Teri, L. (1982b). Depression in adolescence: Its relationship to assertion and various aspects of self-image. *Journal of Clinical Child Psychology, 11*(2), 101–106.

Tharp, R. G. (1965). Marriage roles, child development and family treatment. *American Journal of Orthopsychiatry, 35*, 531–538.

Tilelli, J. A. (1980). Sexual abuse of children: Clinical findings and implications for management. *New England Journal of Medicine, 302*(6), 319–323.

Tizard, B., & Rees, J. (1975). The effect of early institutional rearing on the behavior and affectional relationships of four year old children. *Journal of Child Psychiatry and Psychology, 16*, 61–73.

Toolan, J. M. (1962). Suicide and suicidal attempts in children and adolescents. *American Journal of Psychiatry, 118*, 719–724.

Tooley, K. (1975). The choice of a surviving sibling as "scapegoat" in some cases of maternal bereavement: A case report. *Journal of Child Psychology and Psychiatry, 16*, 331–339.

Towers, R. L. (1989). *Children of alcoholics/addicts.* Washington, DC: National Education Association.

Tuckman, J., & Regan, R. (1966). Intactness of the home and behavioral problems in children. *Journal of Child Psychiatry and Psychology, 7*, 225–233.

Valente, S. M., Saunders, J., & Street, R. (1988). Adolescent bereavement following suicide: An examination of relevant literature. *Journal of Counseling and Development, 67*, 174–177.

Van Eerdewegh, M. M., Bieri, M. D., Parrilla, R. H., & Clayton, P. J. (1982). The bereaved child. *British Journal of Psychiatry, 140*, 23–29.

Varenhorst, B. (1969). Learning the consequences of life's decisions. In J. Krumboltz & C. Thoresen (Eds.), *Behavioral counseling: Cases and techniques.* New York: Holt, Rinehart, & Winston.

Vrcan, L. (1988). The growing threat of gang violence. *School and College, 27*(4), 25.

Vriend, T. (1969). High performing inner city adolescents assist low performing peers in counseling groups. *Personnel and Guidance Journal, 48*, 897–904.

Waldron, S., Shrier, D. K., Stone, B., & Tobin, F. (1975). School phobia and other childhood neurosis: A systematic study of children and their families. *American Journal of Psychiatry, 132*, 802–808.

Walker, B. (1983). Adolescent suicide: A family crisis. *Adolescence, 18*(70), 285–289.

Wallerstein, J. S. (1983). Children of divorce: The psychological tasks of the child. *American Journal of Orthopsychiatry, 53*(2), 59–61, 230–234.

Wallerstein, J., & Kelly, J. (1976). The effects of parental divorce: Experiences in the child in later latency. *American Journal of Orthopsychiatry, 46*, 256–269.

Walters, D. R. (1975). *Physical and sexual abuse of children.* Bloomington: Indiana University Press.

Watters, E. (1991). The devil in Mr. Ingram. *Mother Jones, 16*, 30–33.

Weiner, I. (1970). *Psychological disturbance in adolescence.* New York: Wiley.

Weissman, M. M., Paykel, E. S., & Klerman, G. L. (1972). The depressed woman as a mother. *Social Psychiatry, 7,* 98–108.

Welsh, R. S. (1976a). Severe parental punishment and delinquency: A developmental theory. *Journal of Clinical Child Psychology, 1,* 17–20.

Weston, D., Ludolph, P., Misle, B., Ruffins, S., & Block, J. (1990). Physical and sexual abuse in adolescent girls with borderline personality disorder. *American Journal of Orthopsychiatry, 60*(1), 55–66.

White, H. (1974). Self–poisoning in adolescents. *British Journal of Psychiatry, 124,* 24–35.

Whiting, L. (1976). Defining emotional neglect. *Children Today, 5*(1), 2–5.

Whitman, B. Y., Accardo, P., Boyert, M., & Kendagor, R. (1990). Homelessness and cognitive performance in children: A possible link. *Social Work, 35,* 516–519.

Williams, B. G. (1981). Myths and sexual child abuse: Identification and elimination. *The School Counselor, 29*(2), 103–110.

Williams, C., & Lyons, C. (1976). Family interaction and adolescent suicidal behavior: A preliminary investigation. *Australian & New Zealand Journal of Psychiatry, 10*(3), 243–252.

Williams, G. J. R. (1983). Child protection: A journey into history. *Journal of Clinical Child Psychology, 12*(3), 236–243.

Williamson, J. M., Borduin, C. M., & Howe, B. A. (1991). The ecology of adolescent maltreatment: A multilevel examination of adolescent physical abuse, sexual abuse, and neglect. *Journal of Consulting and Clinical Psychology, 59*(3), 449–457.

Wolfe, R., & Cotler, S. (1973). Undergraduates who attempt suicide compared with normal and psychiatric controls. *Omega, 4*(4), 305–312.

Wolff, S. (1971). Dimensions and clusters of symptoms in disturbed children. *British Journal of Psychiatry, 118,* 429–436.

Woodling, B. A. (1981). Sexual misuse: Rape, molestation, and incest. *Pediatric Clinics of North America, 28*(2), 481–499.

Work, H., & Anderson, H. (1971). Studies in adoption: Requests for psychiatric treatment. *American Journal of Psychiatry, 127,* 124–125.

Wright, L. S. (1982). Parental permission to date and its relationship to drug use and suicidal thoughts among adolescents. *Adolescence, 17*(66), 409–418.

Wyers, N. L. (1987). Homosexuality in the family: Lesbian and gay spouses. *Social Work, 32,* 143–148.

Zimiles, H., & Lee, V. E. (1991). Adolescent family structure and educational progress. *Developmental Psychology, 27*(2), 314–320.

Zinner, E. S. (1987). Responding to suicide in schools: A case study in loss intervention and group survivorship. *Journal of Counseling and Development, 65,* 499–501.

Zussman, J. U. (1980). Situational determinants of parental behavior: Effects of competing cognitive activity. *Child Development, 51,* 792–800.

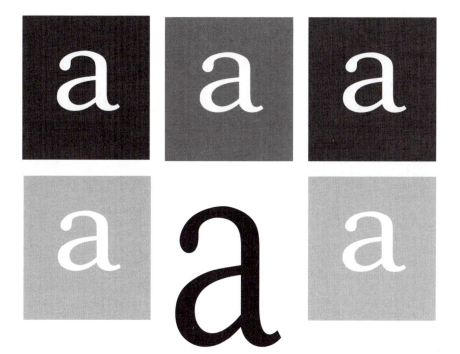

Author Index

Subject Index